Advances in Face Image Analysis: Theory and Applications

Edited By

Fadi Dornaika

University of the Basque Country (UPV/EHU)
IKERBASQUE Foundation for Science
Manuel Lardizabal,
1, 20018 San Sebastián,
Spain

advertisements or ideas contained in the Work.

Limitation of Liability:

In no event will Bentham Science Publishers, its staff, editors and/or authors, be liable for any damages, including, without limitation, special, incidental and/or consequential damages and/or damages for lost data and/or profits arising out of (whether directly or indirectly) the use or inability to use the Work. The entire liability of Bentham Science Publishers shall be limited to the amount actually paid by you for the Work.

General:

1. Any dispute or claim arising out of or in connection with this License Agreement or the Work (including non-contractual disputes or claims) will be governed by and construed in accordance with the laws of the U.A.E. as applied in the Emirate of Dubai. Each party agrees that the courts of the Emirate of Dubai shall have exclusive jurisdiction to settle any dispute or claim arising out of or in connection with this License Agreement or the Work (including non-contractual disputes or claims).

2. Your rights under this License Agreement will automatically terminate without notice and without the need for a court order if at any point you breach any terms of this License Agreement. In no event will any delay or failure by Bentham Science Publishers in enforcing your compliance with this License Agreement constitute a waiver of any of its rights.

3. You acknowledge that you have read this License Agreement, and agree to be bound by its terms and conditions. To the extent that any other terms and conditions presented on any website of Bentham Science Publishers conflict with, or are inconsistent with, the terms and conditions set out in this License Agreement, you acknowledge that the terms and conditions set out in this License Agreement shall prevail.

Bentham Science Publishers Ltd.
Executive Suite Y - 2
PO Box 7917, Saif Zone
Sharjah, U.A.E.
Email: subscriptions@benthamscience.org

BENTHAM
SCIENCE

CONTENTS

FOREWORD

Computer vision is one of the most active research fields in information technology, computer science and electrical engineering due to its numerous applications and major research challenges. Face image analysis constitutes an important field in computer vision and can be a key challenge in developing human-centered technologies. Face image analysis problems have been investigated in computer vision and Human Machine Interaction applications (*e.g.*, identity verification, eye typing, emotion recognition, m-commerce). Making computers understand the contents of images taken by cameras is very challenging, and therefore the computer vision technology faces a lot of challenges. Differed from the biometric problems, *e.g.*, finger-print or iris based recognition; face recognition inherently relies on the uncontrolled environment and inevitably suffers from degrading factors such as illumination, expression, pose and age variations. Image-based age estimation is relatively a new research topic. Estimating human age automatically *via* facial image analysis has lots of potential real-world applications, such as human computer interaction and multimedia communication.

This book presents the reader with cutting edge research in the domain of face image analysis. Besides, the book includes recent research works from different world research groups, providing a rich diversity of approaches to the face image analysis. The material covered in the eleven chapters of the book presents new advances on computer vision and pattern recognition approaches, as well as new knowledge and perspectives.

The chapters, written by experts in their respective field, will make the reader acquainted with a number of topics and some trendy techniques used to tackle many problems related to face images. It is impressive to note that the editor and authors have tried to capture a wide and dynamic topic. I believe readers will not only learn from this book, but it will be of high reference value as well.

Denis Hamad
Université du Littoral Côte d'Opale,
Calais, France

PREFACE

Over the past two decades, many face image analysis problems have been investigated in computer vision and machine learning. The main idea and the driver of further research in this area are human-machine interaction and security applications. Face images and videos can represent an intuitive and non-intrusive channel for recognizing people, inferring their level of interest, and estimating their gaze in 3D. Although progress over the past decade has been impressive, there are significant obstacles to be overcome. It is not possible yet to design a face analysis system with a potential close to human performance. New computer vision and pattern recognition approaches need to be investigated. Face recognition as an essential problem in pattern recognition and social media computing, attracts many researchers for decades. For instance, face recognition became one of three identification methods used in e-passports and a biometric of choice for many other security applications.

The e-Book "Advances in Face Image Analysis: Theory and Applications" is oriented to a wide audience including: i) researchers and professionals working in the fields of face image analysis; ii) the entire pattern recognition community interested in processing and extracting features from raw face images; and iii) technical experts as well as postgraduate students working on face images and their related concepts. One of the key benefits of this E-Book is that the readers will have access to novel research topics. The book contains eleven chapters that address several topics including automatic face detection, 3D face model fitting, robust face recognition, facial expression recognition, face image data embedding, model-less 3D face pose estimation and image-based age estimation.

We would like to express our gratitude to all the contributing authors that have made this book a reality. We would also like to thank Prof. Denis Hamad for writing the foreword and Bentham Science Publishers for their support and efforts. A special thank goes to Dr. Ammar Assoum for providing the latex style file.

Fadi Dornaika
University of the Basque Country
Manuel Lardizabal, 1
20018 San Sebastián, Spain

LIST OF CONTRIBUTORS

Ammar Assoum	LaMA laboratory, Lebanese University, Tripoli, Lebanon
Alireza Behrad	Department of Electrical and Electronic Engineering, Shahed university, Tehran-Qom Exp. Way, 3319118651, Tehran, Iran
Alireza Bosaghzadeh	University of the Basque Country, Manuel Lardizabal, 1, 20018, San Sebastian, Spain
Fadi Dornaika	University of the Basque Country, Manuel Lardizabal, 1, 20018, San Sebastian, Spain Department of Computer Science and Artificial Intelligence, University of the Basque Country, UPV/EHU, San Sebastian, Spain IKERBASQUE, Basque Foundation for Science, Bilbao, Spain
Jon Goenetxea	Vicomtech-IK4, Paseo Mikeletegi, 57, Parque Tecnológicoo, 20009, Donostia, Spain
Jouhayna Harmouch	LaMA Laboratory, Lebanese University, Tripoli, Lebanon
Zhong Jin	School of Computer Science & Engineering, Nanjing University of Sciences and Technology, Nanjing, China
Fawzi Khattar	LaMA Laboratory, Lebanese University, Tripoli, Lebanon
Franck Luthon	IUT de Bayonne Pays Basque, Université de Pau Pays d'Adour,, 2 allée du parc Montaury, 64600, Anglet, France
Waldir Pimenta	Departamento de Informática, University of Minho, Campus de Gualtar, 4710-057, Braga, Portugal
Luis P. Santos	Departamento de Informática, University of Minho, Campus de Gualtar, 4710-057, Braga, Portugal
Shenglan Ben	School of Electronic Science & Engineering, Nanjing University, Nanjing, 210094, China
Sun Wenyun	School of Computer Science & Engineering, Nanjing University, Nanjing, 210094, China
Luis Unzueta	Vicomtech-IK4, Paseo Mikeletegi, 57, Parque Tecnológicoo, 20009, Donostia, Spain
Libo Weng	Department of Computer Science and Artificial Intelligence, University of the Basque Country, UPV/EHU, San Sebastian, Spain School of Computer Science & Engineering, Nanjing University of Sciences and Technology, Nanjing, China

CHAPTER 1

Facial Expression Classification Based on Convolutional Neural Networks

Wenyun Sun, Zhong Jin[*]

School of Computer Science and Engineering, Nanjing University of Science and Technology, Nanjing, China

Abstract: Research trends in Convolutional Neural Networks and facial expression analysis are introduced at first. A training algorithm called stochastic gradient descent with l_2 regularization is employed for the facial expression classification problem, in which facial expression images are classified into six basic emotional categories of anger, disgust, fear, happiness, sadness and surprise without any complex pre-processes involved. Moreover, three types of feature generalization for solving problems with different classifiers, different datasets and different categories are discussed. By these techniques, pre-trained Convolutional Neural Networks are used as feature extractors which work quite well with Support Vector Machine classifiers. The results of experiments show that Convolutional Neural Networks not only have capability of classifying facial expression images with translational distortions, but also have capability to fulfill some feature generalization tasks.

Keywords: Alex-Net architecture, Backpropagation algorithm, CK-Regianini dataset, CK-Zheng dataset, Classification accuracy, CMU-Pittsburgh dataset, Combined features, Convolutional Neural Networks, Deep learning, Facial expression classification, Feature extraction, Feature generalization, Feature representation, Hidden layers, Pre-trained networks, Stochastic Gradient Descent, Supervised feature learning, Support Vector Machine, Trainable parameters, Translational invariance property.

INTRODUCTION

A feature extractor and a classifier are two essential modules in a conventional

---

[*] **Address to Corresponding Author Zhong Jin:** School of Computer Science and Engineering, Nanjing University of Science and Technology, Nanjing, China; Tel: +86 25 84303280 Ext. 3071; Fax: +86 25 84317235; E-mail: zhongjin@njust.edu.cn

Fadi Dornaika (Ed)

image pattern recognition system. A good feature extractor of image could produce a feature representation which has more discriminant information and less correlations than the original pixel data. There are quite a few popular techniques recently, *e.g.*, the Scale-Invariant Feature Transform (SIFT) [1] and the Histogram of Oriented Gradients (HOG) [2]. On the other hand, a highly efficient classifier could perform its job well without any help of complex feature extractors. Nowadays, some highly efficient classifiers and good feature extractors based on deep learning have come out.

Convolutional Neural Networks

Remarkable achievements have been obtained by studies of classifiers for high dimensional image data in the last two decades. More and more attentions have been gotten by Convolutional Neural Networks (CNNs) which have become the representatives among other deep learning methods. Although CNNs were suggested in 1989 [3], efficient training algorithms were absent until the stochastic diagonal Levenberg-Marquardt algorithm for CNNs was proposed by LeCun *et al.* in 1998 [4]. A so-called LeNet-5 was designed by LeCun *et al.* It could classify handwritten digits and letters into categories without complex preprocesses.

There is some theoretical research which brings the state-of-the-art techniques to the classical CNNs recently, *e.g.* rectified linear unit [5], local contrast normalization [6], local response normalization [7] and dropout [8]. On the other hand, engineering studies have never been stopped. Handwritten character recognition [9, 10], natural image processing [7, 11], *etc.* are well-known engineering application of CNNs.

The most interesting work had been done by Krizhevsky *et al.* who won the ImageNet Large Scale Visual Recognition Challenge (ILSVRC) in 2012 [7]. They achieved a top-5 error rate of 16.4% on the classification benchmark, which beat the second place result of 26.1% with handcrafted features.

In ILSVRC 2013, an approach from Zeiler *et al.* [11] improved the performance by visualizing hidden layers of CNNs. They found that Krizhevsky's network has the ability of extracting features of different scale and complexity. This phenomenon shows the feature representation capability of CNNs evidently. A reliable feature extractor could be easily got by cutting the Soft-Max layer off at the end of CNNs and keeping the rest layer's trainable parameters fixed. The features from one of each hidden layers, especially from the last one, could be used as the inputs of any other classifiers. In other words, when a classifier is trained, a feature extractor will be got at the same time. The extractor can be widely used for various purposes. Based on this view of point, Zeiler *et al.* proposed a theory of feature generalization. Abundant feature information is included in nature images which also have a large scale of categories. Thus, a pre-trained feature extracting network for natural images could be applied to the processes of specific data conveniently. Finally, it is notable that these methods we mentioned above are usually implemented and accelerated by Graphics Processing Unit (GPU) based high performance computing techniques.

Facial Expression Analysis

In another domain, the research of classifying facial expressions was started by psychologists. In 1978, facial action coding system (FACS) [12] was proposed by Ekman *et al.* The well-known facial expression image dataset, called Cohn-Kanade (CK) [13, 14], built by the Robotics Institute of Carnegie Mellon University and Department of Psychology of University of Pittsburgh, contains a set of facial expression image sequences and their corresponding action unit (AU) codes.

In 1984, Ekman *et al.* continued their studies, and classified facial expressions into six categories by different emotions, *i.e.*, anger, disgust, fear, happiness, sadness and surprise [15]. In the problem of facial expression analysis, especially in the classification case, feature extractors and classifiers should keep invariant to individuals and perspective projection distortions.

In the recent years, quite a few studies have been devoted to expression classification of static images or image sequences. Some are about specific handcrafted feature extraction algorithms [16, 17], and some are about classifiers which use plan 2-dimensional pixels data as their inputs [18, 19].

In the following sections, a gradient-based learning algorithm and a feature extraction technique are introduced. Then, several experiments are conducted. Finally, the entire studies are concluded, and more interesting work which is required to pay attention to is outlined in the last section.

GRADIENT-BASED LEARNING FOR CNNS

LeNet-5 [4] is a typical case of CNNs. It consists of layers called C1, S2, C3, S4, C5 and F6. Its feedforward process could be outlined as follows:

- Firstly, the input image is transformed by 3-dimensional convolution with six kernels with size of 5^*5^*1, added by bias term, activated by tanh function. The first set of six feature maps called C1 will be got.
- Secondly, a max-polling process is applied to C1, and the second set of feature maps called S2 will be obtained.
- Thirdly, the layers of C3, S4 are generated by the same mechanism.
- Fourthly, two fully connected layers called C5 and F6 are calculated by the same way as conventional neural networks. C5 could be considered as a convolutional layer or as a fully connected layer, since the output of C5 are feature maps with size of 1^*1. In order to enable the classifier to reject unreasonable inputs, finally a Gaussian layer is use for computing the distance between 84-dimesion activation data of F6 and 10 fixed binary codes.
- Finally, training progress could be simply understood as a fitting job with respect to F6 in order to minimize the Gaussian distance between F6 layer's activation and its nearest binary code.

Fig. (**1**) shows the visualization of each layer for an input of digital image. From left to right, there are input layers, C1's kernel, C2's activation, C3's kernel, C4's activation, C5's activation and F6's activation, respectively. The activations of S2 and S4 have the same visualizations as C1's and C3's. In this demonstration, the image is classified into the category of 5 and the Gaussian distance between F6's activation and its nearest cluster center is 0.237.

If we consider x_0 as the inputs, $\{f_1, f_2, \cdots, f_L\}$ as the layers (including a loss layer), $\{w_1, w_2, \cdots, w_L\}$ as the parameters(weights, biases *etc.*) and $\{x_1, x_2, \cdots, x_L\}$ as the layers' output, the feed forward calculation can be described as $x_n = f_n(x_{n-1}, w_n)$, $n \in \{1, 2, \cdots, L\}$.

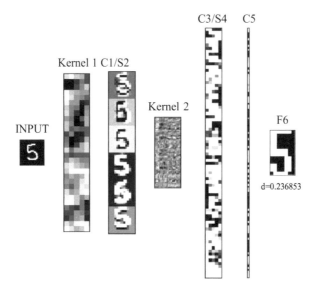

Fig. (1). Visualization of each layer in LeNet-5.

A multiple layered CNN with a loss function can be regarded as a system built by a cascade of transformation modules $\{f_1(x_0, w_1), f_2(x_1, w_2), \cdots, f_L(x_{L-1}, w_L)\}$ whose inputs and outputs are connected one after another.

The training process can be formulated as an optimization problem

$$
\begin{aligned}
\min_{w_1, w_2, \cdots, w_{L-1}} \quad & E(x_0, w_1, w_2, \cdots, w_L) \\
\text{s.t.} \quad & E(x_0, w_1, w_2, \cdots, w_L) = x_L \\
& x_n = f_n(x_{n-1}, w_n)
\end{aligned}
\tag{1}
$$

where (x_0, w_L) is a pair of training data.

Each transformation is differentiable, thus the gradient-based learning algorithm can be employed for training CNNs. The gradients with respect to each transformation inputs and parameters can be formulated as follows:

$$
\frac{\partial E}{\partial x_{n-1}} = \frac{\partial f_n}{\partial x}(x_{n-1}, w_n) \frac{\partial E}{\partial x_n}
\tag{2}
$$

$$\frac{\partial E}{\partial w_n} = \frac{\partial f_n}{\partial w}(x_{n-1}, w_n)\frac{\partial E}{\partial x_n} \tag{3}$$

where $\frac{\partial f_n}{\partial x}(x_{n-1}, w_n)$ is the Jacobian of f_n with respect to x evaluated at the

point $(x_{n-1} \ w_n)$, and $\frac{\partial f_n}{\partial w}(x_{n-1}, w_n)$ is the Jacobian of f_n with respect to w

evaluated at the same point. The Eq.(2) and Eq.(3) are the main ideas of Backpropagation (BP) algorithm. An improved learning algorithm called l_2 regularization is commonly used for anti-overfitting. The new optimization problem is shown as follows:

$$\min_{w_1, w_2, \cdots, w_{L-1}} \quad E'(x_0, w_1, w_2, \cdots, w_L)$$

$$\text{s.t.} \quad E'(x_0, w_1, w_2, \cdots, w_L) = x_L + \lambda\frac{1}{2}\sum_{n=1}^{L-1} \|w_n\|_2^2 \tag{4}$$

$$x_n = f_n(x_{n-1}, w_n).$$

The gradients for the new problem of Eq.(4) can be easily calculated on the base of Eq.(2) and Eq.(3) by

$$\frac{\partial E'}{\partial x_n} = \frac{\partial E}{\partial x_n} \tag{5}$$

$$\frac{\partial E'}{\partial w_n} = \frac{\partial E}{\partial w_n} + w_n. \tag{6}$$

The stochastic gradient descent procedure to solve problem of Eq.(4) is summarized in Algorithm 1.

Algorithm 1 Stochastic Gradient Descent with l_2 Regularization

1: **Input:** teaching data X, teaching labels Y, learning rate α, tolerance ϵ
2: **Initialize:** $w_1, w_2, ..., w_{L-1}$:= tiny random values around zero

  3:   **repeat**

  4:      x_0 := random subset of X ▷ feedforward

  5:      $y_{ground\ truth}$:= corresponding subset of Y

  6:      **for** n := 1 to L **do**

  7:         $x_n := f_n(x_{n-1}, w_n)$

  8:      **for** n := L to 1 **do**   ▷ backpropagation

  9:         calculate $\partial E'/\partial x_n$ by Eq.(2) and Eq.(5)

10:      **for** n := $L-1$ to 1 **do**

11:         calculate $\partial E'/\partial w_n$ by Eq.(3) and Eq.(6)

12:      **for** n := 1 to $L-1$ **do**   ▷ update weights

13:         $w_n := w_n - \alpha \partial E'/\partial w_n$

14:      **until** $E' \leq \epsilon$

15:      **return** $w_1, w_2, ..., w_{L-1}$

The Alex-Net [7] and Zeiler's Net [11] are proposed based on LeNet-5. They may be regarded as the representative of the modern CNNs. They simplified some unnecessary processes of LeNet-5 and made some improvement such as normalization and anti-overfitting mechanisms. In the architecture of the Alex-Net, the layers are divided into two groups in which activations are calculated individually except both in the first layer and the last one. There are no relations between the two groups in order to reduce communication traffic between two GPUs. The overall network has a 150528-dimensional input layer, and the number of neurons in the remaining layers is given by 253440, 186624, 64896, 64896, 43264, 4096, 4096 and 1000 respectively. The way of dividing layer into groups, the number of neurons in each layers and the layer type are all alternative. Thus different architectures could be devised for different problems and for different GPUs. A compromise should be made between reducing the time cost of each epoch and improving the performance of each epoch, so as to make the network converges faster.

In a word, CNNs have four characteristics which are listed as follows:

• Convolution / local receptive field is used for sharing weights.
• Sub-sampling / pooling is used.
• Network has 2-5 convolutional layers and 1-2 fully connected layers followed

by.

- Network can be learnt by hierarchical first order optimization algorithms, *i.e.* BP algorithm.

FEATURE GENERALIZATION

A supervised feature learning technique will be introduced in this section. When the input layer of a pre-trained CNN is set well, the hidden layer includes the representation of the input data. The deeper a hidden layer goes, the more complicated a feature is extracted. It may be difficult to get these meaningful information by simple handcrafted feature extractors. When a classifier is got, a corresponding feature extractor is obtained at the same time. For example, a reliable feature extractor can be got by removing the soft-max layer at the end of a pre-trained neural network.

The pre-trained network can be used in two ways. Both of the them work well, but they still have differences:

- Using parts of the network as a fixed feature extractor with its parameters untouched. The extractor can work together with non-neural techniques.
- Using parts of the parameters as the initial values of a new CNN [11], giving the opportunity to fine tune the transported parameters in another network.

In order to show the flexibility of this technique, the first way is used in this paper. Moreover, multiple datasets and multiply categories are used to investigate the performance of feature generalization. Here, a pseudocode of the basic version of the feature generalization is provided in Algorithm 2.

Algorithm 2 Feature Generalization + SVM Framework

1: **Input:** pre-trained CNN's parameters w_n CNN's layer id k for feature extraction, CNN+SVM training data X, CNN+SVM training labels Y CNN+SVM test data X', CNN+SVM test labels Y'
2: $x_0 := X$ ▷ extract training features
3: **for** $n := 1$ to k **do**
4: $x_n := f_n(x_{n-1}, w_n)$
5: $F := x_k$

  6:    $x_0 := X'$ ▷ extract test features

  7:    **for** $n := 1$ to k **do**

  8:    $x_n := f_n(x_{n-1}, w_n)$

  9:    $F' := x_k$

10:     m := svmtrain(F, Y)   ▷ train SVM

11:    $Y^{\wedge\prime} :=$ svmpredict(m, F')   ▷ test SVM

12:     accuracy := count if($Y^{\wedge\prime} = Y'$) / size(Y')   ▷ evaluate performance

13:    **return** accuracy

It is notable that a feature extractor learnt from expression images will be only helpful to handle facial images, since the deep features contain some image structures of facial organs. These image structures had been demonstrated by Deconv-Net technique [11]. Another thing should be pay attention to is possible that using such a nice feature extractor for sex classification or age fitting problems may be not the best choice. These features have weak capacity of discrimination in these problems. This phenomenon will be shown later.

EXPERIMENTS

In this section, two sets of experiments were carried out:

- Firstly, CNNs were used for classifying facial expression into six basic emotional expression categories, *i.e.*, anger, disgust, fear, happiness, sadness and surprise.
- Secondly, experiments on feature generalization had been done. The Support Vector Machine(SVM) classifiers converged rapidly with data obtained by CNN feature extractors, got good accuracies on test sets.

Datasets

CK-Regianini Dataset

The well-known CK facial expression dataset [13, 14] do not have complete emotion labels. CK-Regianini dataset which had been manually annotated by Regianini [20] was used instead. This dataset contains 97 subjects, and each subject has several expression sequences with resolution of 640^*490. There are totally 487 sequences. The last 4 frames of each sequence which contain stable emotional expression were chosen. There were totally 1948 static images with their basic emotional expression labels for our experiments.

In order to reduce the computation cost, a squared region of interest (top:12 bottom:431 left:110 right:530) was simply specified to crop images in advance. Thus useless background data were mainly removed. Small translational distortions still existed. Finally, the cropped images were resized to 96*96 (see Fig. **2(a)**).

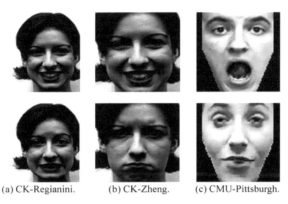

(a) CK-Regianini.   (b) CK-Zheng.   (c) CMU-Pittsburgh.

Fig. (2). Cropped samples.

As shown in Table **1**, these images were divided into training set, validation set and test set by 70%, 15% and 15% respectively. The validation set was just used for observing the progress of training, and selecting the best training snapshot to prevent overfitting. Finally, 1948 samples were divided into 3 sets and 6 categories.

Table 1. Subsets Division of CK-Regianini dataset.

Category	Size		
	Training	Validation	Test
Anger	216	46	46
Disgust	130	27	27
Fear	224	48	48
Happiness	290	61	61
Sadness	228	48	48

(Table 1) contd.....

| Surprise | 280 | 60 | 60 |
| Total | 1368 | 290 | 290 |

CK-Zheng Dataset

CK-Zheng dataset is cropped from CK dataset manually by Zheng *et al.* [19]. It contains 97 subjects. Each subject has several expression sequences with resolution of 96*96. The total count of the sequences is 415.

Similarly, the last 4 frames of each sequence were selected. 1660 static images were divided into training set, validation set and test set by 70%, 15% and 15% respectively.

CK-Zheng dataset and CK-Regianini datasets are basically identical except their cropping methods. Unlike CK-Regianini, all faces in the CK-Zheng dataset are registered carefully (see Fig. **2b**).

CMU-Pittsburgh dataset

CMU-Pittsburgh dataset [21] played an important role in the experiments of feature generalization. It consists of 463 facial expression images with resolution of 60*70. All these images had been carefully annotated and cropped, and the background had been totally removed.

In order to keep the dimensions same in all datasets, CMU-Pittsburgh dataset is additionally resized to 96*96 and kept its aspect ratio unchanged (see Fig. **2c**).

Experiments on CNN-based Facial Expression Classification

This series of experiments was designed for validating the performance of CNNs to solve facial expression classification problem.

Design

Alex-Net architecture was employed with its number of channels in the input layer modified for handling grayscale images. The size of mini-batch was defined as large as possible under the limitation of the memory. l_2 regularization with a weight decay parameter of 0.0005 was used here. Momentum technique was not used. Learning rate was set at 0.01, and it would be scaled by 0.9773 per 100 iterations.

Although, CK-Zheng dataset can be easily handled since it has already been well registered, It was used just for comparing our methods with conventional approaches which reported in Zheng's paper [19]. CK-Regianini dataset was also employed for examining the translational invariance property of the classifier. The classification accuracies were analyzed not only on entire sets but also on each sub-category (see Table **2** and Table **3**).

Table 2. Classification results on CK-Zheng dataset.

Category	Accuracy		
	Training	Validation	Test
Anger	100%	92.68%	97.56%
Disgust	100%	96.30%	100%
Fear	100%	100%	97.62%
Happiness	100%	100%	100%
Sadness	100%	97.44%	100%
Surprise	100%	97.96%	97.96%
Total	100%	97.58%	**98.79%**

Results and Analysis

Two networks were trained on CK-Zheng dataset and CK-Regianini dataset by the method we mentioned above, and converged at epoch 2673 and 1125 respectively. Accuracies of 98.79% and 98.62% on each test set were obtained. The accuracies on each sub-set and each sub-category are listed in Table **2** and Table **3**.

Table 3. Classification results on CK-Regianini dataset.

Category	Accuracy		
	Training	Validation	Test
Anger	100%	100%	100%
Disgust	100%	100%	96.30%

(Table 3) contd.....

Fear	100%	100%	95.83%
Happiness	100%	100%	100%
Sadness	100%	100%	97.92%
Surprise	100%	100%	100%
Total	100%	100%	**98.62%**

The results shown in Table **4** is much better than those reported in Zheng's paper [19]. In total, 4 classification errors occurred on each test set of CK-Zheng dataset and CK-Regianini dataset. The error images, actual labels and predicted labels of these cases are illustrated in Fig. **3**.

Table 4. Results of type I feature generalization (generalizing to different classifier).

Input Data of SVM	Dimension	Accuracy			Time
		Training	Validation	Test	
Layer 8 Features	1000	100%	98.97%	**96.90%**	0.6
Layer 7 Features	4096	100%	98.28%	95.86%	9
Layer 6 Features	4096	100%	96.21%	92.07%	36
Layer 5 Features	1024	100%	84.48%	82.07%	7
Raw Image	9216	100%	21.03%	21.03%	52
Layer 7&8 Features	5096	100%	97.24%	**95.17%**	13
Layer 6&8 Features	5096	100%	94.83%	92.07%	39
Layer 6&7 Features	8192	100%	93.79%	91.72%	70
Layer 6&7&8 Features	9192	100%	92.41%	91.03%	74

Fig. (3). Error cases of classification. Top:CK-Zheng. Bottom:CK-Regianini.

From Table **4** and Table **5**, the following observations can be obtained. The latter one achieved a closed performance to the former one in fewer training epochs. An obvious reason is that the CK-Regianini dataset contains larger facial regions than the CK-Zheng dataset. Moreover, another important reason is that CNNs have the capability to handle translational distortions in the CK-Regianini dataset. A robust classifier which has the property of translational invariance is valuable in engineering applications. For example, a target could be localized by means of classifying the sliding windows [22]. The reason why CNNs also take an essential part in solving the localization problem of ILSVRC is that CNNs have both the abilities of localization and classification which are discussed here.

Table 5. Results of type II feature generalization (generalizing to different classifier & data).

Input Data of SVM	Dimension	Accuracy			Time
		Training	Validation	Test	
Layer 8 Features	1000	62.92%	47.76%	50.75%	0.2
Layer 7 Features	4096	76.90%	46.27%	56.72%	2
Layer 6 Features	4096	98.18%	62.69%	**61.19%**	2
Layer 5 Features	1024	100%	29.85%	28.36%	0.3
Raw Image	9216	100%	20.90%	20.90%	3
Layer 5 & 6 Features	5120	100%	28.36%	26.87%	3
Layer 6 & 7 Features	8192	98.78%	56.72%	**59.70%**	4
Layer 5 & 6 & 7 Features	9216	100%	26.87%	26.87%	5

Experiments on Feature Generalization

Nowadays the research on feature generalization of CNNs is a hot issue. The activations of hidden layers can be considered as a kind of feature representation of the input data. Especially in deep neural networks, deep activations can be easily classified than the original data. Thus, CNNs can be flexibly used as feature extractors. Further research on feature generalization by experiments had been done.

Design

Feature generalization is a very flexible technique. The extractor can be used on different datasets, even different classification problem in which categories are totally different. Or use it in a more complicated problem which has a situation combining different classifiers, different datasets and different categories. For the convenience of our experiments, feature generalization are defined as 3 typical types as follows:

- Type I: Generalizing to a different classifier. A CNN feature extractor is learnt from CK-Regianini dataset. Then features are extracted on the same dataset. Finally an SVM classifier is used for training and testing with these features. This type is truly the most basic one.
- Type II: Generalizing to a different classifier and different data. A CNN feature extractor is learnt from CK-Regianini dataset. Then features are extracted on CMU-Pittsburgh dataset. Finally an SVM classifier is used for training and testing with these features. Two datasets are totally different except they all contain expressions. We hope to be able to extract reliable features no matter how they are located in any specific dataset.
- Type III: Generalizing to a different classifier and classification problems of different category. Sex labels are manually annotated on CK-Regianini dataset. Then a CNN is trained for the sex classification problem. Thus the CNN feature extractor is obtained, and used for extracting features on the same dataset. Finally an SVM classifier is used for training and testing with these features. We extremely hope to get a set of features from the extractor which may be useful for handling wide-ranging problems such as sex classification and expression classification here. It may be a challenge.

3 experiments were made separately for each type by following steps in Algorithm 2. The training procedure in the previous experiments was used to create pre-trained networks as feature extractors. Then these feature extractors were connected to SVM classifiers. Both CK-Regianini dataset and CMU-Pittsburgh dataset were used.

The number of samples in CMU-Pittsburgh dataset is quite small. This dataset was utilized just for proving that feature generalization could improve the performance on small dataset by using a feasible feature extractor learnt from a larger dataset.

Results and Analysis

The results of type I feature generalization are given in Table **4**. The SVM classifier got an accuracy of 96.90% by using features from layer 8 of the CNN. This accuracy rate is the best in single layer cases and combined layers cases. Also it is almost close to the one shown in Table **2** and **3**. We can infer from Table **4** that the performance goes higher and the training process goes faster by using deep features than using input data. On the contrary, shallow features are hard to be well classified. And big sizes of shallow features may also make the SVM training process slower. At worst, unacceptable large memory cost may lead to a failure of training. We attempted to combine features from layer 8 with features from layer 6 or 7, but lower performances were got. Features from layer 8 are dominant in this situation.

The results of type II feature generalization are listed in Table **5**. The SVM classifier got an accuracy of 61.19% by using features from layer 6 of the CNN. The poor accuracy rate is the best in single layer cases and combined layers cases. The best performance is not so nice, but comparing to the accuracy rate of 20.90% which obtained from the case of raw image, the performances increased by 1-2 times in the cases of deep layers. Using the extractor for the new dataset maybe not the best choice, but it is probably an valid one. Similar to type I feature generalization, performance cannot be improved by using features from combined layers in this case too.

Table 6. Results of type II feature generalization (generalizing to different classifier & categories).

Input Data of SVM	Dimension	Accuracy			Time
		Training	Validation	Test	
Layer 8 Features	1000	29.36%	28.18%	24.05%	4
Layer 7 Features	4096	39.02%	32.99%	32.30%	35
Layer 6 Features	4096	82.28%	61.86%	63.92%	26
Layer 5 Features	1024	99.71%	97.25%	**97.94%**	5
Raw Image	9216	100%	21.65%	15.46%	49
Layer 5&6 Features	10624	100%	87.29%	88.66%	88
Layer 6&7 Features	5120	99.71%	97.59%	**98.28%**	38
Layer 5&6&7 Features	14720	100%	87.29%	87.63%	130

The results of type III feature generalization are listed in Table **6**. The SVM classifier got an accuracy of 97.94% by using features from layer 6 of the CNN. It also got an accuracy of 98.28%with features from layer 5 and 6 of the CNN. Using features from combinations of multiple layer improved the performance this time. Similar to Table **5**, the best accuracy rate did not appear in the case of using features from the deepest layer but from a middle layer. The reason may be that, in all layers of a CNN, a layer close to the input layer contains low order features which could be generalized to all different problems (*e.g.* Gabor features in the 1st layer). However, low order features can be hardly separated than higher ones, so they are not the best choice. On the contrary, a layer close to the output layer contains high order features which may have functions for detecting specific targets. High order features are useful for specific problems, and cannot be generalized to other problems easily. So both are not the best choice for type III feature generalization. Optimal features sometimes appear in the middle of these hidden layers. The exact position can be determined by experiments. As shown in Table **6**, the performance is improved by combining features from different layers. But 6 more times of the SVM training time was paid as the price.

The advantages of feature generalization are concluded as follows:

- Firstly, SVM classifiers are not so helpful for us to classify high dimensional image data. However, the performance will be enhanced when a valid feature extractor is employed.
- Secondly, the training time of SVMs in these experiments is 0.6s, 2s and 5s respectively, which is far less than the time for retraining an entire CNN.

All these experiments show that CNNs are not only good classifiers for the facial expression problem, but also good feature extractors for similar problems with different classifiers, different data or different categories.

DISCUSSION

This paper applied CNNs to the problem of facial expression classification, and achieved accuracies rate of 98.79% and 98.62% on two datasets. Compared to the results of conventional approaches on the same dataset [19], ours is better. Three types of feature generalization were examined on similar problems with different classifiers, different data or different categories. These experiments confirmed the validity of the CNN feature extractors.

With the rapid development of CNNs, there are more and more topics on CNN-based expression classification which are needed to be studied, *e.g.*

- Using recurrent networks to solve the classification problem on image sequences. It will make better use of the information in the time domain.
- Optimizing network architecture and training parameters by hyperparameter optimization techniques.
- Localizing and classifying several facial expressions in one image simultaneously, depending on the multiple target detection function of CNNs.

CONFLICT OF INTEREST

The author confirms that author has no conflict of interest to declare for this publication.

ACKNOWLEDGEMENTS

This work is partially supported by National Natural Science Foundation of China under Grant Nos. 61420201, 61472187, 61373063, 61233011, 61125305, 61375007, and by National Basic Research Program of China under Grant No. 2014CB349303. Many thanks to Dr. Hao Zheng for sharing his previous works sincerely.

REFERENCES

[1]   D.G. Lowe, "Distinctive image features from scale-invariant key points", *Int. J. Comput. Vis.,* vol. 60, no. 2, pp. 91-110, 2004.
[http://dx.doi.org/10.1023/B:VISI.0000029664.99615.94]

[2]   N. Dalal, and B. Triggs, "Histograms of oriented gradients for human detection", In: *IEEE Computer Society Conference on Computer Vision and Pattern Recognition*, 2005, pp. 886-893.
[http://dx.doi.org/10.1109/CVPR.2005.177]

[3]   Y. LeCun, B. Boser, J.S. Denker, D. Henderson, and R.E. Howard, "W. Hubbard, and L. D. Jackel, "Backpropagation applied to handwritten zip code recognition", *Neural Comput.,* vol. 1, no. 4, pp. 541-551, 1989.
[http://dx.doi.org/10.1162/neco.1989.1.4.541]

[4]   Y. LeCun, L. Bottou, Y. Bengio, and P. Haffner, "Gradient-based learning applied to document

recognition", *Proceedings of the IEEE,* vol. 86, no. 11, pp. 2278-2324, 1998. [http://dx.doi.org/10.1109/5.726791]

[5]   V. Nair, and G. Hinton, "Rectified linear units improve restricted boltzmann machines", In: *The 27th International Conference on Machine Learning*, 2010, pp. 807-814.

[6]   K. Jarrett, K. Kavukcuoglu, M. Ranzato, and Y. LeCun, "What is the best multi-stage architecture for object recognition?", In: *IEEE 12th International Conference on Computer Vision*, 2009, pp. 2146-2153.
[http://dx.doi.org/10.1109/ICCV.2009.5459469]

[7]   A. Krizhevsky, I. Sutskever, and G.E. Hinton, "Imagenet classification with deep convolutional neural networks", In: *Advances in neural information processing systems.* 2012, pp. 1106-1114.

[8]   G.E. Hinton, N. Srivastava, A. Krizhevsky, I. Sutskever, and R.R. Salakhutdinov, "Improving neural networks by preventing coadaptation of feature detectors", *arXiv:1207.0580,* 2012.

[9]   D.C. Ciresan, U. Meier, J. Masci, L.M. Gambardella, and J. Schmidhuber, "High-performance neural networks for visual object classification", *arXiv:1102.0183,* 2011.

[10]   D. Ciresan, U. Meier, and J. Schmidhuber, "Multi-column deep neural networks for image classification", In: *IEEE Computer Society Conference on Computer Vision and Pattern Recognition*, 2012, pp. 3642-3646.
[http://dx.doi.org/10.1109/CVPR.2012.6248110]

[11]   M.D. Zeiler, and R. Fergus, "Visualizing and understanding convolutional networks", *Computer Vision – ECCV 2014. arXiv:1311. 2901,* 2011.

[12]   P. Ekman, and E. Friensen, *Facial Action Coding System(FACS): Manual.* Consulting Psychologists Press: Palo Alto, 1978.

[13]   T. Kanade, J.F. Cohn, and Y. Tian, "Comprehensive database for facial expression analysis", In: *Fourth IEEE International Conference on Automatic Face and Gesture Recognition*, 2000.
[http://dx.doi.org/10.1109/AFGR.2000.840611]

[14]   P. Lucey, J.F. Cohn, T. Kanade, J. Saragih, Z. Ambadar, and I. Matthews, "The extended cohn-kanade dataset (ck+): A complete dataset for action unit and emotion-specified expression", In: *IEEE Computer Society Conference on Computer Vision and Pattern Recognition*, 2010, pp. 94-101.
[http://dx.doi.org/10.1109/CVPRW.2010.5543262]

[15]   W. Friensen, and P. Ekman, *Emfacs-7: Emotional Facial Action Coding System.* Tech. Rep.: University of California at San Francisico, 1983.

[16]   J. Wang, L. Yin, X. Wei, and W. Sun, "3d facial expression recognition based on primitive surface feature distribution", In: *IEEE Computer Society Conference on Computer Vision and Pattern Recognition*, 2006, pp. 1399-1406.

[17]   T. Ahonen, A. Hadid, and M. Pietikäinen, "Face description with local binary patterns: application to face recognition", *IEEE Trans. Pattern Anal. Mach. Intell.,* vol. 28, no. 12, pp. 2037-2041, 2006.
[http://dx.doi.org/10.1109/TPAMI.2006.244] [PMID: 17108377]

[18]   W. Gu, C. Xiang, Y.V. Venkatesh, D. Huang, and H. Lin, "Facial expression recognition using radial encoding of local gabor features and classifier synthesis", *Pattern Recognit.,* vol. 45, no. 1, pp. 80-91, 2012.

[http://dx.doi.org/10.1016/j.patcog.2011.05.006]

[19]   H. Zheng, *"Facial expression analysis".* Tech. Rep: School of Computer Science and Engineering, Southeast University, Nanjing, China, 2014.

[20]   L. Regianini, "Manual annotations of facial fiducial points on the Cohn Kanade database", *lAIV laboratory, University of Milan, http://lipori.dsi.unimi.it/download.html,* 2009. Tech. Rep.

[21]   S. Dubuisson, F. Davoine, and M. Masson, "A solution for facial expression representation and recognition", *Signal Process. Image Commun.,* vol. 17, no. 9, pp. 657-673, 2002.
[http://dx.doi.org/10.1016/S0923-5965(02)00076-0]

[22]   C. Szegedy, A. Toshev, and D. Erhan, "Deep neural networks for object detection", In: *Advances in Neural Information Processing Systems.* 2013, pp. 2553-2561.

CHAPTER 2

Sparsity Preserving Projection Based Constrained Graph Embedding and Its Application to Face Recognition

Libo Weng[1,2], Zhong Jin[1,*], Fadi Dornaika[2,3]

[1] *School of Computer Science and Engineering, Nanjing University of Science and Technology, Nanjing, China*

[2] *Department of Computer Science and Artificial Intelligence, University of the Basque Country UPV/EHU, San Sebastian, Spain*

[3] *IKERBASQUE, Basque Foundation for Science, Bilbao, Spain*

Abstract: In this chapter, a novel semi-supervised dimensionality reduction algorithm is proposed, namely Sparsity Preserving Projection based Constrained Graph Embedding (SPP-CGE). Sparsity Preserving Projection (SPP) is an unsupervised dimensionality reduction method. It aims to preserve the sparse reconstructive relationship of the data obtained by solving a L_1 objective function. Label information is used as additional constraints for graph embedding in the SPP-CGE algorithm. In SPP-CGE, both the intrinsic structure and the label information of the data are used. In addition, to deal with new incoming samples, out-of-sample extension of SPP-CGE is also proposed. Promising experimental results on several popular face databases illustrate the effectiveness of the proposed method.

Keywords: Affinity matrix, Constrained graph embedding, Dimensionality reduction, Eigenvalue problem, Face recognition, Graph embedding, ISOMAP, Laplacian eigenmaps, Laplacian matrix, Linear discriminant analysis, Locality preserving projection, Locally linear embedding, Multidimensional scaling, Neighborhood preserving embedding, Principal component analysis, Projection matrix, Recognition rate, Semi-supervised learning, Sparse representation, Sparsity preserving projection.

---
* **Address to Corresponding Author Zhong Jin:** School of Computer Science and Engineering, Nanjing University of Science and Technology, Nanjing, China; Tel: +86 25 84303280 Ext. 3071; Fax: +86 25 84317235; E-mail: zhongjin@njust.edu.cn

INTRODUCTION

In many real world applications, such as face recognition and text categorization, the data is usually provided in high dimension space. Moreover, the labels of the original data are usually inadequate and it will spend expensive human labor to acquire the labels. To deal with this problem, semi-supervised dimensionality reduction methods can be used to project the data in the high-dimensional space into a space of fewer dimensions.

In the recent years, researchers have proposed a lot of methods for dimension reduction. Principal Component Analysis [1] (PCA) and Multidimensional Scaling [2] (MDS) are two classic linear unsupervised dimensionality reduction methods. Linear Discriminant Analysis [1] (LDA) is a supervised method. In 2000, Locally Linear Embedding [3] (LLE) and ISOMAP [4] were separately proposed in *science* which laid a foundation of manifold learning. Soon afterwards, M. Belkin *et al.* proposed Laplacian Eigenmaps [5] (LE). He *et al.* proposed both Locality Preserving Projection [6] (LPP), essentially a linearized version of LE, and Neighborhood Preserving Embedding [7] (NPE), a linearized version of LLE. LPP and NPE can be interpreted in a general graph embedding framework with different choices of graph structure.

Sparsity Preserving Projection [8 - 11] (SPP) is an unsupervised learning method. It can be considered as an extension to NPE since the latter has similar objective function. However, SPP utilises sparse representation to obtain the affinity matrix. We extend SPP to the semi-supervised case by integrating the idea of Constrained Graph Embedding [12] (CGE). CGE tries to project the data point with the same labels into one single point in the projection space by a constraint matrix. We propose a method called sparsity preserving projection based constrained graph embedding that can combine the benefits of both SPP and CGE. In SPP-CGE algorithm, the construction of affinity matrix is parameter-free, local structure is preserved and data points with the same label are projected into one point in the projection space.

Since SPP-CGE is essentially a nonlinear method, the projection matrix of SPP-CGE could not be obtained in a direct manner. A traditional way to deal with a new incoming sample is to re-perform the whole algorithm one package again which will be quite time-consuming. A simple way to obtain an approximate mapping matrix is presented to replace the unknown mapping function for data projection.

In this chapter, we propose a new semi-supervised method for dimensionality reduction named SPP-CGE. The chapter is organized as follows. Firstly, the related methods including LPP, NPE, SPP and CGE are introduced. Then, the proposed method and the out-of-sample extension are presented. Finally, some experimental results for face recognition on three databases: Yale [13, 14], ORL and PIE are given.

RELATED WORK

Some mathematical notations are listed and will be used in the next several sections. Let $\mathbf{X} = [\mathbf{x}_1, \mathbf{x}_2, \ldots, \mathbf{x}_n] \in R^{m \times n}$ be the data matrix, where n is the number of training samples and m is the dimension of each sample. Let $\mathbf{y} = [y_1, y_2, \ldots, y_n]^T$ be a one-dimensional map of $\mathbf{X}$. Under a linear projection $\mathbf{y}^T = \mathbf{p}^T \mathbf{X}$, each data point $\mathbf{x}_i$ in the input space R^m is mapped into $y_i = \mathbf{p}^T \mathbf{x}_i$ in the real line. Here, $\mathbf{p} \in R^m$ is a projection axis. Let $\mathbf{Y} \in R^{d \times n}$ be the data projections into a d dimensional space.

Locality Preserving Projection

LPP aims to preserve the local structure of the data by keeping two sample points close in the projection space when they are similar in the original space.

The reasonable criterion of LPP is to optimize the following objective function under some constraints:

$$\min_{\mathbf{p}} \sum_{i,j} (y_i - y_j)^2 W_{ij}, \tag{1}$$

where $\mathbf{W}$ is the affinity matrix associated with the data.

The way to define $\mathbf{W}$ can be alterable. One simple definition is as follows:

$$W_{ij} = \begin{cases} 1, & \mathbf{x}_i \in \delta_k(\mathbf{x}_j) \text{ or } \mathbf{x}_j \in \delta_k(\mathbf{x}_i), \\ 0, & \text{otherwise.} \end{cases} \tag{2}$$

where $\delta_k(\mathbf{x}_i)$ means a set of the k neighbors of $\mathbf{x}_i$.

Another way to define $\mathbf{W}$ is:

$$W_{ij} = exp(-\frac{\|\mathbf{x}_i - \mathbf{x}_j\|^2}{\sigma^2}). \tag{3}$$

where σ^2 is a parameter.

After some simple algebraic formulations, we obtain:

$$\sum_{i,j} (y_i - y_j)^2 W_{ij} = 2\mathbf{p}^T \mathbf{X} \mathbf{L} \mathbf{X}^T \mathbf{p}, \tag{4}$$

where $\mathbf{L} = \mathbf{D} - \mathbf{W}$ is the Laplacian matrix and $\mathbf{D}$ is a diagonal matrix with $D_{ii} = \sum_j W_{ij}$.

With the constraint $\mathbf{p}^T \mathbf{X} \mathbf{D} \mathbf{X}^T \mathbf{p} = 1$, Eq. (1) becomes:

$$\min_{\mathbf{p}} \frac{\mathbf{p}^T \mathbf{X} \mathbf{L} \mathbf{X}^T \mathbf{p}}{\mathbf{p}^T \mathbf{X} \mathbf{D} \mathbf{X}^T \mathbf{p}}. \tag{5}$$

The optimal $\mathbf{p}$ is given by solving the minimum eigenvalue problem:

$$\mathbf{X} \mathbf{L} \mathbf{X}^T \mathbf{p} = \lambda \mathbf{X} \mathbf{D} \mathbf{X}^T \mathbf{p}. \tag{6}$$

The eigenvectors $\mathbf{p}_1, \ldots, \mathbf{p}_d$ corresponding to the d smallest eigenvalues are then used as the columns of the projection matrix $\mathbf{P}$, *i.e.* $\mathbf{P} = [\mathbf{P}_1, \ldots, \mathbf{P}_d]$. The projected samples are obtained by $\mathbf{Y} = \mathbf{P}^T \mathbf{X}$.

Neighborhood Preserving Embedding

NPE also aims to preserve the local structure of the data, but the evaluation of affinity matrix and its objective function differs from that of LPP. NPE tries to keep the neighborhood representation in the projection space.

For each sample, local least squares approximation is used to obtain the representative coefficients by the k nearest neighbors. Let N denote the representative matrix which can be obtained by minimizing the following cost function:

$$\phi(\mathbf{N}) = \sum_{\mathbf{x}_j \in \delta_k(\mathbf{x}_i)} \|\mathbf{x}_i - \sum_j N_{ij}\mathbf{x}_j\|^2. \tag{7}$$

Let $y_i = \mathbf{p}^{\mathrm{T}} \mathbf{x}_i$ be the one dimension projection of $\mathbf{x}_i$. The problem of NPE is given by:

$$\min_{\mathbf{P}} \sum_i (y_i - \sum_j N_{ij} y_j)^2. \tag{8}$$

With constraint $\mathbf{p}^{\mathrm{T}} \mathbf{X}\mathbf{X}^{\mathrm{T}} \mathbf{p} = 1$, Eq. (8) becomes:

$$\min_{\mathbf{P}} \frac{\mathbf{p}^T \mathbf{X}\mathbf{M}\mathbf{X}^T \mathbf{p}}{\mathbf{p}^T \mathbf{X}\mathbf{X}^T \mathbf{p}}, \tag{9}$$

where $\mathbf{M} = \mathbf{I} - \mathbf{N} - \mathbf{N}^{\mathrm{T}} + \mathbf{N}^{\mathrm{T}}\mathbf{N}$ and $\mathbf{I}$ is the identity matrix.

The corresponding minimum eigenvalue problem is given by:

$$\mathbf{X}\mathbf{L}\mathbf{X}^T \mathbf{p} = \lambda \mathbf{X}\mathbf{X}^T \mathbf{p}. \tag{10}$$

The eigenvectors $\mathbf{p}_1, \ldots, \mathbf{p}_d$ corresponding to the d smallest eigenvalues are the columns of the sought linear transform $\mathbf{P}$, *i.e.* $\mathbf{P} = [\mathbf{p}_1, \ldots, \mathbf{p}_d]$. The projected samples are obtained by $\mathbf{Y} = \mathbf{P}^{\mathrm{T}}\mathbf{X}$.

Sparsity Preserving Projection

SPP is similar to NPE, using sparse representation instead of the linear representation of k nearest neighbors to get the weight matrix. For $\mathbf{x}_i$, the representative coefficients are obtained by solving a L_1 problem:

$$\min_{\mathbf{s}_i} \|\mathbf{s}_i\|_1, \text{ s.t. } \mathbf{x}_i = \mathbf{X}\mathbf{s}_i, \tag{11}$$

where $\mathbf{s}_i = [s_{i1}, \ldots, s_{i(i-1)}, 0, s_{i(i+1)}, \ldots, s_{in}]$

The problem of SPP is:

$$\min_{\mathbf{p}} \sum_i (\mathbf{p}^T \mathbf{x}_i - \mathbf{p}^T \mathbf{X} \mathbf{s}_i)^2. \tag{12}$$

With the constraint $\mathbf{p}^T \mathbf{X} \mathbf{X}^T \mathbf{p} = 1$, Eq. (12) becomes:

$$\max_{\mathbf{p}} \frac{\mathbf{p}^T \mathbf{X} \tilde{\mathbf{S}} \mathbf{X}^T \mathbf{p}}{\mathbf{p}^T \mathbf{X} \mathbf{X}^T \mathbf{p}}, \tag{13}$$

where $\tilde{\mathbf{S}} = \mathbf{S} + \mathbf{S}^T - \mathbf{S}^T \mathbf{S}$, and $\mathbf{S} = [\mathbf{s}_1, \ldots, \mathbf{s}_n]^T$.

The corresponding eigenvalue problem is:

$$\mathbf{X} \tilde{\mathbf{S}} \mathbf{X}^T \mathbf{p} = \lambda \mathbf{X} \mathbf{X}^T \mathbf{p}. \tag{14}$$

The eigenvectors $\mathbf{p}_1, \ldots, \mathbf{p}_d$ corresponding to the d smallest eigenvalues are then the columns of the sought linear transform. We have $\mathbf{P} = [\mathbf{p}_1, \ldots, \mathbf{p}_d]$, and $\mathbf{Y} = \mathbf{P}^T \mathbf{X}$.

Constrained Graph Embedding

CGE uses the label information as additional constraints which maps the samples with a same label to one point in the projection space. We assume that the first l samples are with labels from c classes.

In the projection space, a constraint matrix $\mathbf{U}$ is used to keep the samples with a same label in one point. The definition of $\mathbf{U}$ is as follows:

$$\mathbf{U} = \begin{pmatrix} \mathbf{J} & 0 \\ 0 & \mathbf{I}_{n-l} \end{pmatrix} \in \mathbb{R}^{n \times (c+(n-l))}, \tag{15}$$

where the *i*-th row of $\mathbf{J}$ is a indictor vector of $\mathbf{x}_i$:

$$J_{ij} = \begin{cases} 1, & \text{if } \mathbf{x}_i \text{ is labeled from class } j, \\ 0, & \text{otherwise}, \end{cases} \tag{16}$$

where $j = 1,\ldots, c$.

An auxiliary vector $\mathbf{z}$ is adopted to implement the constraint:

$$\mathbf{y} = \mathbf{U}\mathbf{z}, \tag{17}$$

with the above constraint, it is clearly to see that if $\mathbf{x}_i$ and $\mathbf{x}_j$ share the same label, then $y_i = y_j$.

With simple algebraic formulation, we have:

$$\sum_{i,j} (y_i - y_j)^2 W_{ij} = \mathbf{y}^T \mathbf{L} \mathbf{y} = \mathbf{z}^T \mathbf{U}^T \mathbf{L} \mathbf{U} \mathbf{z}, \tag{18}$$

and

$$\mathbf{y}^T \mathbf{D} \mathbf{y} = \mathbf{z}^T \mathbf{U}^T \mathbf{D} \mathbf{U} \mathbf{z}, \tag{19}$$

where the affinity matrix $\mathbf{W}$ is simply calculated as in Eq. (2), $\mathbf{L} = \mathbf{D} - \mathbf{W}$ and $\mathbf{D} = diag(D_{11}, \ldots, D_{nn})$, $D_{ii} = \sum_j W_{ij}$.

The problem of CGE is as follows:

$$\min_{\mathbf{z}} \mathbf{z}^T \mathbf{U}^T \mathbf{L} \mathbf{U} \mathbf{z}, \text{ s.t. } \mathbf{z}^T \mathbf{U}^T \mathbf{D} \mathbf{U} \mathbf{z} = 1. \tag{20}$$

The optimal vector $\mathbf{z}$ is given by the minimum eigenvalue solution to the generalized eigenvalue problem:

$$\mathbf{U}^T \mathbf{L} \mathbf{U} \mathbf{z} = \lambda \mathbf{U}^T \mathbf{D} \mathbf{U} \mathbf{z}. \tag{21}$$

The eigenvectors $\mathbf{z}_1, \ldots, \mathbf{z}_d$ corresponding to the d smallest eigenvalues, yield the auxiliary matrix $\mathbf{Z} = [\mathbf{z}_1, \ldots, \mathbf{z}_d]$. We have $\mathbf{Y} = (\mathbf{U}\mathbf{Z})^T$. $\mathbf{Y}$ is a $d \times n$ matrix and it represents the data projection of $\mathbf{X}$ in d-dimensional space.

SPP BASED CONSTRAINED GRAPH EMBEDDING

In the section, we propose a SPP based Constrained Graph Embedding Based (SPP-CGE). In SPP-CGE, the construction of the affinity matrix is parameterless and the local structure is preserved in the projection space. In addition, the label constraint is also integrated in the algorithm. This constraint merges the sample points with the same label together in the projection space.

SPP-CGE

The affinity matrix is obtained by sparse representation as showed in Eq. (11). In this way, the affinity matrix can be obtained without setting any parameters.

We also want to keep the sparse representation in the projection space. The problem of SPP-CGE is defined as follows:

$$\min_{\mathbf{y}} \sum_i (y_i - \mathbf{y}^T \mathbf{s}_i)^2. \tag{22}$$

Then the same defined constraint matrix $\mathbf{U}$ is used to constraint the projection sample points, *i.e.* let $\mathbf{y} = \mathbf{U}\mathbf{z}$. Then, Eq. (22) becomes:

$$\min_{\mathbf{z}} \sum_i (\mathbf{z}^T \mathbf{U}^T \mathbf{e}_i - \mathbf{z}^T \mathbf{U}^T \mathbf{s}_i)^2, \tag{23}$$

where the i-th item of $\mathbf{e}_i$ is 1, 0 otherwise.

With simple algebraic manipulations, the objective function can be rewritten as:

$$\sum_i (\mathbf{z}^T\mathbf{U}^T\mathbf{e}_i - \mathbf{z}^T\mathbf{U}^T\mathbf{s}_i)^2 = \mathbf{z}^T\mathbf{U}^T(\mathbf{I} - \mathbf{S} - \mathbf{S}^T + \mathbf{S}^T\mathbf{S})\mathbf{U}\mathbf{z} = \mathbf{z}^T\mathbf{U}^T\mathbf{U}\mathbf{z} - \mathbf{z}^T\mathbf{U}^T\tilde{\mathbf{S}}\mathbf{U}\mathbf{z}, \quad (24)$$

where $\tilde{\mathbf{S}} = \mathbf{S} + \mathbf{S}^T\text{-}\mathbf{S}^T\mathbf{S}$.

With the constraint $\mathbf{z}^T\,\mathbf{U}^T\,\mathbf{U}\mathbf{z} = 1$, the objective function Eq. (24) can be re-casted into:

$$\max_{\mathbf{z}} \frac{\mathbf{z}^T\mathbf{U}^T\tilde{\mathbf{S}}\mathbf{U}\mathbf{z}}{\mathbf{z}^T\mathbf{U}^T\mathbf{U}\mathbf{z}}. \qquad (25)$$

The optimal vector $\mathbf{z}$ is given by the maximum eigenvalue solution to the following generalized eigenvalue problem:

$$\mathbf{U}^T\tilde{\mathbf{S}}\mathbf{U}\mathbf{z} = \lambda\mathbf{U}^T\mathbf{U}\mathbf{z}. \qquad (26)$$

The eigenvectors $\mathbf{z}_1, \ldots, \mathbf{z}_d$ corresponding to the d largest eigenvalues, yield the auxiliary matrix $\mathbf{Z} = [\mathbf{z}_1, \ldots, \mathbf{z}_d]$. The data projections of $\mathbf{X}$ in the d-dimensional space is given by:

$$\mathbf{Y} = (\mathbf{U}\mathbf{Z})^T. \qquad (27)$$

Out-of-Sample Extension

The projection matrix of SPP-CGE could not be obtained directly since SPP-CGE provides a nonlinear projection. $\mathbf{Y}$ is the obtained nonlinear projection of the data $\mathbf{X}$. The traditional way to deal with a new incoming sample is to re-perform the whole algorithm again which will be time-consuming.

We assume a linear projection function $\mathbf{y}(\mathbf{x}) = \mathbf{P}^T\,\mathbf{x}$ to approximate the unobtainable original non-linear projection, where $\mathbf{P} = [\mathbf{p}_1, \ldots, \mathbf{p}_d]$. One simple idea to calculate the approximate projection matrix $\mathbf{P}$ is to fit the following function which minimizes the least square error on the existing samples.

$$\mathbf{P} = \arg\min_{\mathbf{P}} \left(\|\mathbf{P}^T\mathbf{X} - \mathbf{Y}\|^2 + \gamma\,\|\mathbf{P}\|^2 \right). \qquad (28)$$

where γ is a positive balance parameter that controls the regularization.

By vanishing the the derivative of the right side w.r.t. $\mathbf{P}$, the optimal $\mathbf{P}$ can be obtained as:

$$\mathbf{P} = (\mathbf{XX}^T + \gamma\mathbf{I})^{-1}\mathbf{XY}^T. \tag{29}$$

For a new incoming sample $\mathbf{x}_{\text{test}}$, $\mathbf{y}_{\text{test}} = \mathbf{P}^{\text{T}}\,\mathbf{x}_{\text{test}}$ is regarded as its approximate projection point in the d-dimensional space.

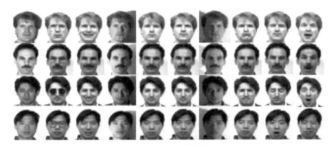

(a) 40 images in Yale.

(b) 40 images in ORL.

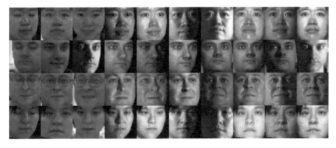

(c) 40 images in PIE.

Fig. (1). Images from the three databases.

EXPERIMENTAL RESULTS

In this section, we evaluate the proposed algorithm on three real face databases: Yale, ORL and PIE. Fig. (**1**) shows some original images from the three databases.

Yale: [1] This database contains 165 face images from 15 people and each person has 11 images. We resize the images to 32×32 for processing.

ORL: [2] This database contains 400 face images from 40 people and each person has 10 images. The size of the original image is 92×112. We resize the images to 32×32 for processing.

PIE: [3] This database contains 1926 images from 68 individuals. The images are resized to 32×32 for processing.

For these databases, grey level images are used. We select the first 50% of the images of each individual as training set, and the remaining for test. In the training set, part of the images are labeled as additional information in different percentages. After dimensionality reduction, nearest neighbor classifier is used for classification on the unlabeled train samples and on the test samples.

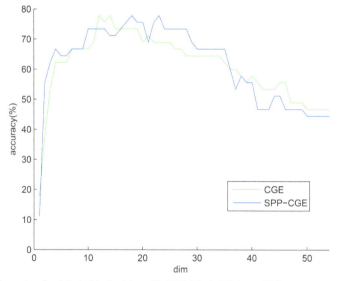

Fig. (2). Recognition rate of unlabeled train data with 20% labeled data on Yale.

Fig. (**2**) shows the recognition rate of the unlabeled train data with 20% labeled data on Yale. In general, the proposed method outperforms the CGE method for all the range of reduced dimension and they have almost the same rate at the peak point.

Fig. (**3**) illustrates the recognition rate of the unlabeled train data with 20% labeled data on ORL. The proposed algorithm outperforms CGE under almost the whole range of the reduced dimension.

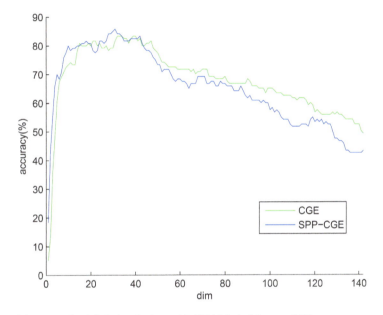

Fig. (3). Recognition rate of unlabeled train data with 20% labeled data on ORL.

Fig. (**4**) shows the recognition rate of the unlabeled training data with 20% labeled data on PIE. In general, the proposed method outperforms the CGE method.

Table **1**, **2** and **3** show the best recognition rates among the whole range of reduced dimension on Yale, ORL and PIE respectively. In general, 30% labeled samples leads to good results on both unlabeled training data and test data which indicates more label information makes a contribution to better recognition rate. As shown in Table **1-3**, the proposed method results in a better recognition rate in both unlabeled train data and the test data on these three databases.

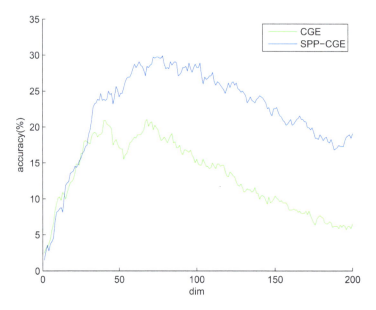

Fig. (4). Recognition rate of unlabeled train data with 20% labeled data on PIE.

Table 1. Recognition rates (%) on Yale.

Methods	Labeled data (20%)		Labeled data (30%)	
	Unlabeled train data (30%)	Test data (50%)	Unlabeled train data (20%)	Test data (50%)
LPP	71.1 (15)	91.6 (41)	**96.6** (15)	93.0 (41)
SPP	71.1 (54)	80.5 (54)	76.6 (37)	80.5 (54)
CGE	77.7 (14)	88.8 (17)	**96.6** (11)	95.8 (12)
SPP-CGE	**77.7** (18)	**95.8** (15)	**96.6** (8)	**97.2** (14)

Table 2. Recognition rates (%) on ORL.

Methods	Labeled data (20%)		Labeled data (30%)	
	Unlabeled train data (30%)	Test data (50%)	Unlabeled train data (20%)	Test data (50%)
LPP	75.8 (22)	**66.5** (35)	**82.5** (57)	68.0 (95)
SPP	48.3 (124)	55.0 (142)	48.3 (124)	60.5 (70)
CGE	83.3 (32)	56.0 (35)	**97.5** (34)	70.0 (40)

(Table 2) contd.....

Methods	Labeled data (20%)		Labeled data (30%)	
	Unlabeled train data (30%)	Test data (50%)	Unlabeled train data (20%)	Test data (50%)
SPP-CGE	85.8 (31)	62.0 (120)	**97.5** (42)	**74.4** (51)

Table 3. Recognition rates (%) on PIE.

Methods	Labeled data (20%)		Labeled data (30%)	
	Unlabeled train data (30%)	Test data (50%)	Unlabeled train data (20%)	Test data (50%)
LPP	18.3 (91)	17.2 (61)	45.2 (182)	26.9 (152)
SPP	22.5 (131)	**36.0** (306)	36.7 (237)	42.4 (155)
CGE	21.0 (68)	21.7 (72)	37.9 (52)	37.5 (44)
SPP-CGE	**30.5** (292)	34.9 (74)	**50.5** (61)	**52.4** (284)

CONCLUSION

In this chapter, a semi-supervised dimensionality reduction method named sparsity preserving projection based constrained graph embedding is proposed. The proposed algorithm uses the idea of SPP, utilizing sparse representation in the observing space for constraints in the projection space. At the same time, to make full use of the label information, the idea of constraint matrix $\mathbf{U}$ to project sample points sharing the same label into one point in CGE method is adopted for further constraining in the projection space.

According to the experimental results, the proposed method outperforms the Constrained Graph Embedding method on several databases. This improvement was significant for challenging face databases. In the experiment, simple color feature is used. Future work may investigate the use of several image descriptors that will be the input of the proposed semi-supervised learning algorithm. The out-of-sample extension may not perform well on some databases, but it is useful to classify a new sample in a simple and efficient way. Thus, future work may investigate enhancing the out-of-sample extension *via* more flexible schemes.

NOTES

[1]http://vision.ucsd.edu/content/yale-face-database

[2]http://www.cl.cam.ac.uk/research/dtg/attarchive/facedatabase.html

[3]http://vasc.ri.cmu.edu/idb/html/face/index.html

CONFLICT OF INTEREST

The author confirms that author has no conflict of interest to declare for this publication.

ACKNOWLEDGEMENTS

This work is partially supported by National Natural Science Foundation of China under Grant Nos. 61420201, 61472187, 61233011, 61125305, 61375007, 61220301, and by National Basic Research Program of China under Grant No. 2014CB349303.

REFERENCES

[1] R.O. Duda, P.E. Hart, and D.G. Stork, *Pattern classification..* John Wiley & Sons, 2012.

[2] I. Borg, and P.J. Groenen, *Modern multidimensional scaling: Theory and applications.* Springer Science & Business Media, 2005.

[3] S.T. Roweis, and L.K. Saul, "Nonlinear dimensionality reduction by locally linear embedding", *Science,* vol. 290, no. 5500, pp. 2323-2326, 2000.
[http://dx.doi.org/10.1126/science.290.5500.2323] [PMID: 11125150]

[4] J.B. Tenenbaum, V. de Silva, and J.C. Langford, "A global geometric framework for nonlinear dimensionality reduction", *Science,* vol. 290, no. 5500, pp. 2319-2323, 2000.
[http://dx.doi.org/10.1126/science.290.5500.2319] [PMID: 11125149]

[5] M. Belkin, and P. Niyogi, "Laplacian eigenmaps for dimensionality reduction and data representation", *Neural Comput,* vol. 15, no. 6, pp. 1373-1396, 2003.
[http://dx.doi.org/10.1162/089976603321780317]

[6] X. He, and P. Niyogi, "Locality preserving projections", *Neural Information Processing Systems,* vol. 16, pp. 234-241, 2003.

[7] X. He, D. Cai, S. Yan, and H-J. Zhang, "Neighborhood preserving embedding", In: *Tenth IEEE International Conference on Computer Vision,* vol. 2. IEEE Computer Society: Washington, DC, USA, 2005, pp. 1208-1213.

[8] L. Qiao, S. Chen, and X. Tan, "Sparsity preserving projections with applications to face recognition",

Pattern Recognit., vol. 43, no. 1, pp. 331-341, 2010.
[http://dx.doi.org/10.1016/j.patcog.2009.05.005]

[9]   X. Song, L. Jiao, S. Yang, X. Zhang, and F. Shang, "Sparse coding and classifier ensemble based multi-instance learning for image categorization", *Signal Process.,* vol. 93, no. 1, pp. 1-11, 2013.
[http://dx.doi.org/10.1016/j.sigpro.2012.07.029]

[10]   H. Cheng, Z. Liu, L. Yang, and X. Chen, "Sparse representation and learning in visual recognition: theory and applications", *Signal Process.,* vol. 93, no. 6, pp. 1408-1425, 2013.
[http://dx.doi.org/10.1016/j.sigpro.2012.09.011]

[11]   J. Yang, L. Zhang, Y. Xu, and J-y. Yang, "Beyond sparsity: The role of l 1-optimizer in pattern classification", *Pattern Recognit.,* vol. 45, no. 3, pp. 1104-1118, 2012.
[http://dx.doi.org/10.1016/j.patcog.2011.08.022]

[12]   X. He, M. Ji, and H. Bao, "Graph embedding with constraints", In: *International Joint Conference on Artificial Intelligence,* vol. 9. IEEE Computer Society: Washington, DC, USA, 2009, pp. 1065-1070.

[13]   O. Arandjelovic, "Gradient edge map features for frontal face recognition under extreme illumination changes", In: *Proceedings of the British machine vision association conference.* BMVA, 2012, pp. 1-11.

[14]   W. Chen, M.J. Er, and S. Wu, "Illumination compensation and normalization for robust face recognition using discrete cosine transform in logarithm domain", *IEEE Trans. Syst. Man Cybern. B Cybern.,* vol. 36, no. 2, pp. 458-466, 2006.
[http://dx.doi.org/10.1109/TSMCB.2005.857353] [PMID: 16602604]

CHAPTER 3

Face Recognition Using Exponential Local Discriminant Embedding

Alireza Bosaghzadeh[1], Fadi Dornaika[1,2,*]

[1] *University of the Basque Country, Manuel Lardizabal, 1, 20018, San Sebastian, Spain*

[2] *IKERBASQUE, Basque Foundation for Science, Bilbao, Spain*

Abstract: Local Discriminant Embedding (LDE) was recently proposed to overcome some limitations of the global Linear Discriminant Analysis (LDA) method. Whenever a small training data set is used, LDE cannot directly be applied to high-dimensional data. This case is the so-called small-sample-size (SSS) problem. The classic solution to this problem was applying dimensionality reduction on the raw data (*e.g.*, using Principal Component Analysis (PCA)). This chapter introduces a novel discriminant technique called "Exponential Local Discriminant Embedding" (ELDE). The proposed ELDE can be seen as an extension of LDE framework in two directions. Firstly, the proposed framework overcomes the SSS problem without discarding the discriminant information that was contained in the null space of the locality preserving scatter matrices associated with LDE. Secondly, the proposed ELDE is equivalent to transforming original data into a new space by distance diffusion mapping (similar to Kernel-based non-linear mapping), and then, LDE is applied in such a new space. As a result of diffusion mapping, the margin between samples belonging to different classes is enlarged, which is helpful in improving classification accuracy. The experiments are conducted on four public face databases, Extended Yale, PF01, PIE and FERET. The results show that the performances of the proposed ELDE are better than those of LDE and many state-of-the-art discriminant analysis techniques.

Keywords: Complete Kernel Fisher discriminant method, Distance diffusion mapping, Distance metric learning, Exponential discriminant analysis, Exponential locality preserving projections, Face recognition, Feature extraction, Generalized eigenvectors, Intrinsic graph, Kernel Fisher discriminant analysis, Kernel Principal component analysis, Linear discriminant analysis, Local discriminant embedding, Matrix exponential, Penalty graph, Principal component

* **Address to Corresponding Author Fadi Dornaika:** University of the Basque Country, Manuel Lardizabal, 1, 20018 San Sebastian, Spain; Tel: +34 943018034; Fax: +34 943 015590; E-mail: fadi.dornaika@ehu.es

analysis, Regularization, Regularized Kernel discriminant analysis, Singular matrix, Small sample size problem.

INTRODUCTION

In most computer vision and pattern recognition problems, the large number of sensory inputs, such as images and videos, are computationally challenging to analyze. In such cases it is desirable to reduce the dimensionality of the data while preserving the original information in the data distribution, allowing for more efficient learning and inference [1 - 4]. There are two main reasons for estimating a low-dimensional representation of high-dimensional data: reducing mea-surement cost of further data analysis and beating the curse of dimensionality. The dimensionality reduction can be achieved either by feature extraction or feature selection. Feature extraction (manifold learning) refers to methods that create a set of new features based on transformations and/or combinations of the original features, while feature selection methods select the most representative and relevant subset from the original feature set. Feature extraction methods can be classified into two main classes: i) linear methods; and ii) non-linear methods. Recently, manifold learning theory has received a lot of attention by researchers and practitioners. Exploiting the findings of manifold learning theory has led to many progresses in face recognition which is known to be a difficult problem in the domain of computer vision [5 - 7].

The non-linear methods such as Locally Linear Embedding (LLE) [8] and Laplacian Eigenmaps [9] focus on preserving the local structures. Isomap [10] is a non-linear projection method that globally preserves the data. It also attempts to preserve the geodesic distances between samples.

The linear techniques have been increasingly important in pattern recognition [2, 11 - 14] since they permit a relatively simple mapping of data onto a lower-dimensional subspace, leading to simple and computationally efficient classification strategies. The classical linear embedding methods (*e.g.*, Principal Component Analysis (PCA), Linear Discriminant Analysis (LDA), and Locally LDA [15] are demonstrated to be computationally efficient and suitable for practical applications, such as pattern classification and visual recognition. PCA projects the samples along the directions of maximal variances and aims to preserve the Euclidean distances between the samples. Unlike PCA which is unsupervised, Linear Discriminant Analysis (LDA) is a supervised technique. One limitation of PCA and LDA is that they only see the linear global Euclidean structure.

In addition to the Linear Discriminant Analysis (LDA) technique and its variants [16 - 18], there is recently a lot of interests in graph-based linear dimensionality reduction. Many dimensionality reduction techniques can be derived from a graph whose nodes represent the data samples and whose edges quantify the similarity among pairs of samples [19, 20]. Recently proposed methods attempt to linearize some non-linear embedding techniques. This linearization is obtained by forcing the mapping to be explicit, *i.e.*, performing the mapping by a projection matrix. For example, Locality Preserving Projection (LPP) [21 - 23] and Neighborhood Preserving Embedding (NPE) [21] can be seen as linearized versions of LE and LLE, respectively. The main advantage of the linearized embedding techniques is that the mapping is defined everywhere in the original space. Some researchers tried to remedy to the global nature of the linear methods (*e.g.*, PCA, LDA and LPP) by proposing localized models [24]. In this work, localized PCA, LDA, or LPP models are built using the neighbors of a query sample. The authors have shown that the obtained localized linear models can outperform the global models for face recognition and coarse head pose estimation problems. In [25], the authors have extended the LPP to the supervised case by adapting the entries of the similarity matrix according to the labels of the sample pair. In [26], the authors have proposed an enhanced supervised variant of LPP. The affinity matrix weights are modified in order to take into account label information as well as the similarities between pairs of samples. Moreover, the optimized criterion integrates uncorrelation and orthogonality constraints. In [27], the authors assessed the performance of the quotient and difference criteria used in LDA.

They also proposed a unified criterion that combines Quotient-LDA and Difference-LDA criteria.

In [28], the authors have proposed a discriminant method called Average Neighborhood Margin Maximization (ANMM). It associates to every sample a margin that is set to the difference between the average distance to heterogeneous neighbors and the average distance to the homogeneous neighbors. The linear transform is then derived by maximizing the sum of the margins in the embedded space. In addition to the above methods, distance metric learning algorithms (*e.g.*, [29, 30]) attempt to directly estimate an induced Mahalanobis distance over the samples. In essence, these methods provide a linear transform since the Euclidean distance in the embedded space is equal to the Mahalanobis distance in the original space. Most of the proposed solutions for estimating the Mahalanobis matrix are not given in closed form. They are iterative and computationally expensive.

Local Discriminant Embedding (LDE) [31] is known as a powerful tool for discriminant analysis that is proposed to overcome some limitations of the global Linear Discriminant Analysis (LDA) method. It extends the concept of LDA to perform local discrimination. In the case of a small training data set, however, LDE cannot directly be applied to high-dimensional data. This case is the so-called small sample size (SSS) problem which occurs when the number of samples is less than the feature dimension. The SSS problem very often occurs when dealing with visual object recognition tasks including the face recognition problem. The classical solution to this problem was applying dimensionality reduction on the raw data (*e.g.*, using PCA).

Contribution and Related Work

In this chapter, we introduce a novel discriminant technique called "Exponential Local Discriminant Embedding" (ELDE). The proposed ELDE can be seen as an extension of LDE framework in two directions. Firstly, the proposed framework overcomes the SSS problem without discarding the discriminant information that was contained in the null space of the locality preserving scatter matrices associated with LDE. Secondly, the proposed ELDE is equivalent to transforming original data into a new space by distance diffusion mapping (similar to Kernel-based non-linear mapping), and then, LDE is applied in such a new space. As a result of diffusion mapping, the margin between samples belonging to different classes is enlarged, which is helpful in improving classification accuracy.

The use of matrix exponential for data embedding was used in two recent works [23, 32]. In [23], the authors propose Exponential Discriminant Analysis (EDA) method that uses the exponential of the global within-class and between class scatter matrices. In [32], the authors propose Exponential Locality Preserving Projections (ELPP). The EDA method can solve the SSS problem but it still inherits the global nature of LDA in the sense that it ignores the local structures of data. Thus, the performance of EDA may not be optimal. The proposed ELPP also solves the SSS problem but it is an un-supervised technique that does not exploit the label information. The resulting learning based on ELPP cannot properly model underlying structure and characteristics of different classes. In contrast, our proposed ELDE is built upon a local discriminant technique, and therefore able to overcome all limitations of EDA, ELPP, and LDE.

The use of Kernels in the frameworks of machine learning [33] and linear embedding techniques was first introduced in the 90's. Subsequent research saw the development of a series of Kernel Fisher Discriminant Analysis (KFD) algorithms (a Kernelized version of the classical LDA). Baudat *et al.* [34] extends the original KFD to deal with a multi-class classification problem. Lu *et al.* [18] generalized Direct LDA (DLDA) [35] using the idea of kernels and presented kernel direct discriminant analysis (KDDA). Their method was demonstrated effective for face recognition, but, as a non-linear version of DLDA, KDDA unavoidably suffers the weakness of DLDA in the sense that it overlooked the regular information provided by the non-null space of the within-class scatter matrix [35] whenever the SSS problem occurs. Yang *et al.* [36] proposed a Complete Kernel Fisher Discriminant method. The implemented method was intended to perform discriminant analysis in double discriminant subspaces: regular and irregular associated with the within-class scatter matrix after KPCA projection.

Because of its ability to extract the most discriminatory non-linear features, KFD and its variants have been found to be very effective in many real-world applications. Although the Kernelized versions can give better results than the linear discriminant methods, the selection of the Kernel type is still an open problem. Furthermore, some KFD methods have many parameters that should be tuned in advance (*e.g.*, the Complete Kernel Fisher Discriminant method [36]).

REVIEW OF LOCAL DISCRIMINANT EMBEDDING (LDE)

This section briefly presents the LDE method [31]. It should be noticed that the Marginal Fisher Analysis (MFA) method [20] and the LDE method are essentially the same.

In [37], the authors proposed another variant of LDE by using a difference criterion instead of a quotient. [38] proposes a variant of LDE in which the similarity between samples is depending on the relative angle instead of the Euclidean distance. In the sequel, capital bold letters denote matrices and small bold letters denote vectors.

Intrinsic Graph and Penalty Graph

The objective of LDE is to estimate a linear mapping that simultaneously maximizes the local margin between heterogeneous samples and pushes the homogeneous samples closer to each other. The expected effect of LDE framework on data is illustrated in Fig. (1). We assume that we have a set of N labeled samples $\{\mathbf{x}_i\}_{i=1}^N \subset \mathbf{R}^D$. In order to discover both geometrical and discriminant structure of the data manifold, two graphs are built: the within class graph G_w(intrinsic graph) and between-class graph G_b(penalty). Let $l(\mathbf{x}_i)$ be the class label of $\mathbf{x}_i$. For each data sample $\mathbf{x}_i$, two subsets, $N_w(\mathbf{x}_i)$ and $N_b(\mathbf{x}_i)$ are generated. $N_w(\mathbf{x}_i)$ contains the neighbors sharing the same label with $\mathbf{x}_i$, while $N_b(\mathbf{x}_i)$ contains the neighbors having different labels. One simple possible way to compute these two sets of neighbors associated with the local sample is the use of two nearest neighbor graphs: one nearest neighbor graph for homogeneous samples (parameterized by K_1) and one nearest neighbor graph for heterogeneous samples (parameterized by K_2). Note that K_1 and K_2 can be different and chosen with empirical values.

Each of the graphs mentioned before, G_w and G_b, is characterized by its corresponding affinity (weight) matrix $\mathbf{W}_w$ and $\mathbf{W}_b$, respectively. The entries of these symmetric matrices are defined by the following formulas:

$$W_{w,ij} = \begin{cases} sim(\mathbf{x}_i, \mathbf{x}_j) & \text{if } \mathbf{x}_j \in N_w(\mathbf{x}_i) \text{ or } \mathbf{x}_i \in N_w(\mathbf{x}_j) \\ 0, & otherwise \end{cases} \qquad (1)$$

$$W_{b,ij} = \begin{cases} 1 & \text{if } \mathbf{x}_j \in N_b(\mathbf{x}_i) \text{ or } \mathbf{x}_i \in N_b(\mathbf{x}_j) \\ 0, & \text{otherwise} \end{cases} \tag{2}$$

where $sim(\mathbf{x}_i, \mathbf{x}_k)$ is a real value that encodes the similarity between $\mathbf{x}_i$ and $\mathbf{x}_k$. Without loss of generality, we assume that $sim(\mathbf{x}_i, \mathbf{x}_k)$ belongs to the interval [0, 1]. Simple choices for this function are the Kernel heat and the cosine.

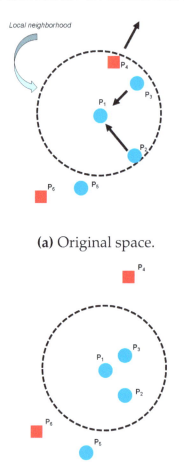

(a) Original space.

(b) Expected mapped space using LDE.

Fig. 1. (a) The center point has three neighbors. The points with the same color and shape belong to the same class. The within-class graph connects nearby points with the same label. The between-class graph connects nearby points with different labels. (b) After Local Discriminant Embedding, the local margins between different classes are maximized, and the distances between local homogeneous samples are minimized.

Optimal Mapping

A linear embedding technique is described by a matrix transform that maps the original samples $\mathbf{x}_i$ into low dimensional samples $\mathbf{A}^T\mathbf{x}_i$. The number of columns of $\mathbf{A}$ defines the dimension of the new subspace. LDE method computes a linear transform, $\mathbf{A}$, that simultaneously maximizes the local margins between heterogenous samples and pushes the homogeneous samples closer to each other (after the transformation). Mathematically, this corresponds to:

$$\min_{\mathbf{A}} \frac{1}{2} \sum_{i,j} \|\mathbf{A}^T (\mathbf{x}_i - \mathbf{x}_j)\|^2 W_{w,ij} \tag{3}$$

$$\max_{\mathbf{A}} \frac{1}{2} \sum_{i,j} \|\mathbf{A}^T (\mathbf{x}_i - \mathbf{x}_j)\|^2 W_{b,ij} \tag{4}$$

Using simple matrix algebra, the above criteria become respectively:

$$\frac{1}{2} \sum_{i,j} \|\mathbf{A}^T (\mathbf{x}_i - \mathbf{x}_j)\|^2 W_{w,ij} = Tr(\mathbf{A}^T \mathbf{X} (\mathbf{D}_w - \mathbf{W}_w) \mathbf{X}^T \mathbf{A}) = Tr\left(\mathbf{A}^T \mathbf{X} \mathbf{L}_w \mathbf{X}^T \mathbf{A}\right) \tag{5}$$

$$\frac{1}{2} \sum_{i,j} \|\mathbf{A}^T (\mathbf{x}_i - \mathbf{x}_j)\|^2 W_{b,ij} = Tr(\mathbf{A}^T \mathbf{X} (\mathbf{D}_b - \mathbf{W}_b) \mathbf{X}^T \mathbf{A}) = Tr\left(\mathbf{A}^T \mathbf{X} \mathbf{L}_b \mathbf{X}^T \mathbf{A}\right) \tag{6}$$

where $Tr(\mathbf{S})$ denotes the trace of the matrix $\mathbf{S}$, $\mathbf{X} = (\mathbf{x}_1, \mathbf{x}_2, \dots, \mathbf{x}_N)$ is the data matrix, $\mathbf{D}_w$ denotes the diagonal weight matrix, whose entries are column (or row, since $\mathbf{W}_w$ is symmetric) sums of $\mathbf{W}_w$, and $\mathbf{L}_w = \mathbf{D}_w - \mathbf{W}_w$ denotes the Laplacian matrix associated with the graph G_w.

Given the two individual optimization objectives, Eq. (3) and Eq. (4), a unified criterion that should be maximized can be formulated as:

$$J = \frac{Tr\left(\mathbf{A}^T \mathbf{X} \mathbf{L}_b \mathbf{X}^T \mathbf{A}\right)}{Tr\left(\mathbf{A}^T \mathbf{X} \mathbf{L}_w \mathbf{X}^T \mathbf{A}\right)} = \frac{Tr\left(\mathbf{A}^T \widetilde{\mathbf{S}}_b \mathbf{A}\right)}{Tr\left(\mathbf{A}^T \widetilde{\mathbf{S}}_w \mathbf{A}\right)} \tag{7}$$

where the symmetric matrix $\widetilde{\mathbf{S}}_b = \mathbf{X}\mathbf{L}_b\mathbf{X}^{\mathbf{T}}$ denotes the locality preserving between class scatter matrix, and the symmetric matrix $\widetilde{\mathbf{S}}_w = \mathbf{X}\mathbf{L}_w\mathbf{X}^{\mathbf{T}}$ denotes the locality preserving within class scatter matrix.

The trace ratio optimization problem (7) can be replaced by the simpler; yet inexact trace form:

$$\max_{\mathbf{A}} Tr\left\{\left(\mathbf{A}^T\mathbf{S}_w\mathbf{A}\right)^{-1}\left(\mathbf{A}^T\mathbf{S}_b\mathbf{A}\right)\right\} \tag{8}$$

The columns of the sought matrix $\mathbf{A}$ are given by the generalized eigenvectors associated with the largest eigenvalues of the following equation:

$$\widetilde{\mathbf{S}}_b\,\mathbf{a} = \lambda\,\widetilde{\mathbf{S}}_w\,\mathbf{a} \tag{9}$$

The Small Sample Size Problem

In many real world problems such as face recognition, both matrices $\mathbf{X}\mathbf{L}_b\mathbf{X}^T$ and $\mathbf{X}\mathbf{L}_w\mathbf{X}^T$ can be singular. This stems from the fact that sometimes the number of images in the training set, N, is much smaller than the number of pixels in each image, D. This is known as the Small Sample Size (SSS) problem. To overcome the complication of singular matrices, original data are first projected onto a PCA subspace or a random orthogonal space so that the resulting matrices $\mathbf{X}\mathbf{L}_b\mathbf{X}^T$ and $\mathbf{X}\mathbf{L}_w\mathbf{X}^T$ are non-singular.

EXPONENTIAL LDE

As can be seen, solving the SSS problem associated with LDE relied on applying a PCA on the raw data. However, PCA eliminates the null space of the total covariance matrix of data [39]. With respect to LDE formulation, one can easily see that the use of PCA stage eliminates the null spaces associated with the locality preserving scatter matrices $\mathbf{X}\mathbf{L}_b\mathbf{X}^T$ and $\mathbf{X}\mathbf{L}_w\mathbf{X}^T$. Therefore, by using PCA as an initial stage in LDE some discriminant information will not be handed over to the framework of LDE.

Matrix Exponential

The matrix exponential is widely used in applications such as control theory. In this section, we briefly introduce the definition and properties of matrix exponential. Let $\mathbf{S}$ be an $n \times n$ square matrix, its exponential is given by:

$$\exp(\mathbf{S}) = \mathbf{I} + \mathbf{S} + \frac{\mathbf{S}^2}{2!} + \ldots + \frac{\mathbf{S}^m}{m!} + \ldots \qquad (10)$$

where $\mathbf{I}$ is the identity matrix with the size of $n \times n$. Matrix exponential has the following properties:

1. $\exp(\mathbf{S})$ is a finite matrix.
2. $\exp(\mathbf{S})$ is a full rank matrix.
3. If $\mathbf{S}$ commutes with $\mathbf{T}$, *i.e.*, $\mathbf{ST} = \mathbf{TS}$, then $\exp(\mathbf{S} + \mathbf{T}) = \exp(\mathbf{S})\exp(\mathbf{T})$.
4. For an arbitrary square matrix $\mathbf{S}$, there exists the inverse of $\exp(\mathbf{S})$.
   This is given by:
   $(\exp(\mathbf{S}))^{-1} = \exp(-\mathbf{S})$
5. If $\mathbf{T}$ is a nonsingular matrix, then $\exp(\mathbf{T}^{-1}\mathbf{ST}) = \mathbf{T}^{-1}\exp(\mathbf{S})\mathbf{T}$.
6. If $\mathbf{v}_1, \mathbf{v}_2, \ldots, \mathbf{v}_n$ are eigenvectors of $\mathbf{S}$ that correspond to the eigenvalues $\lambda_1, \lambda_2, \ldots, \lambda_n$, then $\mathbf{v}_1, \mathbf{v}_2, \ldots, \mathbf{v}_n$ are also eigenvectors of $\exp(\mathbf{S})$ that correspond to the eigenvalues $e^{\lambda_1}, e^{\lambda_2}, \ldots, e^{\lambda_n}$. It is also well known that the matrix is non-singular.

A wide variety of methods for computing $\exp(\mathbf{S})$ were analyzed in [40]. The scaling and squaring method is one of the best methods for computing the matrix exponential [41].

Exponential LDE

The exponential version of LDE is obtained by using the exponential of $\widetilde{\mathbf{S}}_b$ and $\widetilde{\mathbf{S}}_w$. In other words, the eigenvalues of these matrices are replaced with their exponential. This replacement will have two beneficial effects: i) solving the SSS problem, and ii) introducing a distance diffusion mapping that will be explained in the next Section. Thus, the new criterion to be maximized becomes:

$$\max_{\mathbf{A}} Tr \left\{ \left(\mathbf{A}^T \exp(\widetilde{\mathbf{S}}_w) \mathbf{A} \right)^{-1} \left(\mathbf{A}^T \exp(\widetilde{\mathbf{S}}_b) \mathbf{A} \right) \right\} \tag{11}$$

The columns of the sought matrix $\mathbf{A}$ are given by the generalized eigenvectors associated with the largest eigenvalues of the following equation:

$$\exp(\widetilde{\mathbf{S}}_b) \, \mathbf{a} = \lambda \, \exp(\widetilde{\mathbf{S}}_w) \, \mathbf{a} \tag{12}$$

It should be noted that both matrices $\exp(\widetilde{\mathbf{S}}_b)$ and $\exp(\widetilde{\mathbf{S}}_w)$ are full rank matrices. This means that even in the case where the Small Sample Size problem occurs, the linear transform can be estimated without reducing the dimensionality of the data samples. There are many functions in Matlab that can be used to compute $\exp(\widetilde{\mathbf{S}}_b)$ and $\exp(\widetilde{\mathbf{S}}_w)$, and we can also calculate them based on the property 6. However, note that we must normalize scatter matrices $\widetilde{\mathbf{S}}_b$ and $\widetilde{\mathbf{S}}_w$, because $\exp(\widetilde{\mathbf{S}}_b)$ and $\exp(\widetilde{\mathbf{S}}_w)$ may involve large numbers. This normalization is carried out using the Frobenius norms of the matrices.

It should be noticed that LDE involves a two-order moment ($\widetilde{\mathbf{S}}_w$ and $\widetilde{\mathbf{S}}_b$), whereas ELDE is based on a linear combination of different moments (*i.e.*, $\exp(\widetilde{\mathbf{S}}_w)$ and $\exp(\widetilde{\mathbf{S}}_b)$), that include a two-order moment (See Eq. (10)).

The main steps of ELDE algorithm are:

Step 1. Normalize the feature vectors (vectorized images) $\mathbf{x}_1, \mathbf{x}_2, \ldots, \mathbf{x}_N$.

Step 2. Construct the similarity matrices $\mathbf{W}_w$ and $\mathbf{W}_b$ using Eqs. (1) and (2).

Step 3. Construct the locality preserving scatter matrices $\widetilde{\mathbf{S}}_w = \mathbf{X}\mathbf{L}_w\mathbf{X}^T$ and $\widetilde{\mathbf{S}}_b = \mathbf{X}\mathbf{L}_b\mathbf{X}^T$. Then, the optimal projections axes $\mathbf{a}_1, \mathbf{a}_2, \ldots, \mathbf{a}_k$ can be selected as the generalized eigenvectors of (12). These axes correspond to the first largest k eigenvector of $\exp(\widetilde{\mathbf{S}}_b) \, \mathbf{a} = \lambda \, \exp(\widetilde{\mathbf{S}}_w) \, \mathbf{a}$, where $\lambda_1 \geq \lambda_2 \geq \ldots \geq \lambda_k$.

Step 4. Project all samples into the obtained optimal discriminant vectors.

It is worthy to mention that the projection axes (eigenvectors) of LDE and of

ELDE are not equivalent. Indeed, by transforming the generalized eigenvalue decomposition problems of LDE (Eq. (9)) and ELDE (Eq. (12)) to their simple eigenvalue decomposition form, we can easily conclude that the projection axes of LDE are the eigenvectors of $\mathbf{P} = (\widetilde{\mathbf{S}}_w)^{-1}\,\widetilde{\mathbf{S}}_b$ and the projections axes of ELDE are the eigenvectors of $\mathbf{Q} = (\exp(\widetilde{\mathbf{S}}_w))^{-1}\,\exp(\widetilde{\mathbf{S}}_b)$. Since (i) $\mathbf{Q} \neq c\,\mathbf{P}$ (c is a non-zero scalar), (ii) $\mathbf{Q} \neq c\,\mathbf{P}^{-1}$, (iii) $\mathbf{Q} \neq c\,\exp(\mathbf{P})$, and (iv) $\mathbf{P} \neq c\,\exp(\mathbf{Q})$, it follows that the ELDE eigenvectors are not equivalent to the LDE eigenvectors.

THEORETICAL ANALYSIS OF ELDE

Solving the SSS Problem

According to property 6, the matrices $\exp(\mathbf{X}\,\mathbf{L}_b\mathbf{X}^T)$ and $\exp(\mathbf{X}\,\mathbf{L}_w\mathbf{X}^T)$ are full-rank matrices; even in the case where the SSS problem occurs. Indeed, all null eigenvalues of $\mathbf{X}\,\mathbf{L}_b\mathbf{X}^T$ and $\mathbf{X}\,\mathbf{L}_w\mathbf{X}^T$ are mapped to one for their exponential versions. Furthermore, the discriminant information that was contained in the null space of $\mathbf{X}\,\mathbf{L}_b\mathbf{X}^T$ and $\mathbf{X}\,\mathbf{L}_w\mathbf{X}^T$ can be extracted by the ELDE formulation, even when the SSS problem occurs. This is the main reason that explains why the ELDE formulation has more discriminant power than LDE.

Distance Diffusion Mapping

In pattern recognition field, the Kernel trick becomes a well-known tool that tackles the non-linearity of data. The basic idea is to map input data space into a feature space having higher dimension through a kernel-based non-linear mapping $\Phi(\mathbf{x})$. For instance, non-linear Support Vector Machines rely on the Kernel trick in order to classify data that are not linearly separable in the input space [42]. Therefore, ELDE might possess some similar properties of the kernel method. The only difference between ELDE and the kernel method is that ELDE involves the locality preserving scatter matrices, whereas the kernel method maps the feature vectors. However, the scatter matrices are derived from these feature vectors. Hence, ELDE might possess the property of the kernel method.

Similar to the kernel method, for ELDE, there exists a non-linear mapping function Ψ such that the locality preserving scatter matrices are transformed, *i.e.*,

$$\Psi : \quad \mathbb{R}^{D \times D} \longrightarrow \mathbb{R}^{D \times D}$$
$$\widetilde{\mathbf{S}}_b \longrightarrow \Psi(\widetilde{\mathbf{S}}_b) = \exp(\widetilde{\mathbf{S}}_b) = \exp(\mathbf{X} \mathbf{L}_b \mathbf{X}^T)$$
$$\widetilde{\mathbf{S}}_w \longrightarrow \Psi(\widetilde{\mathbf{S}}_w) = \exp(\widetilde{\mathbf{S}}_w) = \exp(\mathbf{X} \mathbf{L}_w \mathbf{X}^T)$$

Recall that LDE finds an optimal projection by simultaneously maximizing the between-class distance and minimizing the within-class distance in local neighborhoods. In the input space, these two distances are given by:

$$d_b = \frac{1}{2} \sum_{i,j} \|\mathbf{x}_i - \mathbf{x}_j\|^2 W_{b,ij} = Tr\left(\mathbf{X} \mathbf{L}_b \mathbf{X}^T\right) = Tr\left(\widetilde{\mathbf{S}}_b\right)$$

$$d_w = \frac{1}{2} \sum_{i,j} \|\mathbf{x}_i - \mathbf{x}_j\|^2 W_{w,ij} = Tr\left(\mathbf{X} \mathbf{L}_w \mathbf{X}^T\right) = Tr\left(\widetilde{\mathbf{S}}_w\right)$$

Since the locality preserving scatter matrices, $\widetilde{\mathbf{S}}_b$ and $\widetilde{\mathbf{S}}_w$, are symmetric and positive semi-definite, they can be written as $\widetilde{\mathbf{S}}_b = \Phi_b^T \Lambda_b \Phi_b$ and $\widetilde{\mathbf{S}}_w = \Lambda_w^T \Phi_w$. Φ_b and Φ_w are two orthogonal matrices. Λ_b and Λ_w are two diagonal matrices that contain the eigenvalues of $\widetilde{\mathbf{S}}_b$ and $\widetilde{\mathbf{S}}_w$, respectively.

Therefore, the above two distances are given by:

$$d_b = \frac{1}{2} \sum_{i,j} \|\mathbf{x}_i - \mathbf{x}_j\|^2 W_{b,ij} = Tr(\widetilde{\mathbf{S}}_b) = \lambda_{b1} + \lambda_{b2} + \ldots + \lambda_{bD} \tag{13}$$

$$d_w = \frac{1}{2} \sum_{i,j} \|\mathbf{x}_i - \mathbf{x}_j\|^2 W_{w,ij} = Tr(\widetilde{\mathbf{S}}_w) = \lambda_{w1} + \lambda_{w2} + \ldots + \lambda_{wD} \tag{14}$$

By using the mappings $\widetilde{\mathbf{S}}_b \to \Psi(\widetilde{\mathbf{S}}_b) = \exp(\widetilde{\mathbf{S}}_b)$ and $\widetilde{\mathbf{S}}_w \to \Psi(\widetilde{\mathbf{S}}_w) = \exp(\widetilde{\mathbf{S}}_w)$, there will be an implicit mapping of samples, in the same input space, such that the distances d_b and d_w are replaced by d'_b and d'_w:

$$d'_b = Tr\left(\exp(\widetilde{\mathbf{S}}_b)\right) = e^{\lambda_{b1}} + e^{\lambda_{b2}} + \ldots + e^{\lambda_{bD}} \tag{15}$$

$$d'_w = Tr\left(\exp(\widetilde{\mathbf{S}}_w)\right) = e^{\lambda_{w1}} + e^{\lambda_{w2}} + \ldots + e^{\lambda_{wD}} \tag{16}$$

Therefore, ELDE, compared with LDE, has a diffusion effect on the distance between samples. Moreover, in general, the distance between samples in different classes is bigger than the related distance between samples in the same class. By assuming that the homogeneous neighborhood size K_1 is roughly close to the heterogeneous neighborhood size K_2, one has $d_b > d_w$. Therefore, for most of the eigenvalues in (13) and (14), one can have the inequality $\lambda_{bi} > \lambda_{wi}$. The latter yields $e^{\lambda_{bi}} > e^{\lambda_{wi}}$.

Since all eigenvalues are non-negative, we can prove that:

$$\frac{e^{\lambda_{bi}}}{e^{\lambda_{wi}}} > \frac{\lambda_{bi}}{\lambda_{wi}},$$

holds true.

We know that $\frac{e^{\lambda_{bi}}}{e^{\lambda_{wi}}} = e^{\lambda_{bi}-\lambda_{wi}}$. Since $\lambda_{bi} > \lambda_{wi} > 0$, we have $\lambda_{bi} - \lambda_{wi} > 0$ and consequently since $\forall x > 0, e^x > 1 + x$ we have

$$e^{\lambda_{bi}-\lambda_{wi}} > 1 + \lambda_{bi} - \lambda_{wi}.$$

Also we have $1 + \lambda_{bi} - \lambda_{wi} > 1 + \frac{\lambda_{bi}-\lambda_{wi}}{\lambda_{wi}}$, since $\lambda_{wi} > 1$ for large eigenvalues.

By transitivity we get,

$$e^{\lambda_{bi}-\lambda_{wi}} > 1 + \lambda_{bi} - \lambda_{wi} > 1 + \frac{\lambda_{bi} - \lambda_{wi}}{\lambda_{wi}}.$$

That gives us,

$$\frac{e^{\lambda_{bi}}}{e^{\lambda_{wi}}} = e^{\lambda_{bi}-\lambda_{wi}} > \frac{\lambda_{bi}}{\lambda_{wi}}.$$

Hence,

$$\frac{e^{\lambda_{bi}}}{e^{\lambda_{wi}}} > \frac{\lambda_{bi}}{\lambda_{wi}}.$$

As shown, there is a difference in diffusion scale between the local within- and between-class distances. The diffusion scale to the between-class distance is larger than the within-class distance. Hence, the margin between heterogeneous samples is enlarged. This is a desired behavior for getting good discrimination. Since the distances (13), (14), (15), and (16) are all defined in the input space, it is clear that ELDE is equivalent to transforming the original data into a new space by distance diffusion mapping, and then, the LDE criterion is applied in such a new space. Fig. (**2**) illustrates a geometrical interpretation of the two processes induced by the proposed ELDE method.

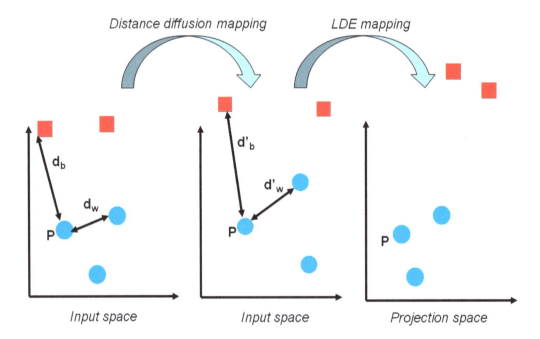

Fig. 2. An illustrative example showing the expected mapping performed by ELDE. First, distances between input samples (homogeneous and heterogeneous) are diffused in the input space. Second, the LDE algorithm is applied on these samples in order to obtain the projection.

PERFORMANCE EVALUATION

We evaluate the performance of the proposed method in tackling the face recognition problem. It is well known that image-based face recognition problem is a test bed for many theoretical developments in pattern recognition and machine learning [43 - 46]. We have used four public face datasets: Extended Yale, PF01, PIE, and FERET.

Face Databases

- **Extended Yale[1]:** We use the cropped version contains 1774 face images of 28 individuals. The images of the cropped version contain illumination variations and facial expression variations. The image size is 192×168 pixels with 256-bit grey scale. The images are rescaled to 32×32 pixels in our experiments.

- **PF01[2]:** It contains the true-color face images of 103 people, 53 men and 50 women, representing 17 various images (1 normal face, 4 illumination variations, 8 pose variations, 4 expression variations) per person. All of the people in the database are Asians. There are three kinds of systematic variations, such as illumination, pose, and expression variations in the database. The images are rescaled to 32×32 pixels in our experiments.

- **PIE[3]:** We use a reduced data set containing 1926 face images of 68 individuals. The images contain poses variations, illumination variations, and facial expression variations. The image size is 32×32 pixels with 256-bit grey scale.

- **FERET[4]:** This set consists of 14051 grayscale images of human heads with poses ranging from frontal to left and right profiles. It has more than 1000 individuals. The images are acquired in a semi-controlled conditions. The proposed method is evaluated on a subset of FERET database, which includes 1400 images of 200 distinct subjects, each subject has seven images. The subset involves variations in facial expression, illumination and pose. In our experiment, the facial portion of each original image is cropped automatically based on the location of eyes and resized to 32×32 pixels.

Recognition Accuracy

We apply our proposed method (ELDE) to face recognition and compare it with the following state-of-art face recognition approaches: Eigenfaces (PCA), Fisherfaces (LDA), Locality Preserving Projections (LPP) [21] (the unsupervised version), Supervised Locality Preserving Projections (SLPP) [47], Exponential Locality Preserving Projections (ELPP) [32], Exponential Discriminant Analysis

(EDA) [23], Average Neighborhood Margin Maximization (ANNM) [28], Maximally Collapsing Metric Learning algorithm (MCML) [29], Complete Kernel Fisher Discriminant method (CKFD) [36], Regularized Kernel Discriminant Analysis (RKDA) [48, 49](a regularized version of the Generalized Discriminant Analysis [34]), and Local Discriminant Em- bedding (LDE) [31].

We stress the fact that only PCA, LPP, and ELPP are unsupervised embedding techniques. For graph-based methods (LPP, SLPP, ELPP, LDE, ANMM, and ELDE), we set the neighborhood size to a predefined range of values, and then we report the top-1 recognition accuracy from the best parameter configuration. The methods suffering from the Small Sample Size problem (LDA, LPP, and LDE) are preceded by a PCA projection. Although MCML does not require the PCA dimensionality pre-stage, we have used the PCA stage before applying the MCML algorithm in order to get tractable computation time for the learning phase. For CKFD and RKDA methods, we used a Gaussian kernel and reported the best recognition accuracy from the best parameter configuration.

We randomly split every data set in ten train/test sets. For each individual, l images were randomly selected as training samples, and the rest were used for testing. The training set was used to learn a face sub-space (a linear transform) using the twelve embedding methods: PCA, LPP, ELPP, LDA, SLPP, EDA, ANMM, MCML, CKFD, RKDA, LDE, and ELDE methods. For a given embedding method, a test image (vectorized form) is first mapped using the linear transform obtained from the training set[5]. For all embedding methods, the classification is carried in the new space using the Nearest Neighbor classifier. We repeated this entire process for every (train/test) split and calculate the average recognition rate over the ten splits. In general, the recognition rates varies with the dimension of the face subspace. Thus, the average recognition rate is given by a curve depicting the rate as a function of the dimension of the new subspace. For every dimension, the average of recognition rates is computed over the 10 splits. The average curve is computed for a range of dimensions (*e.g.*, d_i= 5, 10, 15,..., d_{last}). In our study, the PCA variability is fixed, and hence the recognition rate curves associated with the 10 random splits will not have the same maximum dimension d_{max}. The latter one depends on the training set in the split. Thus, for every dimension d_i in the studied range, the averaging is carried out using only the curves whose d_{max} is equal to or greater than this dimension. For the CKFD method the dimension corresponds to the dimension of the regular and irregular components.

Fig. (**3**) illustrates the recognition rates (*versus* dimension) of the embedding methods obtained with the four face databases. The number of training images was fixed to 5 for Extended Yale, PF01 and FERET databases, and to 15 for PIE face database. These obtained plots are the average over 10 random splits.

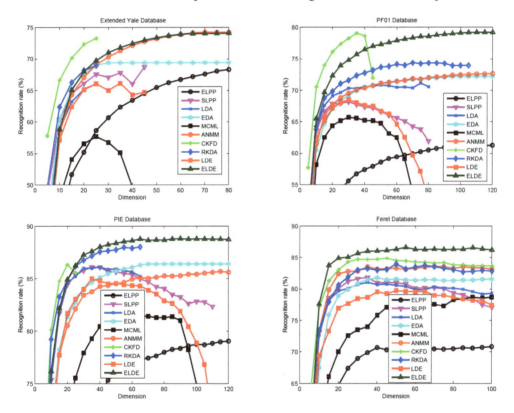

Fig. 3. Recognition rates as a function of the retained dimension of the embedded space obtained with four face databases.

We can observe that (1) ELDE has better performance than LDE over all dimensions, (2) the recognition rate of ELDE increases as the number of dimensions used increases, whereas the performance of LDE (and some other supervised techniques) may worsen by increasing the number of dimensions, (3)

ELDE has much more eigenvectors than LDE. The last property is due to the fact that the ELDE works directly on the raw images, while LDE works on embedded images, (4) the improvement of ELDE over LDE depends on the face database used. For example, this improvement is significant for Extended Yale, PF01, and FERET databases, (5) ELDE is superior to both EDA [23] and ELPP [32], and (6) the next best methods are CKFD, RKDA, and ANMM.

Table 1. Best average recognition accuracy (%) on Extended YALE face set over 10 random splits. Each column corresponds to a fixed number of training images. The number appearing in parenthesis corresponds to the optimal dimensionality of the embedded subspace (at which the maximum average recognition rate has been reported).

Method \ ExtYALE	*3Train*	*5 Train*	*7 Train*
PCA	41.6 (35)	49.1 (40)	58.6 (45)
LPP	55.4 (35)	67.1 (45)	75.4 (45)
ELPP	57.4 (80)	69.6 (125)	78.0 (135)
SLPP	56.0 (35)	68.7 (25)	77.1 (45)
LDA	50.5 (25)	66.3 (27)	73.0 (27)
EDA	55.3 (30)	69.4 (30)	75.9 (30)
MCML	42.6 (25)	57.6 (25)	68.8 (30)
ANMM	**58.9 (40)**	**74.2 (70)**	81.6 (75)
CKFD	58.8 (25)	73.32 (25)	80.7 (25)
RKDA	54.8 (25)	68.9 (25)	76.5 (25)
LDE	53.6 (35)	66.1 (35)	74.0 (45)
ELDE	58.2 (70)	74.0 (75)	81.7 (75)

For some databases, some embedding methods do not have a large number of eigenvectors, this can be explained by the fact that the maximum number of eigenvectors of these methods is directly related to the retained fixed variance of the PCA stage (*e.g.*, SLPP and LDE) or to the number of classes (*e.g.*, LDA, RKDA and CKFD).

The best average performance (best rate in the average curve) obtained by the twelve embedding algorithms as well as the corresponding dimension are summarized in Tables **1**, **2**, **3**, and **4**. In each Table, we studied the recognition accuracy for three different sizes for the training set. In general, the proposed

ELDE has the best recognition rate. In all cases, the performance of ELDE was better than that of LDE method.

Table 2. Best average recognition accuracy (%) on PF01 face set over 10 random splits. Each column corresponds to a fixed number of training images. The number appearing in parenthesis corresponds to the optimal dimensionality of the embedded sub-space (at which the maximum average recognition rate has been reported).

Method \ PF01	*3 Train*	*5 Train*	*7 Train*
PCA	43.2 (55)	50.8 (75)	53.3 (75)
LPP	45.2 (55)	57.0 (75)	59.9 (75)
ELPP	51.5 (135)	61.5 (140)	66.2 (140)
SLPP	57.8 (35)	68.2 (30)	71.3 (30)
LDA	60.5 (55)	71.1 (75)	74.1 (55)
EDA	63.3 (105)	72.2 (110)	75.0 (110)
MCML	55.1 (40)	65.7 (30)	69.3 (45)
ANMM	62.7 (115)	72.5 (115)	75.2 (115)
CKFD	67.67 (55)	79.1 (35)	80.2 (25)
RKDA	61.7 (105)	74.3 (70)	79.1 (70)
LDE	58.6 (35)	68.0 (35)	72.3 (45)
ELDE	**69.5 (115)**	**79.2 (110)**	81.1 (135)

Table 3. Best average recognition accuracy (%) on FERET face subset over 10 random splits. Each column corresponds to a fixed number of training images. The number appearing in parenthesis corresponds to the optimal dimensionality of the embedded subspace (at which the maximum average recognition rate has been reported).

Method \ PIE	*5 Train*	*9 Train*	*15 Train*
PCA	35.2 (85)	46.4 (105)	55.8 (100)
LPP	52.4 (85)	67.4 (95)	81.0 (105)
ELPP	55.4 (140)	71.1 (140)	79.2 (140)
SLPP	61.6 (20)	79.3 (25)	86.1 (30)
LDA	62.9 (55)	79.8 (45)	85.9 (35)
EDA	65.1 (70)	81.2 (70)	86.4 (70)
MCML	55.7 (50)	75.6 (55)	81.6 (55)
ANMM	66.9 (115)	80.5 (115)	85.6 (115)
CKFD	68.0 (60)	82.0 (30)	86.3 (20)

(Table 3) contd.....

Method \ PIE	5 Train	9 Train	15 Train
RKDA	59.7 (20)	80.5 (25)	88.0 (30)
LDE	60.5 (40)	77.4 (45)	85.0 (35)
ELDE	**68.8 (115)**	**84.2 (115)**	**88.8 (65)**

Table 4. Best average recognition accuracy (%) on FERET face subset over 10 random splits. Each column corresponds to a fixed number of training images. The number appearing in parenthesis corresponds to the optimal dimensionality of the embedded subspace (at which the maximum average recognition rate has been reported).

Method \ FERET	5 Train	9 Train	15 Train
PCA	61.3 (100)	65.0 (80)	68.2 (100)
LPP	49.9 (100)	51.9 (100)	55.8 (100)
ELPP	60.8 (90)	67.5 (105)	70.9 (110)
SLPP	68.7 (120)	75.5 (35)	81.8 (35)
LDA	67.3 (100)	75.3 (35)	81.0 (35)
EDA	69.9 (55)	77.8 (40)	81.8 (40)
MCML	69.3 (80)	76.3 (95)	79.6 (105)
ANMM	74.4 (60)	81.8 (100)	83.6 (70)
CKFD	73.6 (50)	81.2 (40)	84.9 (45)
RKDA	72.1 (55)	79.7 (65)	84.0 (50)
LDE	66.3 (100)	74.6 (50)	79.7 (50)
ELDE	74.5 (80)	83.3 (80)	86.6 (55)

Comparison between Regularized LDE and ELDE

There are different methods that can be used to overcome the SSS problem. One of these methods which does not throw away the null space of $\widetilde{\mathbf{S}}_w$ is regularization. In this section, we use a classic regularization scheme to solve the SSS problem of LDE and compare it with the Exponential solution (*i.e.*, ELDE). The general idea of regularization is to remove the singularity of any given singular matrix by adding a regularization term to it. We adopt the regularization by adding a diagonal matrix with small values to the singular matrix $\widetilde{\mathbf{S}}_w$. It removes the singularity problem of $\widetilde{\mathbf{S}}_w$ matrix without reducing the dimensionality of the input data. Therefore, the regularization of LDE (RLDE) consists of estimating the generalized eigenvectors given by:

$$\widetilde{\mathbf{S}}_b \, \mathbf{a} = \lambda \left(\widetilde{\mathbf{S}}_w + \beta \, \text{trace}(\widetilde{\mathbf{S}}_w) \, \mathbf{I} \right) \mathbf{a} \tag{17}$$

where β is a positive scalar and $\mathbf{I}$ is the $D \times D$ identity matrix (same size as $\widetilde{\mathbf{S}}_w$) and D is the feature dimension.

For comparison, we used four databases with two different numbers of training samples. For the RLDE method, we tried different values for β and picked the one with the highest accuracy.

Table 5. Best average accuracy (%) over 10 random splits using RLDE and the proposed ELDE. bold values correspond to the best accuracy among three methods.

Dataset \ Method	Train sample	LDE	RLDE	ELDE
Yale	3 train	88.4	92.7	**93.1**
	7 train	93.7	96.8	**97.2**
PF01	3 train	58.6	68.7	**70.4**
	7 train	72.3	**82.0**	81.1
PIE	5 train	60.5	67.7	**70.5**
	15 train	85.0	87.7	**89.3**
FERET	3 train	66.3	72.0	**74.5**
	5 train	79.7	84.6	**86.6**

In Table **5**, the best results of both the RLDE and ELDE methods are reported. We observe that both RLDE and ELDE methods show higher recognition rates comparing to the LDE method. This proves that PCA removes some dimensions (spaces) which can be useful for discrimination. However, RLDE and ELDE try to use all dimensions to extract more discriminant information. By using all dimensions with either RLDE or ELDE, one can gain better discriminant features, hence higher recognition rates. In all experimental cases, except for PF01 with 7 trains, the Exponential solution (*i.e.*, ELDE method) outperformed the regularization solution (*i.e.*, RLDE). It shows that the use of matrix exponential does not only intend to solve the SSS problem, but can also improve the performance.

CONCLUSION

In this chapter, we have exploited the matrix exponential in Local Discriminant

Embedding (LDE) to overcome Small Sample Size problem that can affect the classical LDE and to implicitly incorporate a similar effect to that of the non-linear Kernel-based embedding. The proposed method is called Exponential Local Discriminant Embedding (ELDE). It has two main advantages. First, it does not suffer form the Small Sample Size problem that often occurs when dealing with visual data sets for which the number of samples is less than the dimension of the sample. Second, the proposed method is equivalent to transforming the scatter matrices to a new space by distance diffusion mapping, and then, the LDE criterion is applied in such a space. With the help of distance diffusion mapping, the margin between samples belonging to different classes is enlarged, which is helpful in improving the performance of classification.

The effectiveness of the proposed method has been demonstrated through experimentation using four public face databases, Extended Yale, PF01, PIE and FERET. The results show that the performances of the proposed ELDE are better than those of LDE and many state-of-the-art discriminant analysis techniques. Although we have concentrated on the face recognition problem, the proposed approach could also be applied to other category of objects characterized by large variations in their appearance.

NOTES

[1]http : //vision.ucsd.edu/ ~ leekc/ExtYaleDatabase/ExtYaleB.html
[2]http : //nova.postech.ac.kr/special/imdb/imdb.html
[3]http : //www.ri.cmu.edu/projects/project_418.html
[4]http : //www.itl.nist.gov/iad/humanid/ f eret/
[5]For Kernel-based methods, the test image is replaced by a vector, formed by the Kernel similarities between the test image and the training images.

CONFLICT OF INTEREST

The author confirms that author has no conflict of interest to declare for this publication.

ACKNOWLEDGMENTS

This work is partially supported by the project EHU13/40. We want to thank

IEEE Transactions for allowing us to reuse some material for this chapter from the following paper: F. Dornaika and A. Bosaghzadeh, "Exponential local discriminant embedding and its application to face recognition", *IEEE Transactions on Cybernetics*, vol. 43, no. 3, pp. 921-934, 2013. DOI: 10.1109/TSMCB.2012.2218234.

REFERENCES

[1]   L. Saul, K. Weinberger, F. Sha, J. Ham, and D. Lee,"Semi-supervised Learning", In: *Spectral methods for dimensionality reduction.* MIT Press, Cambridge, MA, 2006.

[2]   S. Yan, D. Xu, B. Zhang, H.J. Zhang, Q. Yang, and S. Lin, "Graph embedding and extensions: a general framework for dimensionality reduction", *IEEE Trans. Pattern Anal. Mach. Intell.,* vol. 29, no. 1, pp. 40-51, 2007.
       [http://dx.doi.org/10.1109/TPAMI.2007.250598] [PMID: 17108382]

[3]   T. Zhang, D. Tao, X. Li, and J. Yang, "Patch alignment for dimensionality reduction", *IEEE Trans. Knowl. Data Eng.,* vol. 21, no. 9, pp. 1299-1313, 2009.
       [http://dx.doi.org/10.1109/TKDE.2008.212]

[4]   P. Niyogi, "Manifold regularization and semi-supervised learning: Some theoretical analyses", *J. Mach. Learn. Res.,* vol. 14, pp. 1229-1250, 2013.

[5]   M. Brand, "Charting a manifold", In: *Advances in Neural Information Processing Systems 15.* MIT Press, 2003, pp. 985-992. [Online]. Available: http://papers.nips.cc/paper/2165-charting-a-manifold.pdf

[6]   R. Wang, S. Shan, X. Chen, Q. Dai, and W. Gao, "Manifold-manifold distance and its application to face recognition with image sets", *IEEE Trans. Image Process.,* vol. 21, no. 10, pp. 4466-4479, Oct 2012.
       [http://dx.doi.org/10.1109/TIP.2012.2206039] [PMID: 22752133]

[7]   O. Arandjelovic, and R. Cipolla, "Achieving robust face recognition from video by combining a weak photometric model and a learnt gen- eric face invariant", *Pattern Recognit.,* vol. 46, no. 1, pp. 9-23, 2013.
       [http://dx.doi.org/10.1016/j.patcog.2012.06.024]

[8]   S.T. Roweis, and L.K. Saul, "Nonlinear dimensionality reduction by locally linear embedding", *Science,* vol. 290, no. 5500, pp. 2323-2326, 2000.
       [http://dx.doi.org/10.1126/science.290.5500.2323] [PMID: 11125150]

[9]   M. Belkin, and P. Niyogi, "Laplacian eigenmaps for dimensionality re- duction and data representation", *Neural Comput.,* vol. 15, no. 6, pp. 1373-1396, 2003.
       [http://dx.doi.org/10.1162/089976603321780317]

[10]   J.B. Tenenbaum, V. de Silva, and J.C. Langford, "A global geometric framework for nonlinear dimensionality reduction", *Science,* vol. 290, no. 5500, pp. 2319-2323, 2000.
       [http://dx.doi.org/10.1126/science.290.5500.2319] [PMID: 11125149]

[11]   X. Li, S. Lin, S. Yan, and D. Xu, "Discriminant locally linear embedding with high-order tensor data",

IEEE Trans. Syst. Man Cybern. B Cybern., vol. 38, no. 2, pp. 342-352, April 2008.
[http://dx.doi.org/10.1109/TSMCB.2007.911536] [PMID: 18348919]

[12]   A.M. Martinez, and M. Zhu, "Where are linear feature extraction methods applicable?", *IEEE Trans. Pattern Anal. Mach. Intell.,* vol. 27, no. 12, pp. 1934-1944, 2005.
[http://dx.doi.org/10.1109/TPAMI.2005.250] [PMID: 16358412]

[13]   H. Zhang, Y. Zhang, and T. Huang, "Simultaneous discriminative projection and dictionary learning for sparse representation based classification", *Pattern Recognit.,* vol. 46, pp. 346-354, 2013.
[http://dx.doi.org/10.1016/j.patcog.2012.07.010]

[14]   X. Suna, J. Wanga, M. Sheb, and L. Kong, "Sparse representation with multi-manifold analysis for texture classification from few training images", *Image Vis. Comput.,* vol. 32, no. 11, pp. 835-846, 2014.
[http://dx.doi.org/10.1016/j.imavis.2014.07.001]

[15]   T.K. Kim, and J. Kittler, "Locally linear discriminant analysis for multimodally distributed classes for face recognition with a single model image", *IEEE Trans. Pattern Anal. Mach. Intell.,* vol. 27, no. 3, pp. 318-327, 2005.
[http://dx.doi.org/10.1109/TPAMI.2005.58] [PMID: 15747788]

[16]   D-Q. Dai, and P.C. Yuen, "Face recognition by regularized discriminant analysis", *IEEE Trans. Systems, Man, Cybernetics, part B,* vol. 37, no. 4, pp. 1080-1085, Aug 2007.
[http://dx.doi.org/10.1109/TSMCB.2007.895363]

[17]   K. Fukunaga, *Introduction to Statistical Pattern Recognition..* Academic Press: New York, 1990.

[18]   J. Lu, K. Plataniotis, and A. Venetsanopoulos, ""Face recognition using kernel direct discriminant analysis algorithms," IEEE Trans", *Neural Netw.,* vol. 14, no. 1, pp. 117-126, 2003.
[http://dx.doi.org/10.1109/TNN.2002.806629]

[19]   M. Sugiyama, "Dimensionality reduction of multimodal labeled data by local fisher discriminant analysis", *J. Mach. Learn. Res.,* vol. 8, pp. 1027-1061, 2007.

[20]   S. Yan, D. Xu, B. Zhang, and H-J. Zhang, "Graph embedding: A general framework for dimensionality reduction", In: *Int. Conference on Computer Vision and Pattern Recognition,* 2005.

[21]   X. He, S. Yan, Y. Hu, P. Niyogi, and H.J. Zhang, "Face recognition using laplacianfaces", *IEEE Trans. Pattern Anal. Mach. Intell.,* vol. 27, no. 3, pp. 328-340, 2005.
[http://dx.doi.org/10.1109/TPAMI.2005.55] [PMID: 15747789]

[22]   Y. Xu, A. Zhong, J. Yang, and D. Zhang, "LPP solution schemes for use with face recognition", *Pattern Recognit.,* vol. 43, pp. 4165-4176, 2010.
[http://dx.doi.org/10.1016/j.patcog.2010.06.016]

[23]   T. Zhang, B. Fang, Y.Y. Tang, Z. Shang, and B. Xu, "Generalized discriminant analysis: a matrix exponential approach", *IEEE Trans. Syst. Man Cybern. B Cybern.,* vol. 40, no. 1, pp. 186-197, 2010.
[http://dx.doi.org/10.1109/TSMCB.2009.2024759] [PMID: 19651556]

[24]   Y. Fu, Z. Li, J. Yuan, Y. Wu, and T.S. Huang, "Locality versus globality: Query-driven localized linear models for facial image computing", *IEEE Trans. on Circuits and Systems for Video Technololgy,* vol. 18, no. 12, pp. 1741-1752, 2008.
[http://dx.doi.org/10.1109/TCSVT.2008.2004933]

[25]   W. Yu, X. Teng, and C. Liu, "Face recognition using discriminant locality preserving projections", *Image Vis. Comput.,* vol. 24, no. 3, pp. 239-248, 2006.
[http://dx.doi.org/10.1016/j.imavis.2005.11.006]

[26]   W. Wong, and H. Zhao, "Supervised optimal locality preserving projection", *Pattern Recognit.,* vol. 45, no. 1, pp. 186-197, 2012.
[http://dx.doi.org/10.1016/j.patcog.2011.05.014]

[27]   Y. Tao, and J. Yang, "Quotient *vs.* difference: Comparison between the two discriminant criteria", *Neurocomputing,* vol. 18, no. 12, pp. 1808-1817, 2010.
[http://dx.doi.org/10.1016/j.neucom.2009.10.026]

[28]   F. Wang, X. Wang, D. Zhang, C. Zhang, and T. Li, "MarginFace: A novel face recognition method by average neighborhood margin maximization", *Pattern Recognit.,* vol. 42, pp. 2863-2875, 2009.
[http://dx.doi.org/10.1016/j.patcog.2009.04.015]

[29]   A. Globerson, and S. Roweis, "Metric learning by collapsing classes", In: *Conference on Advances in Neural Information Processing Systems*, 2006, pp. 451-458.

[30]   K.Q. Weinberger, and L.K. Saul, "Distance metric learning for large margin nearest neighbor classification", *J. Mach. Learn. Res.,* vol. 10, pp. 207-244, 2009.

[31]   H. Chen, H. Chang, and T. Liu, "Local discriminant embedding and its variants", In: *IEEE International Conference on Computer Vision and Pattern Recognition*, 2005.

[32]   S. Wang, H. Chen, X. Peng, and C. Zhou, "Exponential locality preserving projections for small sample size problem", *Neurocomputing,* vol. 74, no. 17, pp. 3654-3662, 2011.
[http://dx.doi.org/10.1016/j.neucom.2011.07.007]

[33]   B. Schölkopf, and A. Smola, *Learning with Kernels.* MIT Press: Cambridge, Mass, 2002.

[34]   G. Baudat, and F. Anouar, "Generalized discriminant analysis using a kernel approach", *Neural Comput.,* vol. 12, no. 10, pp. 2385-2404, 2000.
[http://dx.doi.org/10.1162/089976600300014980] [PMID: 11032039]

[35]   L. Chen, H. Liao, J. Lin, M. Kao, and G. Yu, "A new LDA-based face recognition system which can solve the small sample size problem", *Pattern Recognit.,* vol. 33, no. 10, pp. 1713-1726, 2000.
[http://dx.doi.org/10.1016/S0031-3203(99)00139-9]

[36]   J. Yang, A.F. Frangi, J.Y. Yang, D. Zhang, and Z. Jin, "KPCA plus LDA: a complete kernel Fisher discriminant framework for feature extraction and recognition", *IEEE Trans. Pattern Anal. Mach. Intell.,* vol. 27, no. 2, pp. 230-244, 2005.
[http://dx.doi.org/10.1109/TPAMI.2005.33] [PMID: 15688560]

[37]   D. Cai, X. He, K. Zhou, J. Han, and H. Bao, "Locality sensitive discriminant analysis", In: *International Joint Conference on Artificial Intelligence*, 2007, pp. 708-713.

[38]   Y. Fu, M. Liu, and T.S. Huang, "Conformal embedding analysis with local graph modeling on the unit hypersphere", In: *IEEE Int. Conference on Computer Vision and Pattern Recognition*, 2007, pp. 1-6.
[http://dx.doi.org/10.1109/CVPR.2007.383410]

[39]   H. Yu, and H. Yang, "A direct LDA algorithm for high-dimensional data: With application to face recognition", *Pattern Recognit.,* vol. 34, no. 10, pp. 2067-2070, 2001.

[http://dx.doi.org/10.1016/S0031-3203(00)00162-X]

[40]   C. Moler, and C.V. Loan, "Nineteen dubious ways to compute the exponential of a matrix, twenty-five years later", *SIAM Rev.,* vol. 45, no. 1, pp. 3-49, 2003.
[http://dx.doi.org/10.1137/S00361445024180]

[41]   N. Higham, "The scaling and squaring method for the matrix exponential revisited", *SIAM J. Matrix Anal. Appl.,* vol. 26, no. 4, pp. 1179-1196, 2005.
[http://dx.doi.org/10.1137/04061101X]

[42]   J. Shawe-Taylor, and N. Cristianini, *Support Vector Machines and other kernel-based learning methods.* Cambridge University Press, 2000.

[43]   O. Arandjelovic, "Gradient edge map features for frontal face recognition under extreme illumination changes", In: *BMVC 2012: Proceedings of the British machine vision association conference.* BMVA Press, 2012, pp. 1-11.

[44]   W. Chen, M.J. Er, and S. Wu, "Illumination compensation and normalization for robust face recognition using discrete cosine transform in logarithm domain", *IEEE Trans. Syst. Man Cybern. B Cybern.,* vol. 36, no. 2, pp. 458-466, 2006.
[http://dx.doi.org/10.1109/TSMCB.2005.857353] [PMID: 16602604]

[45]   J. Wright, A.Y. Yang, A. Ganesh, S.S. Sastry, and Y. Ma, "Robust face recognition *via* sparse representation", *IEEE Trans. Pattern Anal. Mach. Intell.,* vol. 31, no. 2, pp. 210-227, 2009.
[http://dx.doi.org/10.1109/TPAMI.2008.79] [PMID: 19110489]

[46]   X. Zhang, and Y. Gao, "Face recognition across pose: A review", *Pattern Recognit.,* vol. 42, pp. 2876-2896, 2009.
[http://dx.doi.org/10.1016/j.patcog.2009.04.017]

[47]   Z. Zheng, J. Zhao, and J. Yang, "Gabor feature based face recognition using supervised locality preserving projection", *Advanced Concepts for Intelligent Vision Systems,* pp. 644-653, 2006.
[http://dx.doi.org/10.1007/11864349_59]

[48]   D. Cai, X. He, and J. Han, "Efficient kernel discriminant analysis *via* spectral regression", In: *International Conference on Data Mining,* 2007, pp. 427-432.
[http://dx.doi.org/10.1109/ICDM.2007.88]

[49]   D. Cai, X. He, and J. Han, "Speed up kernel discriminant analysis", *International Journal on Very Large Data Bases,* vol. 20, no. 1, pp. 21-33, 2011.
[http://dx.doi.org/10.1007/s00778-010-0189-3]

CHAPTER 4

Adaptive Locality Preserving Projections for Face Recognition

Fadi Dornaika[1,2,*], Ammar Assoum[3]

[1] *University of the Basque Country, San Sebastian, Spain*

[2] *IKERBASQUE, Basque Foundation for Science, Bilbao, Spain*

[3] *LaMA Laboratory, Lebanese University, Tripoli, Lebanon*

Abstract: This chapter addresses the graph-based linear manifold learning for object recognition. In particular, it introduces an adaptive Locality Preserving Projections (LPP) which has two interesting properties: (i) it does not depend on any parameter, and (ii) there is no correlation between mapped data. The main contribution consists in a parameterless computation of the affinity matrix built on the principle of meaningful and Adaptive neighbors. In addition to the framework of LPP, these two properties have been integrated to the framework of two graph-based embedding techniques: Orthogonal Locality Preserving Projections (OLPP) and Supervised LPP (SLPP). After introducing adaptive affinity matrices and the uncorrelated mapped data constraint, we perform recognition tasks on six public face databases. The results show improvement over those of classic methods such as LPP, OLPP, and SLPP. The proposed method could also be applied to other kinds of objects.

Keywords: Affinity matrix, Classification, Dimensionality reduction, En- hanced Locality Preserving Projections, Face recognition, Graph-based linear embedding, Label information, Laplacian eigenmaps, Laplacian matrix, latent points, Linear discriminant analysis, Locality preserving projections, Nearest neighbor classifier, Orthogonal locality preserving projections, Parameter-less locality preserving projections, Pearson's coefficient, principal component analysis, Projection directions, Recognition rate, Supervised locality preserving projections.

* **Address to Corresponding Author Fadi Dornaika:** University of the Basque Country, Manuel Lardizabal, 1, 20018 San Sebastian, Spain; IKERBASQUE, Basque Foundation for Science, Bilbao, Spain; Tel: +34 943018034; Fax: +34 943 015590; E-mail: fadi.dornaika@ehu.es

INTRODUCTION

When dealing with pattern recognition and computer vision problems, the large amount of input data, such as images and videos, are computationally challenging to manipulate. In these cases it is preferable to reduce the dimensionality of the data without radically altering the original information in the data distribution. This would mostly result in more efficient learning and inference. If the variance of the multivariate data is faithfully represented as a set of parameters, the data can be considered as a set of geometrically related points lying on a smooth low-dimensional manifold. The fundamental issue in dimensionality reduction is how to model the geometry structure of the manifold and produce a faithful embedding for data projection. A large number of approaches have been proposed for computing the embedding. The linear methods, such as multidimensional scaling (MDS) [1] and principal component analysis (PCA) are characterized by their efficiency in observing the Euclidean structure. Unlike PCA which is unsupervised, linear discriminant analysis (LDA) is a supervised technique.

In pattern recognition, linear dimensionality reduction (LDR) techniques have been increasingly used [2, 3] since they allow to build a relatively simple mapping of data onto a lower-dimensional subspace. Recently, manifold learning theory has received a lot of attention by researchers and practitioners. Exploiting the findings of manifold learning theory has led to many progresses in face recognition which is known to be a difficult problem in the domain of computer vision [4 - 6]. The linear methods of dimensionality reduction have the advantage over the non-linear ones in that the embedding function of the former is defined everywhere in the input space, while for the latter, it is only defined for a set of data samples. Several linear dimensionality reduction algorithms are based on a graph whose nodes consist of the data samples and whose edges represent the similarity among these samples [7]. For example, the Locality Preserving Projections (LPP) [8, 9] is a typical graph-based method used for Linear Dimensionality Reduction. LPP is a linearized version of Laplacian Eigenmaps [10] and has been successfully applied in many practical problems such as speech recognition [11], face recognition [12] and age estimation [13]. In order to avoid possible singularities, LPP is generally preceded by a PCA step.

Several extensions to the LPP method have been proposed in the literature. For example, Xu *et al.* [14] added new features to improve the original LPP by i) introducing linear transforms prior to LPP, and ii) changing the original quotient-based criterion to a new difference-based one. Furthermore, although LPP is a unsupervised LDR technique, it is shown that, in some cases it can outperform some supervised techniques such as LDA [15]. This is mainly due to the fact that LPP preserves the locality structures of data. Orthogonal LPP (OLPP) [16] is an other extension of LPP that uses its criterion in order to provide orthogonal projection directions. Moreover, [8] proposes a regularized version of LPP that solves the singularity of the matrix $\mathbf{XDX}^T$. Although the LPP method intrinsically preserves the manifold structure of the input data, its ability to discriminate between different classes is little because of its unsupervised nature. Indeed, the estimation of the linear transform that maps the input data through the LPP framework does not take into account the label information. That is why, a supervised version of LPP (SLPP) is proposed in order to overcome this limitation [17]. The key idea of SLPP is that the computation of the affinity matrix is based on the intraclass neighborhood of each point, *i.e.*, the nearest neighbors belonging to the same class as its.

In this chapter, we propose an improved version of LPP that offers two interesting advantages: i) it is entirely parameter-free, and ii) there is no correlation between mapped data. The chapter is organized as follows. Section 1 describes briefly the original linear mapping of LPP. Section 2 depicts the proposed adaptive LPP. Section 3 summarizes the experimental results for face recognition experiments conducted on five face databases. In the sequel, capital bold letters denote matrices and small bold letters denote vectors.

LOCALITY PRESERVING PROJECTIONS

We assume that we have a set of N samples $\{\mathbf{x}_i\}_{i=1}^N \subset \mathbb{R}^D$. We Construct a neighborhood graph on these data, such as a full mesh, a k-nearest-neighbor or ε-ball graph. The weight A_{ij} of each edge $\mathbf{x}_i \sim \mathbf{x}_j$ is computed by a symmetric affinity function $A_{ij} = K(\mathbf{x}_i; \mathbf{x}_j)$, typically Gaussian, *i.e.*,

$$A_{ij} = \exp\left(-\frac{\|\mathbf{x}_i - \mathbf{x}_j\|^2}{\beta}\right)$$

where β is usually set to square of the standard deviation of the whole dataset of samples $\{\mathbf{x}_i\}_{i=1}^N$. $\mathbf{A}$ denotes the symmetric affinity matrix constructed from weights $\{A_{ij}\}_{i,j=1}^N$.

Our goal is to find latent points $\{\mathbf{y}_i\}N_{i=1} \subset \mathrm{R}^L$ that minimize $\frac{1}{2}\sum_{i,j}(y_i - y_j)^2 A_{ij}$. This minimization prevents from placing far apart latent points that correspond to similar observed points. For simplicity's sake, we present hereafter the case of one dimensional mapping in which the original data set $\{\mathbf{x}_i\}$ $N_{i=1}$ is mapped to a line.

Let $\mathbf{z} = (y_1, y_2, \ldots, y_N)^T \in \mathbb{R}^N$ be the column vector corresponding to such a map. A criterion that can be reasonably used to choose a good map is to optimize the following objective function under some constraints:

$$\min \frac{1}{2} \sum_{i,j} (y_i - y_j)^2 A_{ij} \tag{1}$$

The minimization of (1) imposes a heavy penalty when the neighboring points $\mathbf{x}_i$ and $\mathbf{x}_j$ are mapped far apart. Using simple algebra formulation, we can write the function (1) as

$$\frac{1}{2} \sum_{i,j} (y_i - y_j)^2 A_{ij} = \mathbf{z}^T \mathbf{D} \mathbf{z} - \mathbf{z}^T \mathbf{A} \mathbf{z} = \mathbf{z}^T \mathbf{L} \mathbf{z} \tag{2}$$

where $\mathbf{D}$ denotes the diagonal weight matrix, whose entries are column (or row, since $\mathbf{A}$ is symmetric) sums of $\mathbf{A}$, and $\mathbf{L} = \mathbf{D} - \mathbf{A}$ is the Laplacian matrix corresponding to $\mathbf{A}$.

In the LPP formulation, the latent data are simply obtained through a linear mapping of the original data. Thus, we can express the one dimensional map $\mathbf{z}$ by:

$$\mathbf{z} = \mathbf{X}^T \mathbf{w} \tag{3}$$

where $\mathbf{X} = (\mathbf{x}_1, \mathbf{x}_2, \ldots, \mathbf{x}_N)$ and $\mathbf{w}$ denote respectively the data matrix, and the projection direction. By combining the equations (3) and (2) and by imposing the constraint $\mathbf{z}^T \mathbf{Dz} = 1$ in order to set an arbitrary scale, we can reduce the minimization problem to finding:

$$\min_{\mathbf{w}} \mathbf{w}^T \mathbf{XLX}^T \mathbf{w} \ s.t. \ \mathbf{w}^T \mathbf{XDX}^T \mathbf{w} = 1 \tag{4}$$

The projection direction $\mathbf{w}$ that minimizes the objective function is determined by the minimum eigenvalue solution to the generalized eigenvalue problem:

$$\mathbf{XLX}^T \mathbf{w} = \lambda \, \mathbf{XDX}^T \mathbf{w} \tag{5}$$

In the case of multi-dimensional mapping, each data sample $\mathbf{x}_i$ is mapped into a vector $\mathbf{y}_i$. The projection directions matrix ($\mathbf{W} = (\mathbf{w}_1, \mathbf{w}_2, \ldots, \mathbf{w}_L)$) consists of the concatenation of generalized eigenvectors $\{\mathbf{w}_{i=1}\}N$ sorted in ascendant order according to their eigenvalues, $0 \leq \lambda_1 \leq \lambda_2 \leq \ldots \leq \lambda_L$. Then, the mapping of $\mathbf{x}$ is given by $\mathbf{y} = \mathbf{W}^T \mathbf{x}$.

In real world applications such as face recognition, the original dimensionality D of the data is usually greater than the number of the samples, N. This issue is referred to as the Small Sample Size (SSS) problem. It will result in a singularity in both matrices $\mathbf{XDX}^T$ and $\mathbf{XLX}^T$ that will prevent the generalized eigen-equation to be directly solved.

A possible solution for the SSS problem is to project the original data to a random orthogonal space or to a PCA subspace before applying LPP, so that the singularity of the matrix $\mathbf{XDX}^T$ is removed. The global transform will thus be given by $\mathbf{W} = \mathbf{W}_{rand} \mathbf{W}_{LPP}$ or $\mathbf{W} = \mathbf{W}_{PCA} \mathbf{W}_{LPP}$ where $\mathbf{W}_{rand}$ consists of an orthogonal random matrix with a sufficient number of columns. The use of random projection has shown an effectiveness and a performance equivalent to that of PCA yet with the obvious advantage that the corresponding transform does not need a training set.

Shortcomings of LPP: The original LPP suffers from two shortcomings. The first one is related to the selection of parameters. Indeed, two parameters need to be set before the computation of the affinity matrix **A**: (i) the width of the Gaussian Kernel β, and (ii) the neighborhood size needed to build the graphs. In practice, the width parameter, is set to the average of pairwise distances over the training set even if this choice is not always the optimal one. On the other hand, the neighborhood size, set in advance to the same value for all samples, has also an impact on the manifold learning. The second shortcoming is due to the eigenvectors that are derived from the generalized eigenvalue problem of (5). Indeed, these eigenvectors can be statistically correlated and may have some redundancy in the information they contain.

ENHANCED AND PARAMETERLESS LPP

To overcome the shortcomings mentioned above, we propose a novel LPP paradigm with two interesting properties: (i) being entirely parameter-free, and (ii) there is no correlation between mapped data. The first property means that the computation of the affinity matrix does not need any parameter in advance while the second one is achieved through an adequate modification of the constraint used in the optimization. We proceed as follows.

The computation of the affinity matrix is based on the normalized Pearson correlation[1] and adaptive neighborhood. If p_{ij} denotes the Pearson's coefficient between two arbitrary samples $\mathbf{x}_i$ and $\mathbf{x}_j$, then we can transform them to similarities that belong to the interval [0, 1] using the equation:

$$\bar{p}_{ij} = \frac{p_{ij} - min(p_{ij})}{1 - min(p_{ij})}$$

Let m_i denotes the average similarity of a given sample $\mathbf{x}i$ in the training data set to all other samples. Then, the $(i, j) - th$ element of the affinity matrix **A** will be given by:

$$A_{ij} = \begin{cases} \bar{p}_{ij} & if \ \bar{p}_{ij} > m_i \ or \ \bar{p}_{ij} > m_j \\ 0, & otherwise \end{cases} \tag{6}$$

Unlike the classic LPP in which the neighborhoods of sample points (the adjacency matrix) are determined either through k-NN graph or ε-ball neighborhood, our proposed method picks the neighbors according to the local sample point x_i and its similarities with all other samples. Neighbors of each sample are determined in an adaptive way. Indeed, for k-NN based graphs, each row (respectively column) in the affinity matrix $\mathbf{A}$, will contain at least k non-zero entries. However, with our adaptive method the number of neighbors is no more constant and varies depending on the structure of the data. The strategy we use to build the adjacency matrix can be considered as an adaptive ε-ball neighborhood in which the radius of the ball will adapt depending on the similarity between the sample and the rest of the data. Note that there are mainly two differences between the classic ε-ball neighborhood construction method and ours: (1) the ε-ball method needs a user-defined input value which is the ball radius ε, and (2) this value remains constant for all data samples, whereas in our strategy, we use an adaptive threshold that may change according to the local sample. Thus, our strategy constructs the graph of LPP in a parameter-free and adaptive way for all databases without the need for any parameter tuning.

The second improvement we brought to classic LPP was to remove any correlation that may exist between mapped data by imposing specific related constraints [18]. Indeed, let $\mathbf{S}$ denote the total scatter matrix corresponding to the data matrix $\mathbf{X}$, then the global scatter matrix associated with the linear mapping $\mathbf{w}^T\mathbf{x}$ is given by $\mathbf{w}^T\mathbf{S}\,\mathbf{w}$. Requiring the absence of any correlation between the mapped data yields the constraint $\mathbf{W}^T\mathbf{S}\mathbf{W} = \mathbf{I}$ ($\mathbf{I}$ is the identity matrix).

According to the foregoing, the new enhanced LPP graph is the solution of

$$\min_{\mathbf{W}}(\mathbf{w}^T\mathbf{X}\mathbf{L}\mathbf{X}^T\,\mathbf{w}) \ s.t. \ \mathbf{w}^T\mathbf{S}\mathbf{w} = 1 \qquad\qquad (7)$$

The columns of the searched transform matrix $\mathbf{W}$ correspond to the generalized eigenvectors defined by:

$$\mathbf{X}\,\mathbf{L}\mathbf{X}^T\,\mathbf{w} = \lambda\,\mathbf{S}\,\mathbf{w}$$

The eigenvectors are sorted in ascendant order according to the corresponding eigenvalues, $0 \leq \lambda_1 \leq \lambda_2 \leq \ldots \leq \lambda_L$. In the sequel, the LPP of Eqs. (5) and (7) will be referred to as the "parameterless LPP" method and "enhanced LPP" method respectively.

Despite the similarity that can be observed in the mathematical expressions of the objective functions in Eqs. (4) and (7), two main differences should be highlighted between them. First, the computation of the Laplacian matrix, **L**, is not the same. Indeed, the graph corresponding to eq. (4) is built using a k-NN neighborhood graph, whereas the one corresponding to eq. (7) is adaptively built according to the samples. Thus, we can expect to have a better data representation when using this scheme. Second, the constraints imposed in both objective functions are not the same. In fact, the projection directions related to the objective function of eq. (4) are computed by introducing a normalization process that uses the volume of the graph (sum of all weights). Thus, eq. (4) enhances the locality preserving and at the same time maximizes a weighted variance. However, the projection directions computed according to the objective function of eq. (7) require the non-existence of correlation between the data projected along the different projection axes.

PERFORMANCE EVALUATION

Face Databases

The proposed parameterless and enhanced LPP methods have been tested on six face datasets: UMIST, Yale, Extended YaleB, PF01, PIE, and FERET. It is well known that image-based face recognition problem is a test bed for many theoretical developments in pattern recognition and machine learning [19, 20].

UMIST: It consists of 575 images of 20 individuals. In our experiments, the images are rescaled to 56×46 pixels.

Yale: It contains 165 grayscale images of 15 persons. Each person has 11 images. Each image is cropped then resized to 48×32 pixels.

Extended Yale B: The original database contains 16128 grayscale face images of 28 human subjects. For our experiments we use a subset of the cropped version that contains only 1774 images. They are rescaled to 48×42 pixels in our experiments.

PIE: We use a reduced subset of the 750,000 images that constitute this huge database. This contains 1926 images of 68 subjects. The image size is 32×32 pixels with 256-bit grayscale.

PF01: This database is composed of true-color face images of 103 people, 53 men and 50 women, representing 17 various observations (with illumination, pose and expression variations) per person.

FERET: In our experiments, we use a subset of 3010 images equally distributed over 301 subjects. The images are rescaled to 96×64 pixels.

For all face datasets, we use PCA as a preprocessing step. The obtained projection is then embedded using the linear transform corresponding to the different LPP variants. For all methods, the classification is carried in the new space using the Nearest Neighbor classifier.

Experimental Results

Before presenting the quantitative evaluation of classification, it would be worthy to study the effect of using the constraint about uncorrelated output. To this end, we use a synthetic example. The synthetic data set is formed by 600 points that live in a 2D space (See Fig. **1a**). Using this set, an enhanced LPP is carried out. The obtained output data (a set of 600 2D points) are plotted in Fig. (**1b**). As can be seen, the total covariance of the data is a diagonal matrix, meaning that the second component is independent of the first component.

Fig. (**2**) depicts the recognition rate of PCA, classic LPP, parameterless LPP, and enhanced LPP obtained with the Extended YaleB and PIE face data sets as a function of the dimension. Fig. (**2a**) corresponds to the Extended YaleB face data set and Fig. (**2b**) corresponds to the PIE face data set. These rates are computed as an average over 10 random splits. For the classic LPP, we have kept the K value that gave the best results.

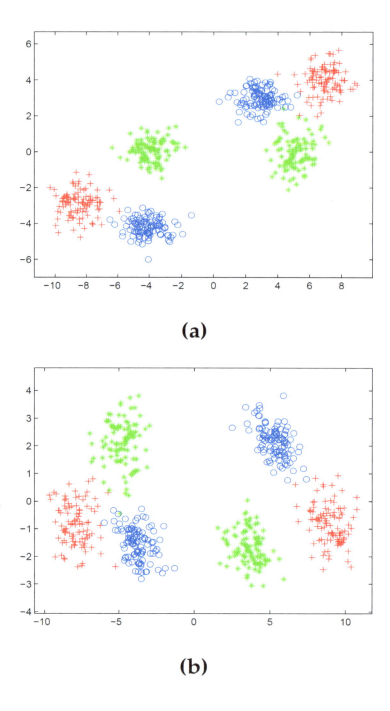

(a)

(b)

Fig. (1). (a) Input data. **(b)** Mapped data using the enhanced LPP (uncorrelated output).

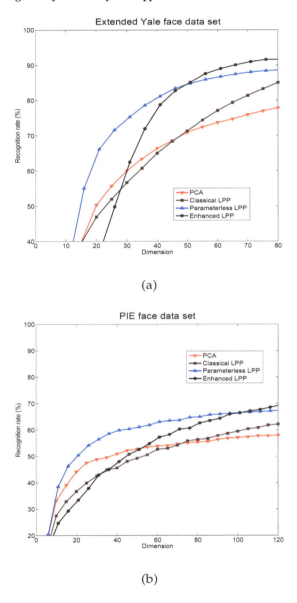

(a)

(b)

Fig. (2). Recognition accuracy as a function of the retained dimension for the Extended YaleB and PF01 face data sets. The used mapping methods are: PCA, LPP, Parameterless LPP, and enhanced LPP. Top: Extended YaleB face data set. Bottom: PF01 face data set.

Table **1** illustrates the best mean recognition rates obtained with five face data sets. The used mapping methods are: Random Projection (RP), PCA, classic LPP, parameterless LPP and enhanced LPP. The averages are computed over 10 splits of the data set for which the training/test percentage was set to 70% − 30%. In Table 1 and subsequent tables, LPP-1 denotes the Parameter-less LPP and LPP-2 denotes the Enhanced LPP.

Table 1. Mean of the recognition rate (%) of different methods on five face databases. The results are averaged over 10 random splits of the data set for which the training/test percentage was set to 70% − 30%. LPP-1 denotes the Parameter-less LPP and LPP-2 denotes the Enhanced LPP.

Face data set	RP	PCA	classic LPP	LPP-1	LPP-2
UMIST	97.9	**98.0**	97.9	**98.0**	**98.0**
Yale	80.2	80.0	79.3	82.0	**83.0**
Extended YaleB	85.2	78.0	85.6	88.7	**91.6**
PF01	48.0	48.4	48.5	**51.0**	50.0
PIE	59.7	58.0	62.3	67.5	**69.4**

Table **2** illustrates the same recognition rates where the training/test percentage was set to 30% − 70%. These depicted recognition rates correspond to the maximum dimension used by each method. As can be seen, the proposed versions of LPP gave better results than PCA and the classic LPP. For UMIST data set the improvement is negligible since this data set does not contain a lot of variabilities.

Table 2. Mean of recognition rate (%) of different methods on five face databases. The results are averaged over 10 random splits of the data set for which the training/test percentage was set to 30% - 70%.

Face data set	RP	PCA	classic LPP	LPP-1	LPP-2
UMIST	91.0	**92.4**	91.6	91.7	92.1
Yale	71.1	71.8	73.8	72.7	**74.5**
Extended YaleB	78.0	73.0	80.6	82.8	**86.4**
PF01	38.0	55.4	55.8	56.7	**56.9**
PIE	56.5	54.0	59.4	61.7	**63.1**

Table **3** shows the mean of the recognition rate (%) on FERET face database using the classic LPP with three neighborhood sizes (first three columns) and the two proposed variants of LPP (last two columns). The averages are computed over 10 splits of the data set for which the training/test percentage was set to 70% − 30%.

Table 3. Mean of the recognition rate (%) on FERET face database using the classic LPP with three neighborhood sizes (first three columns) and the two proposed variants of LPP (last two columns). The results are averaged over 10 random splits of the data set for which the training/test percentage was set to 70% − 30%. The total number of the training images was 2107 images.

	LPP (K=13)	LPP (K=20)	LPP (K=50)	LPP-1	LPP-2
FERET	48.2	47.4	45.9	58.1	52.5

Table **4** shows the mean of the recognition rate (%) on FERET face database using the classic LPP with three neighborhood sizes (first three columns) and the two proposed variants of LPP (last two columns). The averages are computed over 10 splits of the data set for which the training/test percentage was set to 30% − 70%.

Table 4. Mean of the recognition rate (%) on FERET face database using the classic LPP with three neighborhood sizes (first three columns) and the two proposed variants of LPP (last two columns). The results are averaged over 10 random splits of the data set for which the training/test percentage was set to 30% − 70%. The total number of the training images was 903 images.

	LPP (K=5)	LPP (K=9)	LPP (K=13)	LPP-1	LPP-2
FERET	33.2	32.5	31.9	40.3	36.3

We can observe that in general the proposed schemes (parameterless LPP and enhanced LPP) have performed better than the classic LPP. They have not required any tedious setting for the parameters. We can also observe that the performance of the enhanced LPP can be slightly worse than that of the parameterless LPP for PF01 and FERET. This can be explained by the fact that both methods use the same dimension given by PCA so that the total scatter matrix for large databases used by the enhanced LPP cannot be very accurate. As can be seen the improvement obtained by the proposed enhanced LPP depends on the data set used.

We have also computed the recognition rates using disjoint test sets. To this end, we use 4-fold cross validation procedure. The obtained recognition rates for UMIST, Yale, Extended YaleB, PF01, PIE, and FERET are depicted respectively in Table **5**, **6**, **7**, **8**, **9**, and **10**. By inspecting these results, we can observe that the proposed LPP algorithms (parameterless LPP and enhanced LPP) perform better than the classic LPP. The average recognition rates associated with 4-fold cross validation are close to those obtained with 10 random splits using 70% of training data. The obtained standard deviations are large since the number of folds is relatively small.

Table 5. Recognition rate (%) of different methods on UMIST data set. The results correspond to 4-fold cross validation (4 disjoint test sets).

UMIST	Classic LPP	LPP-1	LPP-2
fold1	71.8	76.3	82.2
fold2	92.5	94.0	94.1
fold3	89.6	93.3	93.3
fold4	70.5	71.7	70.6
Mean (std. dev.)	81.1 (11.5)	83.9 (11.5)	**85.1** (11.0)

Table 6. Recognition rate (%) of different methods on YALE data set. The results correspond to 4-fold-cross validation (4 disjoint test sets).

Yale	Classic LPP	LPP-1	LPP-2
fold1	73.3	83.3	83.3
fold2	73.3	76.7	73.3
fold3	96.6	93.3	96.7
fold4	89.3	89.3	92.0
Mean (std. dev.)	83.1 (11.7)	85.7 (7.2)	**86.3** (10.2)

Table 7. Recognition rate (%) of different methods on Extended Yale B data set. The results correspond to 4-fold-cross validation (4 disjoint test sets).

Extended YaleB	Classic LPP	LPP-1	LPP-2
fold1	94.5	96.3	97.3
fold2	70.0	65.7	70.1
fold3	90.7	89.3	93.9
fold4	61.2	58.6	66.1
Mean (std. dev.)	79.1 (16.0)	77.3 (17.8)	**81.8** (16.0)

Table 8. Recognition rate (%) of different methods on PF01 data set. The results correspond to 4-fold-cross validation (4 disjoint test sets).

PF01	Classic LPP	LPP-1	LPP-2
fold1	76.6	78.9	75.2
fold2	46.0	49.0	41.6
fold3	31.7	41.3	34.3
fold4	64.5	70.6	68.0
Mean (std. dev.)	54.7 (19.8)	**60.0** (17.7)	54.8 (19.8)

Table 9. Recognition rate (%) of different methods on PIE data set. The results correspond to 4-fold-cross validation (4 disjoint test sets).

PIE	Classic LPP	LPP-1	LPP-2
fold1	47.4	53.7	51.1
fold2	68.8	73.3	73.2
fold3	60.4	67.1	65.2
fold4	69.8	76.4	77.2
Mean (std. dev.)	61.6 (10.4)	**67.6** (10.0)	66.7 (11.5)

Table 10. Recognition rate (%) of different methods on FERET data set. The results correspond to 4-fold-cross validation (4 disjoint test sets).

FERET	Classic LPP	LPP-1	LPP-2
fold1	21.1	32.9	24.9
fold2	48.6	63.3	55.65
fold3	58.6	67.4	61.3
fold4	45.0	49.5	46.7
Mean (std. dev.)	43.3 (15.9)	**53.3** (15.6)	47.1 (15.9)

Fig. (**3**) illustrates nine misclassified probe images using the enhanced LPP. These examples corresponding to PIE, PF01 and FERET databases, respectively. The left column depicts the probe images and the right one depicts the Nearest Neighbor image found in the embedded space. As can be seen, the combined effect of pose and lighting can be a serious perturbing effect for face recognition.

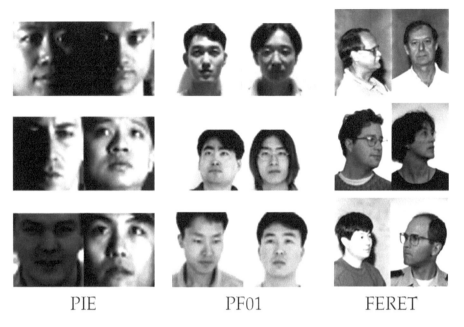

PIE   PF01   FERET

Fig. (3). Some misclassified images for the enhanced LPP. In every row, the left image is the probe image, and the right one is the most similar one using the Nearest Neighbor classifier in the embedded space.

We have measured the CPU time associated with the classic computation of the graph and the proposed adaptive computation. To this end, 173 training images from UMIST face data set were considered. The corresponding CPU times were 1.7s for the classic k-NN based graph and 2.7s for the adaptive scheme. We performed the experiments using a non-optimized MATLAB code running on a PC equipped with an 860 core-i7 CPU running at 2.8 GHz.

Performance Comparison for OLPP and SLPP

We have also integrated the proposed enhancements into the frameworks of OLPP and SLPP. We have also studied the effect of using the adaptive affinity matrix in OLPP and SLPP. Table **11** illustrates the performance obtained by OLPP based on the classic graph and on the proposed adaptive affinity matrix. Table **12** illustrates the performance obtained by SLPP based on the classic graph and on the proposed adaptive affinity matrix. As can be seen, introducing an adaptive affinity matrix will improve the performance of recognition on average. We have observed that for the supervised case this improvement is very small. This can be explained by the fact that the use of labels in the affinity matrix provided very useful information.

Table 11. Mean recognition rate (%) of different methods on five face databases. The results are averaged over 10 random splits of the data set for which the training/test percentage was set to 30% - 70%.

Face data set	Classic OLPP	Parameterless OLPP
UMIST	83.4	**85.6**
Yale	68.4	**72.3**
Extended YaleB	**70.6**	69.7
PF01	55.0	**56.8**
PIE	59.2	**60.2**
FERET	42.5	**43.1**

Table 12. Mean recognition rate (%) of different methods on five face databases. The results are averaged over 10 random splits of the data set for which the training/test percentage was set to 30% - 70%.

Face data set	Classic SLPP	Parameterless SLPP
UMIST	94.8	**95.6**
Yale	81.3	**84.3**
Extended YaleB	**96.2**	96.1
PF01	87.4	**88.1**
PIE	79.9	**80.2**
FERET	55.5	**56.3**

CONCLUSION

We proposed a new parameterless and enhanced Locality Preserving Projection method. It is well known that a well-designed graph and proper weights of edges tend to result in good performance of LPP. But LPP is going to work well only when the conditions are strictly satisfied. The affinity matrix computation does not need any parameter setting. The constraint imposed in the optimization makes the obtained mapped data uncorrelated. Experimental results show that the proposed approaches gave better results than the classic LPP. In general, the second variant of LPP (enhanced LPP) gave the best results. However, we observed that for large databases (such as FERET database) the results of the parameterless LPP can be better than the results of the enhanced LPP. In practice, if there is no prior hint on which method should be used for computing the embedding, one possible solution consists in using both embedding methods. To classify a probe image, it is embedded using both transforms. Then, the Nearest Neighbor classifier is utilized in both spaces. The decision can be guided by the best distance found. Although we concentrated on the face recognition problem, the proposed approaches could also be applied to other category of objects. The proposed approaches can also be used for data visualization and clustering.

NOTES

1 http://en.wikipedia.org/wiki/Correlation_and_dependence.

CONFLICT OF INTEREST

The author confirms that author has no conflict of interest to declare for this publication.

ACKNOWLEDGMENTS

We want to thank Elsevier for allowing us to reuse material for this chapter from our following paper: F. Dornaika and A. Assoum, "Enhanced and parameterless locality preserving projections for face recognition," *Neurocomputing*, ISSN: 0925-2312, vol. 99, pp. 448-457, 2013, doi:10.1016/j.neucom.2012.07.016.

REFERENCES

[1]   I. Borg, and P. Groenen, *Modern Multidimensional Scaling: theory and applications.* Springer-Verlag New York, 2005.

[2]   A.M. Martinez, and M. Zhu, "Where are linear feature extraction methods applicable?", *IEEE Trans. Pattern Anal. Mach. Intell.,* vol. 27, no. 12, pp. 1934-1944, 2005.
[http://dx.doi.org/10.1109/TPAMI.2005.250] [PMID: 16358412]

[3]   S. Yan, D. Xu, B. Zhang, H.J. Zhang, Q. Yang, and S. Lin, "Graph embedding and extensions: a general framework for dimensionality reduction", *IEEE Trans. Pattern Anal. Mach. Intell.,* vol. 29, no. 1, pp. 40-51, 2007.
[http://dx.doi.org/10.1109/TPAMI.2007.250598] [PMID: 17108382]

[4]   M. Brand, *Charting a manifold in Advances in Neural Information Processing Systems 15,* 2003 pp.

985-992. Available from: [http://papers.nips.cc/paper/2165-charting-a-manifold.pdf]

[5]   R. Wang, S. Shan, X. Chen, Q. Dai, and W. Gao, "Manifold-manifold distance and its application to face recognition with image sets", *IEEE Trans. Image Process.,* vol. 21, no. 10, pp. 4466-4479, 2012.
[http://dx.doi.org/10.1109/TIP.2012.2206039] [PMID: 22752133]

[6]   O. Arandjelovic, and R. Cipolla, "Achieving robust face recognition from video by combining a weak photometric model and a learnt generic face invariant", *Pattern Recognit.,* vol. 46, no. 1, pp. 9-23, 2013.
[http://dx.doi.org/10.1016/j.patcog.2012.06.024]

[7]   B.Z. Yan, D. Xu, and H-J. Zhang, "Graph embedding: A general framework for dimensionality reduction", In: *Int. Conference on Computer Vision and Pattern Recognition*, 2005.

[8]   J. Liu, and Y-P. Tan, "Regularized locality preserving projections and its extensions for face recognition", *IEEE Trans. Systems, man and Cybermetrics, Part B: Cybermetrics,* vol. 40, 2010.

[9]   L. Zhang, L. Qiao, and S. Chen, "Graph-optimized locality preserving projections", *Pattern Recognit.,* vol. 43, pp. 1993-2002, 2010.
[http://dx.doi.org/10.1016/j.patcog.2009.12.022]

[10]   M. Belkin, and P. Niyogi, "Laplacian eigenmaps for dimensionality reduction and data representation", *Neural Comput.,* vol. 15, no. 6, pp. 1373-1396, 2003.
[http://dx.doi.org/10.1162/089976603321780317]

[11]   Y. Tang, and R. Rose, "A study of using locality preserving projections for feature extraction in speech recognition", In: *International Conference on Acoustics, Speech and Signal Processing*, 2008, pp. 1569-1572.
[http://dx.doi.org/10.1109/ICASSP.2008.4517923]

[12]   J. Shermina, "Application of Locality Preserving Projections in Face Recognition", *International Journal of Advanced Computer Science and Applications,* vol. 1, no. 3, 2010. [IJACSA].

[13]   W-L. Chao, J-Z. Liu, and J-J. Ding, "Facial age estimation based on label-sensitive learning and age-oriented regression", *Pattern Recognit.,* vol. 46, no. 3, pp. 628-641, 2013.
[http://dx.doi.org/10.1016/j.patcog.2012.09.011]

[14]   Y. Xu, A. Zhong, J. Yang, and D. Zhang, "LPP solution schemes for use with face recognition", *Pattern Recognit.,* vol. 43, pp. 4165-4176, 2010.
[http://dx.doi.org/10.1016/j.patcog.2010.06.016]

[15]   X. He, S. Yan, Y. Hu, P. Niyogi, and H-J. Zhang, "Face recognition using laplacianfaces", *IEEE Trans. Pattern Anal. Mach. Intell.,* vol. 27, no. 3, pp. 328-340, 2005.
[http://dx.doi.org/10.1109/TPAMI.2005.55] [PMID: 15747789]

[16]   D. Cai, X. He, J. Han, and H.J. Zhang, "Orthogonal laplacianfaces for face recognition", *IEEE Trans. Image Process.,* vol. 15, no. 11, pp. 3608-3614, 2006.
[http://dx.doi.org/10.1109/TIP.2006.881945] [PMID: 17076419]

[17]   Z. Zheng, Z. Zhao, and Z. Yang, "Gabor feature based face recognition using supervised locality preserving projection", In: *Advanced Concepts for Intelligent Vision Systems.* 2006, pp. 644-653.
[http://dx.doi.org/10.1007/11864349_59]

[18]   Z. Jin, J. Yang, Z. Hu, and Z. Lou, "Face recognition based on uncorrelated discriminant transformation", *Pattern Recognit.,* vol. 34, no. 7, pp. 1405-1416, 2001.
[http://dx.doi.org/10.1016/S0031-3203(00)00084-4]

[19]   O. Arandjelovic, "Gradient edge map features for frontal face recognition under extreme illumination changes", In: *BMVC 2012: Proceedings of the British Machine Vision Association Conference.* BMVA Press, 2012, pp. 1-11.

[20]   W. Chen, M.J. Er, and S. Wu, "Illumination compensation and normalization for robust face recognition using discrete cosine transform in logarithm domain", *IEEE Trans. Syst. Man Cybern. B Cybern.,* vol. 36, no. 2, pp. 458-466, 2006.
[http://dx.doi.org/10.1109/TSMCB.2005.857353] [PMID: 16602604]

CHAPTER 5

Face Recognition Using 3D Face Rectification

Alireza Bosaghzadeh[1,*], Mohammadali Doostari[2], Alireza Behrad[2]

[1] *University of the Basque Country, San Sebastian, Spain*

[2] *Shahed University, Tehran, Iran*

Abstract: While face recognition algorithms have shown promising results using gray level face images, their accuracy deteriorate if the face images are not frontal. As the head can move freely, it causes a key challenge in the problem of face recognition. The challenge is how to automatically and without manual intervention recognize non-frontal face images in a gallery with frontal face images. The rotation is a linear problem in 3D space and can be solved easily using the 3D face data. However, the recognition algorithms based on 3D face data gain less recognition rates than the methods based on 2D gray level images. In this chapter, a sequential algorithm is proposed which uses the benefits of both 2D and 3D face data in order to obtain a pose invariant face recognition system. In the first phase, facial features are detected and the face pose is estimated. Then, the 3D data (Face depth data) and correspondingly the 2D image (Gray level face data) are rotated in order to obtain a frontal face image. Finally, features are extracted from the frontal gray level images and used for classification. Experimental results on FRAV3D face database show that the proposed method can drastically improve the recognition accuracy of non-frontal face images.

Keywords: 3D rotation, Biometric, Depth data, Dimensionality reduction, Ellipse fitting, Eigen problem, Eigenface, Face recognition, Facial features, Fisherface, Feature extraction, Gray level image, IRAD contours, Linear Discriminant Analysis, Least mean square, Manifold learning, Mean filter, Mean curvature, Nearest Neighbor classifier, Pose estimation.

INTRODUCTION

A lot of researchers has focused on face recognition as it has a variety of applications in surveillance systems, law enforcement, human-computer interfaces

---

* **Address to Corresponding author Alireza Bosaghzadeh:**University of the Basque Country, Paseo Manuel Lardizabal, 1, 20018, San Sebastian, Spain; Tel: +34 943015060; Fax: +34 943015590; E-mail: alireza.bosaghzadeh@ehu.es

and access controls [1]. Also, it observes a lot of attention in the biometric area since capturing a face image is passive and non intrusive compared to other biometrics like fingerprint or iris. Variations in illumination conditions, aging, facial expressions and face pose make this task difficult [2 - 10].

Different algorithms were proposed to overcome these variations. Wang *et al.* [11] used a set of images with different variations in lightening and head movement for training. They model each image set as a manifold and proposed a manifold-manifold distance to compare the distance between each two manifolds. Arandjelovic *et al.* [12] proposed a "re-illumination" algorithm to solve the lightening condition variations. They obtained high recognition rates on databases with large variation in capturing conditions.

Among different variations, since the head can move easily, the face pose variation is one of the most important challenges. Although, most of the available face recognition techniques obtain high recognition rates on frontal faces [13, 14], their results deteriorate if the face is not frontal. Thus, handling the pose variations between the gallery face images and the test image is an extremely important factor for many practical application scenarios. A variety of methods have been proposed specifically to address the pose invariance face recognition [15 - 19].

To cover the possible appearances under all horizontal rotations, Singh *et al.* [20] construct a panoramic view of a face by using a mosaicing scheme. They use frontal view and rotated views to generate the panoramic view. In the recognition phase, the synthesised face mosaics were matched with face images in arbitrary poses by a SVM classifier.

In [18], a 3D Generic Elastic Model is used to construct the 3D model of each subject using only a single 2D image, which can match the images in the same pose as the test image. Before matching, a linear regression approach is used to estimate the pose of the test image. Then, all 3D models are rendered in different poses around the estimated pose and the rendered images are used for matching against the test query. Finally, by normalized correlation matching, the distances between the test query and the synthesized images are computed.

In [21], the authors proposed a method to synthesize a frontal view from a non-frontal face image. They divide the face into overlapping patches and estimate the local warp in order to obtain the frontal view of the patches. To find the optimal warps, they use a discrete Markov random fields and a belief propagation method in order to formulate the optimization problem as a discrete labeling algorithm.

In [17], a multi-pose face recognition approach using fusion of scale invariant features (FSIF) is proposed. They fuse some scale invariant features extracted by scale invariant features transforms (SIFT) from several different poses of 2D face images. Finally, Linear Discriminant Analysis (LDA) dimensionality reduction is used to extract the optimum features for classification.

The authors in [22] combine two feature descriptors namely Gabor Wavelet and enhanced LBP features for feature extraction. Then, they use a generalized neural network for classification. Their method is efficient only for slight variations in pose and deteriorates with large pose variations. Later in [19], they use higher-order moments of curvelet as features and a curvelet neural network for classification. The experimental results show that their proposed method achieve higher accuracy for pose invariant face recognition than standard back propagation neural network.

PROPOSED METHOD

In this chapter, we introduce a novel pose invariant face recognition technique which can overcome the rotation problem in face recognition. As pose variation is non-linear in two-dimensional (2D) space but linear in three-dimensional (3D) space, we solve the pose variation problem in the 3D space and then use it to map 2D data. The proposed method uses only frontal images for training and performs matching on test images with pose variations. It has a sequential procedure to eliminate the effect of pose variation in the test data. In the first step, preprocessing tasks are done on the data to remove noises from the 3D face data. In the second phase, facial features in the 3D image are located. In the third step, the 3D rotation of the face (*i.e.*, face pose) is estimated. Knowing the face pose, 3D face data and correspondingly the gray level face image are rotated in order to obtain the frontal face image. Finally, gray level images are used for feature extraction and classification.

FACE DATABASE

We use FRAV3D face database[1] which has data from 105 Caucasian adult subjects (81 males/24 women). The capturing process was conducted under controlled conditions with the absence of daylight illumination. In order to cover possible variations of lighting, gesture and face pose, a total of 16 acquisitions were taken from each individual in different face turns and illumination conditions. In details, there are 4 frontal images, 2 with positive and 2 with negative rotation about y-axis, one with positive and one with negative rotation about the x-axis, one looking up and one looking down image, one with open mouth, one with a smile and two with illumination variations. One of the advantages of this database comparing to other databases is that between every two captures, only one perturbation parameter was changed. For each acquisition, a BMP file contained colored image of 400×400 pixels (2D image) and a VRML file of depth data (3D data) is provided. In Fig. (**1**), 16 samples of one subject can be seen which contains the gray level image (2D data) and the depth data (3D data).

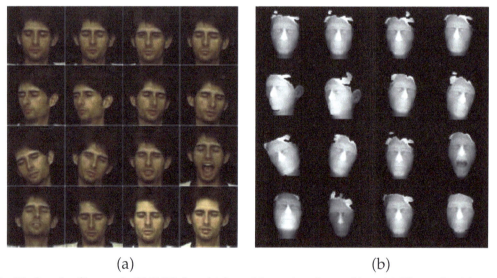

(a)   (b)

Fig. (1). Sample of images in FRAV3D face database. 16 samples of one subject, **(a)** 2D gray level images and **(b)** 3D depth data.

PREPROCESSING

In the first step, because of some artifacts and noises that might happen with the presence of hair and occlusions in the process of capturing depth data, it is important to preprocess the 3D data. In the FRAV3D database, there are two types of noise in the depth data, holes and spikes. Hole is referred to an area in the data where there is no depth information available. Depending on the capturing technology, holes might happen because of the presence of an obstacle between the sensor and the face or because of some special colors in the object (*e.g.*, black color like hair and bear). To remove the holes in the data, we use cubic inter-polation. We filled the holes by using the available data around them and applying cubic interpolation. In Fig. (**2a**), we can see a 3D face with holes in the eyebrows, eyelashes and around nose area. In Fig. (**2b**), the same face after hole filling is shown.

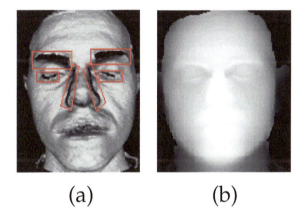

(a)   (b)

Fig. (2). (a) 3D depth data before preprocessing with holes in the eyebrows, eyelashes and around nose area. **(b)** Same depth data after filling the holes.

The second noise is spike which is a single point or a small area with a very different depth value than the surrounding area. In Fig. (**3a**), we can see a face surface with spikes in the are below the nose and eyebrows. To remove this noise, we look in a window of 3 × 3. If there is a big difference between the center point and the neighbor values, we remove the center point and estimate it with cubic interpolation. In Fig. (**3b**), we can see the same face surface after removing the spikes.

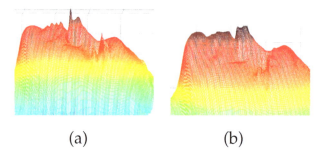

(a)   (b)

Fig. (3). Spike noise in the face surface. **(a)** A face surface with spike noise below the nose and eyebrows. **(b)** A face surface after removing the spikes.

Apart from the two above mentioned noises, there might exist some disparities in the face surface. To remove them and obtain a smooth surface, after eliminating holes and spikes, we filter the whole surface with a mean filter.

FACIAL FEATURE DETECTION

After processing the face surface, the next step is to detect the facial features. Since tip of the nose is the center and the highest protruding point on a face surface, it plays an important role in face normalization, face registration, face modelling, facial features extraction, pose estimation and face recognition.

Different techniques have been proposed to locate the nose tip. In [23], the authors quantify the rotations about the y-axis and then rotate the face surface around this axis. In each rotation, the closest point to the camera is selected as a candidate for nose location. Then, the exact location of the nose is selected from the candidates. This method can locate the nose only if the rotation is around y-axis and if there is rotation in other axes it will be computationally expensive. A similar method was also proposed in [24].

They rotate the input image around the y-axis in step of 3° to generate 2D profiles. Then they use a circle whose center travels along the profile to detect nose tip candidates. Finally, the detection of real nose tip is carried out by calculating the cardinal point fitness and spike fitness. Since this method relies on the accurate and complete 2D left-and-right-most face profiles, it is likely to fail in self-occlusion 3D faces caused by pose variation.

The proposed method to locate the nose tip is based on mean curvature (H). As the nose has a hill structure, the area around the nose tip will have high curvature. We use this property to locate the nose tip in a 3D face surface. Since this property of the nose and also the mean curvature are rotation invariant, the proposed method is invariant to face surface rotation and can locate the nose in faces with different rotations. It should be mentioned that a similar method was also proposed by [25] which locate the inner eye points and nose tip by Gaussian curvature (K) and mean curvature (H). However, our proposed method only uses the mean curvature and does not need the Gaussian curvature.

To locate the nose, first we calculate the mean curvature of the face surface. We can see a face surface in Fig. (**4a**) and its mean curvature in Fig. (**4b**). As we can see it is difficult to find a region which has a high curvature. To overcome this problem, we use the mean filter. Using the mean filter on one hand will eliminate the small areas with high curvature values and on the other hand will prominent the location of the nose (area with high curvature). Also the mean filter is a low-pass filter which can reduce the effect of noise. In Fig. (**4c**), the mean curvature image after filtering is showed. As we can see, by applying the mean (average) filter, the areas with high curvature values are magnified. Another areas in the surface which are magnified are the inner eyes which has valley shapes (*i.e.*, areas with high negative mean curvature). As we can see in Fig. (**4c**) the two inner eye areas are also magnified.

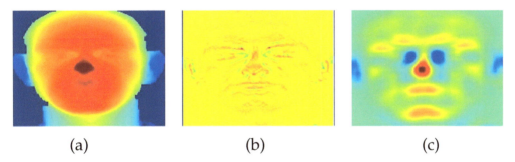

(a)   (b)   (c)

Fig. (4). Facial feature detection process. (**a**) An example of face surface. (**b**) mean curvature image. (**c**) mean curvature image after applying the mean filter. As we can see the nose tip and inner eye points are magnified.

By having the filtered image, we look into an area with high mean curvature values (nose area) where two areas with high negative mean curvature values (inner eyes) are located above it. Finally, the tip of the nose is set to the point with the highest mean curvature value.

The results obtained on FRAV3D face database show that the proposed method is able to locate the nose tip and inner eyes with high accuracy. In Fig. (**5**), we illustrate 12 sample images with facial features being marked with a red plus. As we can see, even with face rotation or facial expression (*e.g.*, laughing or open mouth), the proposed method was able to locate the nose tip.

In general, the proposed method only uses the mean curvature, does not need a training phase and unlike [23, 24] locates the facial features in different pose angles without the need for surface rotation.

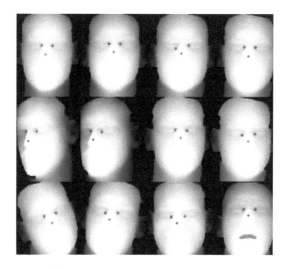

Fig. (5). 12 face surfaces that the facial features are marked.

POSE ESTIMATION

Head pose estimation is a very important task which is useful in many real life applications such as human-computer interaction (HCI), gaze direction estimation, driver fatigue prediction and face recognition [26]. A lot methods have been proposed to address this problem using gray level images [27 - 30] and depth data [31 - 33]. Unlike gray level images, depth data are less affected by illumination variation. The authors in [32] present an algorithm for recovering the six degree of freedom of motion of a head. To estimate the head pose, they use a least-squares minimization of the difference between the measured rate of change of depth at a point and the rate predicted by the depth rate constraint equation. The method in [33], generates and evaluates many pose hypotheses in parallel using graphic processing units (GPUs). A real time head detection and head pose estimation from a low quality depth data is proposed in [34] which uses discriminative random regression forests. They use Kinect sensor and build their own database for evaluation.

The proposed method for pose estimation is an automatic method which needs neither parameter adjustment nor training data.

The procedure for pose estimation is as followed.

- Calculate IRAD contours centered at the nose tip.
- Fit an ellipse to one of these contours and estimate the rotation about the z-axis .
- Estimate the yaw angle (rotation around y-axis) by comparing the depth difference in the right and left side of the contour.
- Estimate the pitch angle (rotation around x-axis) by evaluating the the depth difference between the top and bottom of the face.

In the following, we will describe each step in details.

IRAD Contours

The idea of IRAD^2 contour was proposed by Pears *et al.* [35, 36]. IRAD contour is a space curve on a 3D surface with a fix distance relative to a predefined reference point. Thus, it can be considered as the intersection of a sphere (with radius r and center point p) with an object surface. If the surface is flat, the contours will form circles with radius r, but for non-planar surfaces they will form different shapes [36]. Since these contours are obtained by using polar distance, they are invariant to the rotation of surface. Hence, even with the surface rotation, the obtained contour points will remain the same.

In our work, we set the center of the sphere at the nose tip. The reason for this choice is that, as we explained in the previous section, the nose tip can be easily detected even if the face surface has rotations. To calculate the IRAD image of a face surface, we use Eq. (1) where x_{nose}, y_{nose} and z_{nose} are the location of the nose and x, y and z are the face surface points in x, y and z axes, respectively.

$$IRAD(x,y) = \sqrt{(x - x_{nose})^2 + (y - y_{nose})^2 + (z - z_{nose})^2} \tag{1}$$

In Fig. (**6**), a face surface with the obtained IRAD image along with some of the contours with specific radiuses are illustrated.

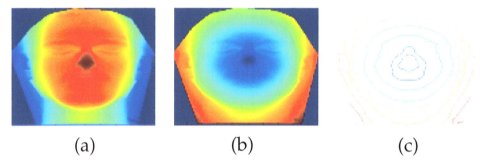

| (a) | (b) | (c) |

Fig. (6). Isoradios image. (**a**) a sample face surface, (**b**) the IRAD image, the points with same distance from the nose tip have the same value, (**c**) sample of some contours with specific distances.

In order to estimate the face rotation, we use a contour with a specific distance. This distance neither should be too large which might get out of the face surface, nor too small that due to occlusion will not have enough points to estimate the rotation. We empirically set this distance to 2.5 cm from the nose tip.

Ellipse Fitting And Roll Correction

To estimate the rotation about the z-axis, we fit an ellipse to the contour points and look at the long diameter of it. In case there is no rotation about the z-axis, the long diameter of the ellipse should be vertical. In other words, the deviation of the long diameter from a vertical line shows the roll.

$$ax^2 + bxy + cy^2 + dx + ey = 1 \tag{2}$$

The general equation of an ellipse is as:

where a, b, c, d and e are the parameters and x and y are the ellipse coordinates.

By setting the x and y as the contour points, we estimate the ellipse parameters by Least Mean Square error. In Fig. (**7**), a contour on the face surface and the fitted ellipse are shown. As it is clear from the image, the long diameter of the ellipse has a deviation from a vertical line.

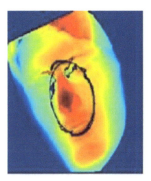

Fig. (7). A face surface where a specific contour points are selected. Also points of a fitted ellipse are demonstrated on the surface.

Having the ellipse parameters, we can find the deviation of the long diameter from a vertical line by using Eq. (3) where arctan is the inverse tangent function and a, b and c are the parameters of the fitted ellipse. After estimating the roll angle, we rotate the face surface such that the deviation from the z-axis becomes zero (*i.e.*, the roll rotation becomes zero).

$$\theta_z = \arctan \frac{b}{c - a} \tag{3}$$

Yaw Correction

Next step is to correct the yaw angle by rectifying the rotation of the face around the y-axis. We consider a face without the yaw angle, if corresponding points on the left and right side of the face have the same depth values. For this purpose, we use the contour points located on the right and left sides of the face surface. We take the average of the depth of the contour points on the right and left side of the face and estimate the yaw angle by Eq. (4) where z_{left} and z_{right} are the depth average and x_{left} and x_{right} are the average of x-coordinate values on the left and right side of the face surface, respectively.

$$\theta_y = \text{atan} \frac{z_{left} - z_{right}}{x_{left} - x_{right}} \qquad \qquad \textbf{(4)}$$

It should be mentioned that to estimate the yaw angle, it is not necessary to rotate all the face surface and only the rotation of the selected IRAD contour which was used to estimate the roll is enough.

After estimating the yaw angle, we rotate the face surface in order to rectify the face rotation around the y-axis.

Pitch Correction

The final step for face alignment is to normalize the rotation about the x-axis. For this purpose we use the area below the nose tip and the saddle point area between the inner eye corners. As there is not a clear criterion for a face surface without rotation about the x-axis, we consider a face surface without pitch, if the area below the nose tip and the saddle point area between the inner eye corners have the same depth values. To calculate the pitch, we use the Eq. (5) where z_2 and z_1 are the depth and y_2 and y_1 are the coordinates in y-axis of saddle point and the area below the nose, respectively.

$$\theta_x = \text{atan} \frac{z_2 - z_1}{y_2 - y_1} \qquad \qquad \textbf{(5)}$$

In order to overcome the misalignments that might happen in the process of landmark detection, we use the average values calculated in an area of 5×5 pixels around the saddle point area between the eyes and the area below the nose.

Table 1. The accuracy of the pose estimation method. Each row shows the percentage of the samples with a specific or lower pose estimation error.

	about z-axis	about y-axis	about x-axis
Less than 10° error	98.21%	99.52%	98.81%
Less than 6° error	94.88%	98.81%	92.33%
Less than 3° error	77.46%	95.00%	67.24%

Accuracy Of The Pose Estimation Method

To calculate the accuracy of the proposed pose estimation method, we manually mark four points on the face, one on the right and one on left side, one on the saddle point between the inner eyes and one on the area below the nose. Then, we recalculate the face pose for each axis according to the mentioned criteria. If the proposed method has correctly estimated the pose, the rotated face should be frontal and the calculated pose according to the manually selected points should be zero. In other words, the obtained angles from the manually selected points, show the error of the proposed pose estimation method. For evaluation, we use all 3D face images in the FRAV3D databases which correspond to the 14 images of 105 subjects. In Table **1**, we report the percentage of samples with pose estimation errors less than 10, 6 and 3 degrees. Also in Fig. (**8**), we plot the percentage of samples having less than a specific error in the pose estimation.

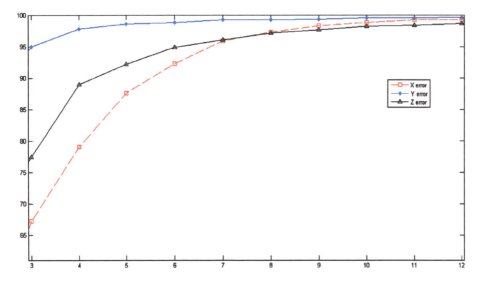

Fig. (8). Percentage of face images and their corresponding pose estimation error.

ROTATION AND POST PROCESSING

Having the pose of each face image, the next step is to rotate it and obtain the frontal face image. Considering α, β and γ as the required rotations about the x, y and z axes, respectively, we use the rotation matrix in Eq. (6). The last row and column are added to the rotation matrix in order to rotate the gray scale image without affecting the rotation of depth data. Hence, our data matrix has 4 columns where the forth one is the gray level data corresponding to each vertex. In Fig. (**9**), we demonstrate two gray scale images before and after alignment.

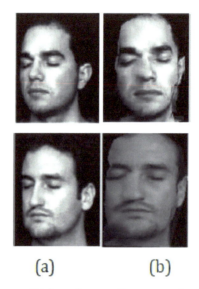

(a)   (b)

Fig. (9). **(a)** Original gray level images. **(b)** Same images after constructing frontal faces.

After constructing the frontal face image, we do illumination normalization and masking. We normalize gray level images to have values between 0 and 255 and then mask them to remove the unwanted area around the face.

$$R = \begin{bmatrix} \cos\beta\,\cos\gamma & -\cos\beta\,\sin\gamma & \sin\beta & 0 \\ \sin\alpha\,\sin\beta\,\cos\gamma + \cos\alpha\,\sin\gamma & -\sin\alpha\,\sin\beta\,\sin\gamma + \cos\alpha\,\cos\gamma & -\sin\alpha\,\cos\beta & 0 \\ -\cos\alpha\,\sin\beta\,\cos\gamma + \sin\alpha\,\sin\gamma & \cos\alpha\,\sin\beta\,\sin\gamma + \sin\alpha\,\cos\gamma & \cos\alpha\,\cos\gamma & 0 \\ 0 & 0 & 0 & 1 \end{bmatrix} \quad (6)$$

EXPERIMENTS

Having the frontal face images, the final step is to extract features from these rotated face images and classify them. Different linear [37 - 39] and nonlinear [40, 41] manifold learning methods are proposed for dimensionality reduction and feature extraction. The benefit of linear techniques over nonlinear ones is that they allow a simple mapping of data onto the embedding space, leading to classification methods which are computationally efficient and simple.

We use two linear techniques, namely, Principal Component Analysis (PCA) and Linear Discriminant Analysis (LDA) to extract features from the gray level face images.

PCA aims to preserve the Euclidean distances between the samples and projects the samples along the directions of maximal variances. It tries to find a linear mapping matrix $\mathbf{A}$ that maximizes where $\text{cov}(\mathbf{X})$ is the covariance matrix of the data matrix $\mathbf{X}$. The linear mapping $\mathbf{A}$ can be obtained by using the eigenvectors associated with the largest eigenvalues of the eigen problem:

$$\text{trace}(\mathbf{A}^T\text{cov}(\mathbf{X})\mathbf{A}), \tag{7}$$

$$\text{cov}(\mathbf{X})\mathbf{A} = \mathbf{A}\Lambda, \tag{8}$$

where Λ is the diagonal matrix of eigenvalues.

Unlike PCA which is an unsupervised technique, LDA is a supervised method. The objective function of PCA which is projecting the data along the maximum variance, may not be adequate for classification. However, in LDA the goal is to find projection directions onto which the within-class scatter $(\mathbf{S}_w)$ is minimized while the between-class scatter $(\mathbf{S}_b)$ is maximized. The within-class scatter matrix shows the sum of the variation of data in each class and is given by:

$$\mathbf{S}_w = \sum_{c=1}^{C}\sum_{i\in c}(\mathbf{x}_i - \bar{\mathbf{x}}_c)(\mathbf{x}_i - \bar{\mathbf{x}}_c)^T, \qquad \bar{\mathbf{x}}_c = \frac{1}{N_c}\sum_{i\in c}\mathbf{x}_i, \tag{9}$$

where C is the number of classes, N_c is the number of samples in class c and $\bar{\mathbf{x}}_c$ is the average of data in each class. The between-class scatter matrix shows the distribution of heterogeneous data and is estimated by calculating the covariance matrix between the center of classes and the center of the whole data as:

$$\mathbf{S}_b = \sum_{c=1}^{C} N_c(\bar{\mathbf{x}}_c - \bar{\mathbf{x}})(\bar{\mathbf{x}}_c - \bar{\mathbf{x}})^T, \qquad \bar{\mathbf{x}} = \frac{1}{N}\sum_{i}\mathbf{x}_i, \tag{10}$$

where $\bar{\mathbf{x}}$ is the average of all samples. The linear mapping $\mathbf{A}$ can be obtained by using the eigenvectors associated with largest eigenvalues of the eigen problem:

$$(\mathbf{S}_w)^{-1}\mathbf{S}_b\mathbf{A} = \mathbf{A}\Lambda, \tag{11}$$

where Λ is the diagonal matrix of eigenvalues.

After calculating the projection matrices of PCA and LDA, we project the data into the obtained embedding spaces and use nearest neighbor classifier for classification.

The goal of the experiments is to evaluate the improvement obtained by applying the proposed 3D face rectification technique. We select the frontal face images plus the two images with illumination variations for training and the non-frontal face images for testing.

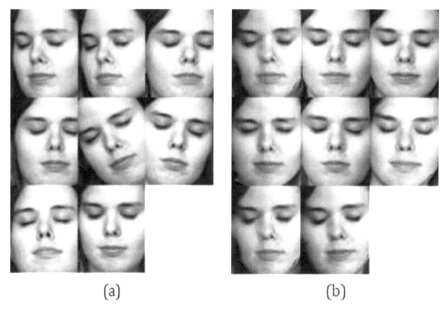

(a)   (b)

Fig. (10). (a) Eight non-frontal images before rotation rectification. **(b)** Same eight images after rotation rectification.

We conduct two experiments. In the first experiment, the non-frontal images are used as test to see the classification accuracy before any face rectification. A set of non-frontal images corresponding to a person can be seen in Fig. (**10a**). In the second experiment, we rectify the rotation of the face images using the proposed 3D face rectification method and then use them as the test data. A set of these rectified images corresponding to the same person are demonstrated in Fig. (**10b**). By comparing the recognition accuracy in the first and second experiment, we can evaluate the improvement obtained by the proposed method. As there are eight pose variations, we report eight recognition rates corresponding to each pose separately.

In Table **2**, we report the results obtained by the PCA dimensionality reduction followed by the nearest neighbor classifier which is called Eigenface. Comparing the results of before and after pose rectification, we observe that the average classification accuracy has increased more than 51% which shows the enhancement caused by the proposed method even when we use an unsupervised manifold learning method.

Table 2. Recognition rate on FRAV3D face database using Eigenface method (PCA) before and after 3D face rectification. Each row correspond to the images with a specific rotation angle. The last row shows the average recognition rate over all rotated images.

	Before rectification	After rectification
Rotation about y-axis	31.13%	53.33%
Rotation about y-axis	30.18%	61.68%
Rotation about y-axis	41.50%	91.58%
Rotation about y-axis	41.50%	89.71%
Rotation about x-axis	3.77%	85.84%
Rotation about x-axis	9.43%	83.80%
Rotation about z-axis	46.22%	85.85%
Rotation about z-axis	16.98%	83.96%
Average recognition rate	27.59%	79.46%

Table **3** shows the results obtained by the supervised method Fisherface (*i.e.*, LDA followed by nearest neighbor classifier). We observe the same behaviour when we use the images rectified by the proposed method. For instance, the average accuracy has improved more than 60% by using the rectified images.

Table 3. Recognition rate on FRAV3D face database using Fisherface method (LDA) before and after 3D face rectification. Each row correspond to the images with a specific rotation angle. The last row shows the average recognition rate over all rotated images.

	Before rectification	After rectification
Rotation about y-axis	36.79%	80.00%
Rotation about y-axis	28.30%	82.24%
Rotation about y-axis	31.13%	97.19%
Rotation about y-axis	32.07%	94.92%
Rotation about x-axis	8.49%	93.39%
Rotation about x-axis	15.09%	94.28%
Rotation about z-axis	70.75%	88.68%
Rotation about z-axis	34.90%	96.23%
Average recognition rate	32.19%	90.87%

Comparing the results of Tables **2** and **3** shows that in all of the rotation variations, the recognition rate has increased drastically after image rectification with the proposed method. Also we observe that in general, the improvement in recognition rate is higher when the rectified faces had rotations about the x-axis and z-axis than the rotation about the y-axis. This is due to the fact that in the rectification process, the images with rotation about the z-axis can be reconstructed completely, since there is no occlusion in the images. Besides, for rotation about the x-axis, there is not big occlusions in the face and the gray scale image can be constructed properly. However, in the rotation about the y-axis there are occluded parts in the face which can not be constructed properly and should be estimated. For instance, as we observed in Fig. (**9b**) the area on the left side of the nose and left side of the face were occluded and the proposed method failed to reconstruct them properly.

CONCLUSION

In this chapter, we present a new method for pose invariant face recognition using 3D face rectification. The proposed method needs neither manual intervention nor training data. It automatically detects the facial features, estimates the face pose, rotates and constructs the frontal face image. It uses the 3D data to estimate the face pose, rotate the depth and gray level data and obtain a frontal face image.

However, in the face recognition part it only uses the 2D (gray level) data. The recognition rates obtained by fisherface method showed that the proposed method was able to increase the accuracy of the recognition task about 60% on average.

For future work, we will use both depth data and gray level image to extract facial features, since there are accurate methods which can detect the facial features using gray level images. In addition, if we consider a symmetric texture assumption on the left and right side of the face, in the rotation about the y-axis, we can use the texture in the not occluded parts of the face to estimate the texture in the occluded parts and increase the quality of the constructed face. Furthermore, fusion of depth (3D) with gray level (2D) data for feature extraction can improve the recognition accuracy.

NOTES
[1]http://frav.escet.urjc.es/databases/FRAV3D
[2]IsoRADious

CONFLICT OF INTEREST

The author confirms that author has no conflict of interest to declare for this publication.

ACKNOWLEDGMENTS

Declared none.

REFERENCES

[1]   A. Suruliandi, K. Meena, and R. Reena Rose, "Local binary pattern and its derivatives for face recognition", *Computer Vision, IET,* vol. 6, no. 5, pp. 480-488, 2012.
[http://dx.doi.org/10.1049/iet-cvi.2011.0228]

[2]   Q. Chen, J. Yao, and W. Cham, "3d model-based pose invariant face recognition from multiple views", *Computer Vision, IET,* vol. 1, no. 1, pp. 25-34, 2007.
[http://dx.doi.org/10.1049/iet-cvi:20060014]

[3]   S. Nikan, and M. Ahmadi, "Local gradient-based illumination invariant face recognition using local phase quantisation and multi-resolution local binary pattern fusion", *Image Processing, IET,* vol. 9, no. 1, pp. 12-21, 2015.
[http://dx.doi.org/10.1049/iet-ipr.2013.0792]

[4]   G. Ghinea, R. Kannan, and S. Kannaiyan, "Gradient-orientation-based pca subspace for novel face

recognition", *Access, IEEE,* vol. 2, pp. 914-920, 2014.
[http://dx.doi.org/10.1109/ACCESS.2014.2348018]

[5]   Y. Cheng, Z. Jin, C. Hao, and X. Li, "Illumination invariant face recognition with particle swarm optimization", In: *Data Mining Workshop (ICDMW)*, December 2014, pp. 862-866.

[6]   A. Shafie, F. Hafiz, and Y. Mustafah, "Face recognition using illumination-invariant local patches", In: *Intelligent and Advanced Systems (ICIAS), 2014 5th International Conference*, June 2014, pp. 1-6.
[http://dx.doi.org/10.1109/ICIAS.2014.6869544]

[7]   W. Lin, M. Chen, K. Widder, Y. Hu, and N. Boston, "Fusion of multiple facial regions for expression-invariant face recognition", *Multimedia Signal Processing, 2007. MMSP 2007. IEEE 9th Workshop ,* pp. 426-429
[http://dx.doi.org/10.1109/MMSP.2007.4412907]

[8]   I. Mpiperis, S. Malassiotis, and M. Strintzis, ""Bilinear models for 3-d face and facial expression recognition," Information Forensics and Security", *Information Forensics and Security, IEEE Transactions,* vol. 3, no. 3, pp. 498-511, September 2008.

[9]   M. Faraji, and X. Qi, "Face recognition under varying illumination with logarithmic fractal analysis", *Signal Processing Letters, IEEE,* vol. 21, no. 12, pp. 1457-1461, December 2014.
[http://dx.doi.org/10.1109/LSP.2014.2343213]

[10]   O. Arandjelovic´, "Unfolding a face: From singular to manifold", In: *Computer Vision âA´ S, ACCV 2009,* vol. 5996. Springer: Berlin Heidelberg, 2010, pp. 203-213. Ser. Lecture Notes in Computer Science.
[http://dx.doi.org/10.1007/978-3-642-12297-2_20]

[11]   R. Wang, S. Shan, X. Chen, Q. Dai, and W. Gao, "Manifold-manifold distance and its application to face recognition with image sets", *IEEE Trans. Image Process.,* vol. 21, no. 10, pp. 4466-4479, 2012.
[http://dx.doi.org/10.1109/TIP.2012.2206039] [PMID: 22752133]

[12]   O. Arandjelovic´, and R. Cipolla, "Achieving robust face recognition from video by combining a weak photometric model and a learnt generic face invariant", *Pattern Recognit.,* vol. 46, no. 1, pp. 9-23, 2013.
[http://dx.doi.org/10.1016/j.patcog.2012.06.024]

[13]   M. Aroussi, M. Hassouni, S. Ghouzali, M. Rziza, and D. Aboutajdine, "Local appearance based face recognition method using block based steerable pyramid transform", *Signal Processing.,* vol. 91, no. 1, pp. 38-50, 2011.
[http://dx.doi.org/10.1016/j.sigpro.2010.06.005]

[14]   B. Zhang, Y. Gao, S. Zhao, and J. Liu, "Local derivative pattern versus local binary pattern: face recognition with high-order local pattern descriptor", *IEEE Trans. Image Process.,* vol. 19, no. 2, pp. 533-544, 2010.
[http://dx.doi.org/10.1109/TIP.2009.2035882] [PMID: 19887313]

[15]   K. Okada, and C. Malsburg, "Pose-invariant face recognition with parametric linear subspaces", In: *Automatic Face and Gesture Recognition. Proceedings. Fifth IEEE International Conference*, May 2002, pp. 64-69.

[16]   H. Hanselmann, H. Ney, and P. Dreuw, "Pose-invariant face recognition with a two-level dynamic

programming algorithm", In: *Pattern Recognition and Image Analysis,* vol. 7887. Springer: Berlin Heidelberg, 2013, pp. 11-20. Ser. Lecture Notes in Computer Science.
[http://dx.doi.org/10.1007/978-3-642-38628-2_2]

[17]   I. Wijaya, K. Uchimura, and G. Koutaki, "Multi-pose face recognition using fusion of scale invariant features", *Proceedings of the 2011 2nd International Congress on Computer Applications and Computational Science,* vol. 144, pp. 207-213, 2012.
[http://dx.doi.org/10.1007/978-3-642-28314-7_28]

[18]   U. Prabhu, J. Heo, and M. Savvides, "Unconstrained pose-invariant face recognition using 3d generic elastic models", *IEEE Trans. Pattern Anal. Mach. Intell.,* vol. 33, no. 10, pp. 1952-1961, 2011.
[http://dx.doi.org/10.1109/TPAMI.2011.123] [PMID: 21670487]

[19]   P. Sharma, R. Yadav, and K. Arya, "Pose-invariant face recognition using curvelet neural network", *Biometrics, IET,* vol. 3, no. 3, pp. 128-138, 2014.
[http://dx.doi.org/10.1049/iet-bmt.2013.0019]

[20]   R. Singh, M. Vatsa, A. Ross, and A. Noore, "A mosaicing scheme for pose-invariant face recognition", *IEEE Trans. Syst. Man Cybern. B Cybern.,* vol. 37, no. 5, pp. 1212-1225, 2007.
[http://dx.doi.org/10.1109/TSMCB.2007.903537] [PMID: 17926704]

[21]   H.T. Ho, and R. Chellappa, "Pose-invariant face recognition using Markov random fields", *IEEE Trans. Image Process.,* vol. 22, no. 4, pp. 1573-1584, 2013.
[http://dx.doi.org/10.1109/TIP.2012.2233489] [PMID: 23247858]

[22]   P. Sharma, K. Arya, and R. Yadav, "Efficient face recognition using wavelet-based generalized neural network", *Signal Process.,* vol. 93, no. 6, pp. 1557-1565, 2013. [special issue on Machine Learning in Intelligent Image Processing.].
[http://dx.doi.org/10.1016/j.sigpro.2012.09.012]

[23]   X. Lu, and A. Jain, "Automatic feature extraction for multiview 3d face recognition", In: *Automatic Face and Gesture Recognition. FGR 2006. 7th International Conference*, April 2006, pp. 585-590.

[24]   X. Peng, M. Bennamoun, and A. Mian, "A training-free nose tip detection method from face range images", *Pattern Recognit.,* vol. 44, no. 3, pp. 544-558, 2011.
[http://dx.doi.org/10.1016/j.patcog.2010.09.015]

[25]   K.I. Chang, K.W. Bowyer, and P.J. Flynn, "Multiple nose region matching for 3D face recognition under varying facial expression", *IEEE Trans. Pattern Anal. Mach. Intell.,* vol. 28, no. 10, pp. 1695-1700, 2006.
[http://dx.doi.org/10.1109/TPAMI.2006.210] [PMID: 16986549]

[26]   E. Murphy-Chutorian, and M.M. Trivedi, "Head pose estimation in computer vision: a survey", *IEEE Trans. Pattern Anal. Mach. Intell.,* vol. 31, no. 4, pp. 607-626, 2009.
[http://dx.doi.org/10.1109/TPAMI.2008.106] [PMID: 19229078]

[27]   J. Kaminski, D. Knaan, and A. Shavit, "Single image face orientation and gaze detection", *Mach. Vis. Appl.,* vol. 21, no. 1, pp. 85-98, 2009.
[http://dx.doi.org/10.1007/s00138-008-0143-1]

[28]   F. Dornaika, and B. Raducanu, "Three-dimensional face pose detection and tracking using monocular videos: tool and application", *IEEE Trans. Syst. Man Cybern. B Cybern.,* vol. 39, no. 4, pp. 935-944,

2009.
[http://dx.doi.org/10.1109/TSMCB.2008.2009566] [PMID: 19336335]

[29]   N. Pyun, H. Sayah, and N. Vincent, "Adaptive haar-like features for head pose estimation", In: *Image Analysis and Recognition*, vol. 8815. Springer: Berlin Heidelberg, 2014, pp. 94-101. Ser. Lecture Notes in Computer Science.
[http://dx.doi.org/10.1007/978-3-319-11755-3_11]

[30]   X. Liu, H. Lu, and D. Zhang, "Head pose estimation based on manifold embedding and distance metric learning", In: *Computer Vision âA S, ACCV 2009*, vol. 5994. Springer: Berlin Heidelberg, 2010, pp. 61-70. Ser. Lecture Notes in Computer Science.
[http://dx.doi.org/10.1007/978-3-642-12307-8_6]

[31]   S. Malassiotis, and M.G. Strintzis, "Robust real-time 3d head pose estimation from range data", *Pattern Recognit.*, vol. 38, no. 8, pp. 1153-1165, 2005.
[http://dx.doi.org/10.1016/j.patcog.2004.11.020]

[32]   F. Kondori, S. Yousefi, H. Li, S. Sonning, and S. Sonning, "3d head pose estimation using the kinect", In: *Wireless Communications and Signal Processing (WCSP), 2011 International Conference*, Nov 2011, pp. 1-4.
[http://dx.doi.org/10.1109/WCSP.2011.6096866]

[33]   M. Breitenstein, D. Kuettel, T. Weise, L. Van Gool, and H. Pfister, "Realtime face pose estimation from single range images", In: *Computer Vision and Pattern Recognition, 2008. CVPR 2008. IEEE Conference*, June 2008, pp. 1-8.
[http://dx.doi.org/10.1109/CVPR.2008.4587807]

[34]   G. Fanelli, T. Weise, J. Gall, and L. Van Gool, "Real time head pose estimation from consumer depth cameras", In: *Pattern Recognition*, vol. 6835. Springer: Berlin Heidelberg, 2011, pp. 101-110.Ser. Lecture Notes in Computer Science.
[http://dx.doi.org/10.1007/978-3-642-23123-0_11]

[35]   T. Heseltine, *"Face recognition: Two-dimensional and three-dimensional techniques"*, Ph.D. dissertation, The University of York, Department of Computer Science, September 2005.

[36]   N.E. Pears, and T. Heseltine, "Isoradius contours: New representations and techniques for 3d face registration and matching", *3rd Int. Symp. on 3D Data Processing, Visualization, and Transmission, Chapel Hill, NC, USA*, pp. 176-183, 2006.
[http://dx.doi.org/10.1109/3DPVT.2006.85]

[37]   F. Dornaika, and A. Bosaghzadeh, "Exponential local discriminant embedding and its application to face recognition", *IEEE Trans. Cybern.*, vol. 43, no. 3, pp. 921-934, 2013.
[http://dx.doi.org/10.1109/TSMCB.2012.2218234] [PMID: 23144037]

[38]   F. Wang, X. Wang, D. Zhang, C. Zhang, and T. Li, "marginface: A novel face recognition method by average neighborhood margin maximization", *Pattern Recognit.*, vol. 42, no. 11, pp. 2863-2875, 2009.
[http://dx.doi.org/10.1016/j.patcog.2009.04.015]

[39]   M. Sugiyama, "Dimensionality reduction of multimodal labeled data by local fisher discriminant analysis", *J. Mach. Learn. Res.*, vol. 8, pp. 1027-1061, 2007.

[40]   M. Belkin, and P. Niyogi, "Laplacian eigenmaps for dimensionality reduction and data representation",

Neural Comput., vol. 15, no. 6, pp. 1373-1396, 2003.
[http://dx.doi.org/10.1162/089976603321780317]

[41]   M. Brand, "Charting a manifold", In: *Advances in Neural Information Processing Systems 15..* MIT Press, 2003, pp. 985-992.

CHAPTER 6

3D Face Recognition

Alireza Behrad[*]

Department of Electrical and Electronic Engineering, Shahed University, Tehran-Qom Exp. Way, 3319118651, Tehran, Iran

Abstract: 3D face recognition algorithms are a group of methods which utilize 3D geometry of face and facial feature for recognition. In comparison with 2D face recognition algorithms that employ intensity or color based features, they are generally robust against lighting condition, head orientation, facial expression and make-up. 3D face recognition has several advantages. Firstly, the shape and the related features of 3D face can be acquired independent from lighting condition. Secondly, the pose of 3D face data can be easily corrected and used for subsequent pose invariant feature extraction. Thirdly, 3D face data are less affected by skin color, face cosmetic and similar face reflectance factors. 3D face recognition may include several stages such as 3D image acquisition, face localization, feature extraction and face recognition. In this article, different algorithms and the pipeline for 3D face recognition are discussed.

Keywords: 3D Face matching, 3D Face recognition, 3D Face registration, 3D Image acquisition, 3D Surface descriptors active triangulation, Biometric identifiers, Curvature descriptors, Face alignment, Face analysis, Face recognition face segmentation, Facial features, Facial landmarks, Feature extraction, Head pose estimation, Human identification, Laser scanner, Nose tip detection, Range images.

INTRODUCTION

Recently the use of biometric information for verification and identification has been getting more and more importance. Generally, biometric information includes various information regarding the human's body, feature or characteristics like height, hair color, finger print, face shape, *etc*. However, some

---

[*] **Address to Corresponding Author Alireza Behrad:** Electrical and Electronic Engineering Department, Faculty of Engineering, Shahed University, Tehran-Qom Exp. Way, 3319118651, Tehran, Iran; Tel: (+98-21) 51212070; Fax: (+98-21) 51212020; E-mail: behrad@shahed.ac.ir

Fadi Dornaika (Ed)

biometrics can be easily changed and cannot be used as unique feature for identification or verification. A biometric identifier is defined as a unique, distinctive and measurable identifier that can be used as a means to describe, verify or identify a person. Fingerprint, iris, palm print and hand motion are general biometric identifiers.

Recently face recognition is increasingly employed as a tool for human identification and verification. Face recognition is defined as a process for identification or verification of a human person based on the characteristics of face. For humans, faces are the most important characteristic for human recognition and we generally know and recognize each other based on the face information. Face recognition is an identification tool at distance. It means that the subject under the identification can be in an arbitrary place unaware of identification process. Because of exclusive characteristics of face recognition systems, they are widely used in security system for human identification and verification. In addition to human recognition, facial features can be used in various applications like human computer interface, age, gender or race analysis, expression determination and so forth.

Face recognition algorithms may be based on 2D or 3D information of the face. 2D face recognition algorithms use intensity or textured based information for the sake of face recognition [1 - 3]. On the contrary, 3D face recognition algorithm use 3D model of face or 3D shape information for face recognition [4 - 6]. Some algorithms also employ mixture of 2D-3D information to enhance the efficiency of face recognition algorithms [7 - 9]. 3D face recognition has several advantages. Firstly, the shape and the related features of 3D face can be acquired independent from lighting condition. Secondly, the pose of 3D face data can be easily corrected and used for subsequent pose invariant feature extraction. Thirdly, 3D face data are less affected by skin color, face cosmetic and similar face reflectance factors.

There are some limitations with 3D face recognition comprising 3D face acquisition, change of face shape with age and expression to name a few. The acquisition of 3D or range images is the main limitation of 3D face recognition algorithms. Laser scanners are general equipment to capture 3D images; however they may damage eyes and are not proper for real-time applications. Therefore, stereo imaging or methods like shape from shading are generally employed to capture 3D face images.

Face localization is the first stage in 3D face recognition. Depending on 3D face acquisition equipment, the 3D face image may include various noises like spikes, holes and distortions; therefore different preprocessing algorithms may be applied to improve the quality of 3D data for further processing. When the noise-free 3D image is obtained, the registration algorithm is employed for the alignment of the 3D faces. The registration stage generally requires facial feature extraction which is an important step for efficient face recognition. Finally, feature extraction algorithm is utilized to extract proper features for recognition.

In this article, various stages for 3D face recognition are discussed and different algorithms for each stage are explained. The rest of this article is organized as follows. In the next section, 3D face acquisition systems are discussed. Section 3 describes various 3D face representation approaches. Section 4 deals with some preprocessing steps for 3D face recognition. Section 4 presents some existing algorithms for 3D face alignment. Various 3D face recognition algorithms appear in section 5 and we conclude the article in section 6.

3D FACE ACQUISITION

Laser scanners are mostly used equipment for capturing 3D images. Laser scanners may be constructed based on the phase shift, time-of-flight and active triangulation principles. In phase shift approach, laser beam with sinusoidally modulated optical power is sent toward the target. Then the phase shift between the sent and reflected light is measured to calculate the distance between laser source and the target. In addition to phase shift, it is also necessary to have the number of full cycles that a light wave undergoes during the transmitted path. In time-of-flight approach, a very short laser pulse is sent to the target and the return light is detected to measure the round-trip time. The round-trip time together with light speed in the medium is utilized to measure the distance between the target and laser emitting device. Time-of-light approach is a suitable method for long-distance measurement. However for near distances, laser scanning based on active triangulation is employed for 3D reconstruction which results in more precise measurement. Fig. (**1**) shows general block scheme of a 3D laser scanner based on active triangulation. As shown in the figure, the scanner includes a laser emitting device to send a laser beam to the target. Then the image of the beam is captured using a camera. In this approach, the 3D position of laser beam on the target is calculated as [10]:

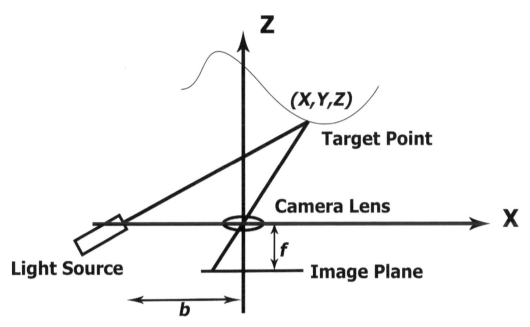

Fig. (1). 3D laser scanner using active triangulation.

$$\begin{pmatrix} X \\ Y \\ Z \end{pmatrix} = \frac{b}{f\cot\alpha - x} \begin{pmatrix} x \\ y \\ f \end{pmatrix} \tag{1}$$

where b is the distance between camera and laser emitting source which is called baseline, f is the focal length of camera, (x, y) are the coordinates of laser point in the camera image and α is the angle between laser direction and image plane.

Laser based approaches are generally accurate; however they are not safe for capturing 3D image of face and may damage the eye. Additionally the capture time is high. Stereovision or binocular imaging utilizes two or several cameras for

3D capture of the scene. 3D face systems using stereovision can capture at a faster rate, however they produce 3D face images with lower accuracy. Fig. (**2**) shows stereo system with parallel optical axes. To find detailed information for the image point (x_l, y_l) on the left image it is necessary to find the corresponding point on the right image (x_r, y_r). Then depth or Z coordinate of the image point in 3D space is calculated as [11]:

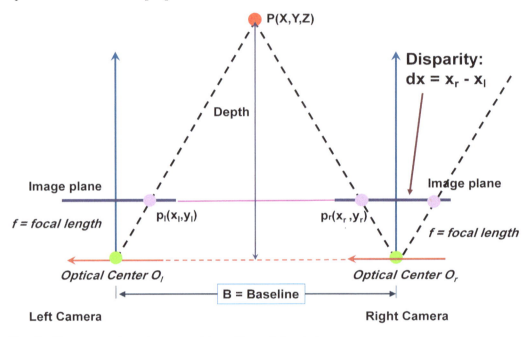

Fig. (2). 3D reconstruction using stereo vision with parallel optical axes.

$$Z = f \frac{B}{dx} \qquad (2)$$

where f is focal of the cameras, B or baseline is the distance between two stereo camera and dx or disparity is defined as:

$$dx = x_r - x_l \qquad (3)$$

The main source of error for stereovision systems is matching error. Therefore, proper algorithms for extraction and matching of distinctive local features are required. Some algorithms like active stereovision systems also employ structured light pattern to enhance the accuracy of the captured 3D data.

Stereo vision can only produce 3D face information for common field of view two stereo cameras. To create 3D depth map for whole face area, 3D face images are captured using stereo cameras from different views of face. Then a 3D image registration or mosaicing algorithm [12, 13] is deployed to construct full 3D model of face. In [13] a 3D face registration algorithm is proposed based on Thin Plate Spline (TPS) transformation and deformable model. Consider reference 3D face H_1 and target 3D face H_2 which are defined as:

$$H_k = \{p_{ki} \mid p_{ki} = (x_{ki}, y_{ki}, z_{ki}), i = 1, \ldots, N_k, K = 1, 2\} \tag{4}$$

where N_k is the number of face points on H_k. TPS transformation, f, is determined by matching corresponding points M_k on H_k as:

$$M_k = \{L_{ki} \mid L_{ki} = (x_{ki}, y_{ki}, z_{ki}), i = 1, \ldots, M, K = 1, 2\} \tag{5}$$

$$L_{2j} = f(L_{1j}), j = 1, \ldots, M, K = 1, 2\} \tag{6}$$

where M is the number of control points subject to $M \leq N_k$. Additionally, the f function should minimize the blending energy function $E(f)$ which is defined as:

$$E(f) = \int_{R^3} \left(\left(\frac{\partial^2 f}{\partial x^2}\right)^2 + \left(\frac{\partial^2 f}{\partial y^2}\right)^2 + \left(\frac{\partial^2 f}{\partial z^2}\right)^2 + 2\left(\frac{\partial^2 f}{\partial xy}\right)^2 + 2\left(\frac{\partial^2 f}{\partial xz}\right)^2 + 2\left(\frac{\partial^2 f}{\partial yz}\right)^2 \right) \tag{7}$$

TPS transformation can be decomposed into components including affine transformation **d**, and non-affine transformation **w** as follows:

$$f(\mathbf{P}) = \mathbf{Pd} + \mathbf{Kw} \tag{8}$$

where **P** are face points H_1 with homogeneous coordinate form as $(x, y, z, 1)$, **d** is a 4×4 affine transformation matrix and **w** is a 4×4 matrix representing the non-affine deformation and **K** is TPS kernel. In [13] the following energy function is defined and minimized to obtain **d**, **w** and λ.

$$E(\mathbf{d}, \mathbf{w}, \lambda) = \frac{1}{M} \sum_{j=1}^{M} \| L_{2j} - f(L_{1j}) \| + \lambda E(f) \tag{9}$$

As mentioned before, the calculation of **d** and **w** requires some control points on H_1 and their corresponding points on H_2. Control points on H_1 may be selected manually or randomly or based on the local shape information of face. In [13] Farthest Point Sampling (FPS) Strategy is employed for evenly distributed control point extraction on the face. In each stage of this algorithm, a farthest point to the currently selected control points is selected as the new control point. To find the farthest point, the surface of face is tessellated by Voronoi diagram using the selected control points.

Various algorithms may also be employed to find corresponding for control points. Iterative Closest Point (ICP) algorithm [14] is a generally used algorithm to find corresponding for control points. In ICP algorithm, it is assumed that two 3D surfaces **M** and **S** are related to each other under a rigid transformation **T** as follows:

$$\mathbf{S} = \{s_1, s_2, \ldots, s_{Ns}\} \tag{10}$$

$$\mathbf{M} = \{m_1, m_2, \ldots, m_{Nm}\} \tag{11}$$

$$\mathbf{M}_i = \mathbf{T}(s_i) \tag{12}$$

where s_i and m_i are the coordinates of different points in 3D surfaces **S** and **M**, respectively, N_s and N_m are the number of points in 3D surfaces **S** and **M**, respectively, and **T** is the transformation function. ICP algorithm aims to conjointly find corresponding points and the transformation matrix between two 3D surfaces as follows [14]:

- Let $\|\mathbf{s} - \mathbf{m}\|$ denote the Euclidean distance between point $\mathbf{s} \in \mathbf{S}$ and $\mathbf{m} \in \mathbf{M}$.
- Let also $CP(\mathbf{s}, \mathbf{M})$ be the closest point in **M** to the surface point **s** and $DCP(\mathbf{s}, \mathbf{M})$ is defined as $\|\mathbf{s} - CP(\mathbf{s}, \mathbf{M})\|$.
- Let $\mathbf{T}^{[0]}$ be an initial estimate of the transformation between two surfaces.

- Repeat for $k = 1, ..., kmax$ or until convergence:
    - Compute the set of correspondences $C = \cup^{Ns}_{i=1}\{(s_i, CP(T^{[k-1]}(s_i),M))|$ $D_{CP}(T^{[k-1]}(s_i),M) < d_{th}\}$ where d_{th} is a threshold to obtain corresponding points.
    - Compute the new transformation function $\mathbf{T}^{[k]}$ that minimizes the mean square error between point pairs in $\mathbf{C}$.

3D FACE REPRESENTATION

The output of 3D face capturing systems are generally defined by X, Y and Z values that is defined as a point cloud. Point clouds define a large set of 3D points from the surface of the face that are generated by 3D face scanners.

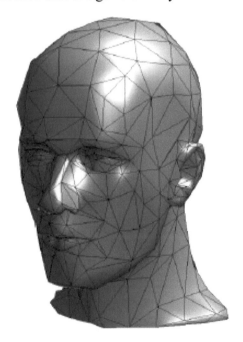

Fig. (3). Triangular mesh model on a synthetic 3D face.

Although some face recognition algorithms have utilized this format of data for feature extraction and face recognition, some others used different surface representation algorithms. There is a close relation between the feature extraction approach and algorithm for face representation. In other word, the face representation algorithm should provide a suitable platform for feature extraction.

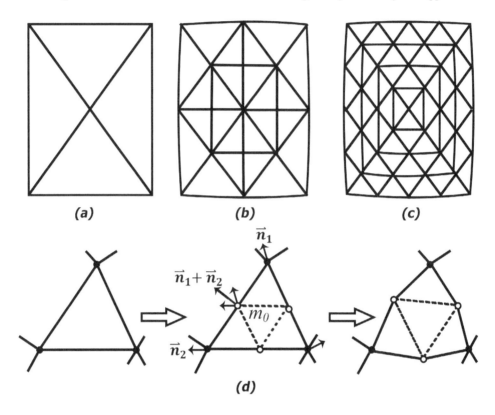

Fig. (4). Various stages of mesh generation algorithm [17]; (a) basic mesh M_0, (b),(c) dividing each triangle into smaller triangles, (d) updating node positions.

3D meshes like polygon or triangular mesh models are one the mostly used approaches for face representation [15 - 19]. A 3D mesh model is a collection of polygons or triangles consisting 3D points and edges that connect them. Fig. (**3**) shows a triangular mesh model on a synthetic 3D face. Several algorithms have been proposed for converting a point cloud to 3D surface model like Delaunay triangulation. Delaunay triangulation preserves empty circle criteria which means for any edge of the triangulated mesh it is possible to find a circle containing edges' ending points but not including other points. Incremental approach is one of the efficient approaches for Delaunay triangulation. In this approach, first a large triangle is considered to contain all node points. Then the points are added into mesh one by one preserving the Delaunay empty circle criteria.

In [17] triangulated mesh is used for 3D face representation and recognition. Fig.

(4) shows various stages of mesh generation using this algorithm. In this approach, face area and nose tip is detected and the basic mesh M_0 (Fig. **4a**) is constructed. Then in each stage of the algorithm, every triangle is divided into four new triangles (Fig. **4b** and **4c**). To fit the 3D face data using the generated mesh, the mesh vertices are updated in two stages. In the first stage, the location of vertex m is updated as:

$$\Delta m = kd \, \|n_1\text{-}n_2\|(\mathrm{n}_1 + \mathrm{n}_2) \tag{13}$$

$$m = m_0 + \Delta m \tag{14}$$

where k is a positive factor, n_1 and n_2 are the normal of two corresponding vertices as shown in Fig. (**4d**) and d denotes the length of edge. To align the generated mesh with points of 3D face, the following energy function is defined and minimized:

$$E(\alpha) = E_{dis}(x_i, \alpha) + \omega E_{smooth}(\alpha) \tag{15}$$

where x_i and α denote the location of face points and mesh nodes respectively and ω is positive weight regulating smoothness energy function. $E_{dis}(x_i, \alpha)$ and $E_{smooth}(\alpha)$ are defined as:

$$E_{dis}(x_i, \alpha) = \sum_{i=1}^{N} w_i d^2(x_i, \alpha) \tag{16}$$

$$E_{smooth}(\alpha) = \sum_{k=1}^{n} \left\| v_k - \frac{1}{m_k} \sum_{i=1}^{m_k} v_{ki} \right\|^2 \tag{17}$$

In [19] spiral facets are used for 3D mesh generation and face representation. In this algorithm the closed contour of the face is covered by triangular facets called Fout. To fill gaps between Fouts, the second group of triangles is used that are called Fgaps. Fig. (**5**) shows face triangulation using spiral facet. As shown in the figure, in each stage Fouts and Fgaps construct a ring. By iteration of the algorithm a spiral facets are constituted for face representation and recognition.

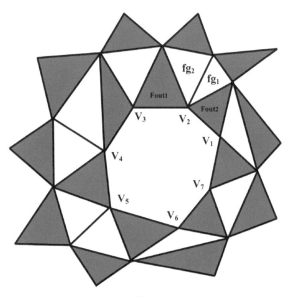

Fig. (5). Face triangulation using spiral facets. Grey and white facets denote Fout and Fgap facets respectively [19].

PREPROCESSING

Inaccuracy and errors in the matching process of stereovision system especially in non-textured area cause spiky noise in the generated 3D face data. Moreover, the 3D face model only includes a set of points in 3D space that are visible in both of the stereo images. This means that any areas that are occluded from either of the cameras will produce gaps or holes in 3D face model. Median filtering is a widely used approach for removing spikes. Median filter is a nonlinear filter which its output is determined by median of neighboring pixels defined by centering a window on the pixel. To fill holes, interpolation algorithms like bilinear, bicubic or nearest neighbor methods are employed.

In addition to filling hole and removing speckle noise, some existing 3D face recognition algorithm detect face area in 3D image before feature extraction and applying face recognition algorithm [20, 21]. The reason for this preprocessing stage is to remove hair and neck areas for robust feature extraction or 3D data registration.

Nose tip detection is variously used as a means to crop central part of 3D face for the next stages of 3D face recognition. Several existing work utilize curvature descriptors like mean (H) and Gaussian (K) curvatures or HK segmentation for nose tip detection. Mean and Gaussian curvatures are defined as:

$$2H = \frac{(1 + h_x^2)h_{yy} - 2h_x h_y h_{xy}(1 + h_y^2)h_{xx}}{(1 + h_x^2 + h_y^2)^{3/2}} \qquad (18)$$

$$K = \frac{h_{xx}h_{yy} - h_{xy}^2}{(1 + h_x^2 + h_y^2)^2} \qquad (19)$$

Table **1** shows patch shape classification using H and K curvatures [11]. Since H and K are sensitive to noise, smoothing filter to remove noise is inevitable for the calculation of H and K values.

Table 1. Patch shape classification using H and K curvatures [11].

H	K	Surface Patch Shape
0	0	Plane
0	+	Concave Cylindrical
0	-	Convex Cylindrical
+	+	Concave Elliptic
+	-	Convex Elliptic
-	-, 0, +	Hyperbolic

In [22] a multi-stage algorithm is used for nose tip detection. In the first stage of this algorithm, the concept of Effective Energy (EE) is used to select some candidates as nose tip. The EE for a point P on the face is defined as:

$$d_i = (P_i\text{-}P).Np = \|P_i\text{-}P\|cos(\theta) \qquad (20)$$

where d_i is EE for point P_i in the neighborhood of P, N_P is normal to face on point P, P_i is a face point in the neighborhood of P and θ is the angle between N_P and $(P_i - P)$. To calculate N_P, the covariance matrix for the set of neighborhood points $\Omega = \{x_1, x_2, ..., x_n\}$ is calculated as:

$$Q = \sum_{x_i \in \Omega} (x_i - \bar{x})(x_i - \bar{x})^T \tag{21}$$

Then by calculation of the eigenvectors and eigenvalues of the covariance matrix, the eigenvector corresponding to smallest eigenvalue is considered as normal vector.

By considering the neighboring set for a point P as $NB(P) = \{p_1, p_2, ..., p_n\}$ and the corresponding EE set as $EE(P) = \{d_1, d_2, ..., d_n\}$, the point P is a candidate for nose tip only if $\forall\ d_i < 0$.

In the second stage of the algorithm, the mean and variance of EE set is calculated as:

$$\mu = \frac{1}{n} \sum_{i=1}^{n} d_i \tag{22}$$

$$\sigma^2 = \frac{1}{n} \sum_{i=1}^{n} (d_i - \mu)^2 \tag{23}$$

These two features are used to train a Support Vector Machine (SVM) classifier for refining candidate nose tip points. Applying SVM classifier does not remove all false points. Therefore in the third stage of the algorithm, three areas with more dense points are opted and the average coordinate is selected as nose tip location.

Detection of facial features like nose tip in the rotated or profile face is the main challenge of face recognition algorithm. To handle the problem, Peng *et al.* [23] utilized projected right most and left most boundaries of the rotated face for nose tip detection. To this end, 3D face is rotated by various rotation angles between -90 to 90 degrees and the projection of the face on the xy plane is calculated. Then the contours of right most and left most pixels for the positive and negative rotation angles are respectively extracted. Fig. (**6**) shows a right most contour for a 3D face. To detect candidate nose points, contour points are scanned by a disk-shaped structure and the number of circle points overlapping with the face area, $n+$, as well as the number of circle points that are located outside the face, $n-$, are calculated. Then the following metric is calculated for all points on the contour points.

$$D = n^{+} - n^{-} \tag{24}$$

As shown in Fig. (**6**), D metric shows a minimum in nose tip and similar points. Therefore by applying a threshold and finding local minimums some candidate nose tips are extracted. The extracted nose tips are further refined by voting algorithm based on histogram of detected points for various rotation angles. This refining stage cannot remove all falsely detected points. Therefore, two other metrics called cardinal point fitness and spike fitness are calculated to identify nose tip.

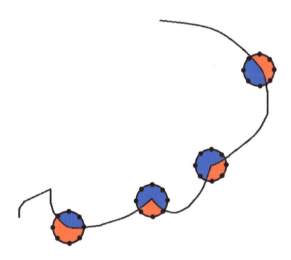

Fig. (6). A right most face contour and scanning contour point using a disk-shaped structure [23].

3D FACE ALIGNMENT

Unlike 2D image, 3D face models can be rotated in different orientations. This property brings the capability of rotating 3D face models for facial landmarks or features alignment prior to face recognition algorithm. Face alignment algorithm makes the face recognition algorithm invariant to face translation, rotation and scale.

Considering different views for 3D face images, the coordinates of face points in two 3D face images are related by:

$$P_2 = RP_1 + T \tag{25}$$

where P_1 and P_1 are 3D face points, R is rotation matrix and T is translation vector. The aim of face alignment algorithm is to estimate rotation matrix, R, and translation vector, T, to align two 3D face images. Some existing algorithms for face alignment extracted facial features like nose tip to calculate face translation and rotations in yaw, pith and roll orientations. Also some algorithms [7, 24] utilized Iterative Closest Points (ICP) to find transformation between two 3D face models. In [25] and [26] symmetry plane of face is detected as a means to calculate and compensate for face rotation and translation. Symmetry plane of face is defined as the plane that divides the face into two approximately identical parts. In [25], the face surface is cut by various planes which are called cutting plane. The intersection of cutting plane with face surface constructs a profile which is called face profile. Special face profile, which is the intersection of face surface with symmetry plane, is called central profile. The central profile exhibits some properties which can be employed for symmetry plane. This properties is summarized as follows [25]:

- Normal vectors of points in central profile lie on symmetry plane.
- Central profile is the most protrusive profile of the face. Protrusion of the face point, p_i and , p_{i+1} on a face profile is defined as:

$$g_i = \arccos(\vec{t}_i \bullet \vec{t}_{i+1}) \tag{26}$$

where $\vec{t}_i$ is the projection of normal vector p_i on the cutting plane.

- Its length should be comparable to face height.
- It is the symmetry plane of 3D face. The symmetry degree for a face profile is defined as the average of symmetry degrees of face points, p_i, on the face profile. Symmetry degree for a face point p_i on a face profile is defined as:

$$g_i = \arccos(n \bullet \vec{p}_i) \tag{27}$$

where n is the normal vector of cutting plane and $\vec{p}_i$ is the normal vector of face profile on p_i.

In this algorithm, the symmetry plane for frontal face is defined as Y-O-Z plane as shown in (Fig. **7a**). Therefore, the symmetry plane for non-frontal face can bet obtained by rotating this plane around Z and Y axis by γ and β angles as well as translating by ρ from the origin (Fig. **7b**). These three parameters are used to generate various cutting planes and by defining an objective function based on symmetry and protrusion of corresponding profiles the symmetry plane is extracted by using Hough voting algorithm.

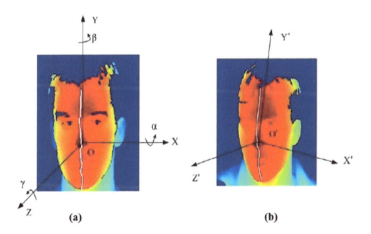

Fig. (7). Symmetry planes for frontal and non-frontal faces: **(a)** frontal face, **(b)** non-frontal face [25].

FACE RECOGNITION

The final stage of 3D face recognition algorithm is feature extraction and identification using the extracted features. Various algorithms have been proposed for feature extraction and face recognition using 3D face data. Some existing approach utilized an extension of general 2D face recognition algorithm for 3D face recognition and face analysis. In [27], eigen surface approach for 3D face recognition. In this approach, each 3D face is converted into vector form and Principal Component Analysis (PCA) approach is employed to reduce the size of feature vector. PCA approach calculates the eigenvalues and eigenvectors of covariance matrix for feature vectors. Then K largest eigenvalues and the corresponding eigenvector are selected for feature extraction. For face recognition, the input face is projected to feature space by using the selected eigenvectors of covariance matrix. Then a distance calculation metric is employed for face recognition.

In [28] Fisher face approach is used for face recognition. Fisher face approach is successfully used in several 2D face recognition algorithms. This algorithm is based on Linear Discriminant Analysis (LDA) which extract features to maximize the determinant of between-class scatter matrix simultaneously with minimizing the determinant of within-class scatter matrix. In [29] histogram of 3D face values is used as features for 3D face recognition. Since the histogram shows the global features of the face, the face area is divided into several stripes. Then the histogram for each strip is calculated as features.

Curvature based features are also employed for 3D face recognition [30, 31]. These features are generally invariants to face rotation. Curvature of a face point shows the blending of 2D curve obtained by the intersection of a plane with face surface at that point. Although various planes can be defined to intersect with the face point, two curves with minimum and maximum curvatures have special importance. It is shown that the curvature of other curves can be calculated using minimum and maximum curvatures. In other word the local shape of face surface can be described with two minimum and maximum curvatures. Mean and Gaussian curvature values which are calculated using Eqs. 18 and 19 are related to minimum and maximum curvature using the following equations:

$$H = -\frac{k_1 + k_2}{2} \tag{28}$$

$$K = k_1 k_2 \tag{29}$$

where k_1 and k_2 are minimum and maximum curvatures respectively.

In [30], 3D surface descriptors based on mean and Gaussian curvatures are employed for face segmentation. Then 86 descriptors are obtained from the segmented regions such as areas, distances, angles, curvature average of a region.

Subsequently, a feature selection algorithm is employed to extra strong features for face recognition.

Profile based algorithms are another group of approaches for face recognition [32 - 34]. In the profile based approaches, the face area is cut with several planes and the resultant 2D curves are used for feature extraction and face recognition. In [33] radial curves passing through nose point is used for face recognition under occlusion and expression. Fig. (8) shows typical radial curves for faces with various face expressions. As discussed in this paper, face expression or occlusion only changes some parts of radial curves and hence the method can be efficiently used for face recognition under face expression. In this approach, first necessary preprocessing is applied to remove noise and fill holes. Then the nose tip is detected and initial registration is applied for head pose estimation and compensation. Consequently, radial curves are extracted for 3D face matching. By applying pose compensation algorithm, occluded parts of face may result in incomplete radial curves; therefore quality filter is applied to remove some incomplete radial curves. In this approach elastic distance computation using geodesic distance is used for curve matching. In [35] local features based on curvelet transform are used for 3D face matching and face recognition. In this paper Fast Distcrete Curvelet Transform (FDCT) in four scales are applied to input image to detect local features. FDCT is defined as [36]:

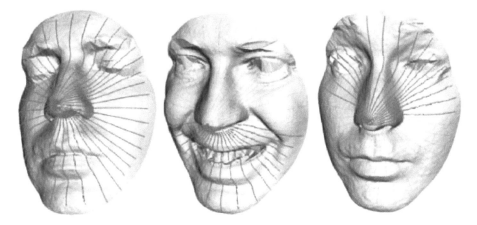

Fig. (8). Radial curves for face with various face expression [33].

$$c_{s,g,i,j} = \sum_{0 \le x_1, x_2 < N} f(x_1, x_2) \varphi_{s,g,i,j}(x_1, x_2) \qquad \textbf{(30)}$$

where $c_{s,g,i,j}$ are discrete curvelet coefficients, s, g and (i, j) denote scale, sub-band and position of face pixels respectively. After applying curvelet transform, by applying a two-stage thresholding algorithm salient feature points are extracted. To match feature points, a feature representation based on local information curvelet coefficients are defined. To this end, 5×5 patches centered on feature points, are used to employ local information based on curvelet coefficients. Then the feature vector are scaled by using a Gaussian weighting function. Additionally, to add the rotation invariance property to extracted features, the feature vectors are rearranged based on their orientation. When the features and their descriptors are extracted, they are used for face recognition using 3D face matching algorithm.

CONCLUDING REMARKS

By advances in 3D face acquisition systems and the emerging recent facilities for capturing 3D data of face, face recognition algorithms have become more common for human identification. 3D face recognition utilizes various shape and geometric features of the face for human identification. These algorithms are robust against environment illumination and face pose. In this article various stages of 3D face recognition algorithms including face acquisition, pre-processing, face alignment and face recognition were discussed. Although, 3D face recognition handle some existing problems of 2D face recognition algorithm, there are some challenges with 3D face recognition algorithms such as change of face shape under expression. Also growing a moustache or a beard or wearing glasses increases the difficulty of 3D face recognition algorithm which can be considered as future research areas. Furthermore, the use of 3D and 2D (texture) information of face in a combined manner can handle some existing challenges of both areas.

CONFLICT OF INTEREST

The author confirms that author has no conflict of interest to declare for this publication.

ACKNOWLEDGEMENTS

The author would like to thank Prof. Fadi Dornaika for his useful comments on the structure of this article.

REFERENCES

[1]   A. Wagner, J. Wright, A. Ganesh, Z. Zhou, H. Mobahi, and Y. Ma, "Toward a practical face recognition system: robust alignment and illumination by sparse representation", *IEEE Trans. Pattern Anal. Mach. Intell.,* vol. 34, no. 2, pp. 372-386, 2012.
[http://dx.doi.org/10.1109/TPAMI.2011.112] [PMID: 21646680]

[2]   Y. Wen, L. He, and P. Shi, "Face recognition using difference vector plus kpca", *Digit. Signal Process.,* vol. 22, no. 1, pp. 140-146, 2012.
[http://dx.doi.org/10.1016/j.dsp.2011.08.004]

[3]   V.M. Patel, T. Wu, S. Biswas, P.J. Phillips, and R. Chellappa, "Dictionary-based face recognition under variable lighting and pose", *IEEE Transactions on Information Forensics and Security,* vol. 7, no. 3, pp. 954-965, 2012.
[http://dx.doi.org/10.1109/TIFS.2012.2189205]

[4]   B. Gokberk, A. Ali Salah, L. Akarun, R. Etheve, D. Riccio, and J-L. Dugelay, "3d face recognition", In: D. Petrovska-Delacréaz, B. Dorizzi, G. Chollet, Eds., *Guide to Biometric Reference Systems and Performance Evaluation. http://dx.doi.org/10.1007/978-1-84800-292-0_9.* Springer: London, 2009, pp. 263-295. [Online]
[http://dx.doi.org/10.1007/978-1-84800-292-0_9]

[5]   Y. Lei, M. Bennamoun, and A.A. El-Sallam, "An efficient 3d face recognition approach based on the fusion of novel local low-level features", *Pattern Recognit.,* vol. 46, no. 1, pp. 24-37, 2013.
[http://dx.doi.org/10.1016/j.patcog.2012.06.023]

[6]   D. Smeets, J. Keustermans, D. Vandermeulen, and P. Suetens, "meshSIFT: Local surface features for 3d face recognition under expression variations and partial data", *Comput. Vis. Image Underst.,* vol. 117, no. 2, pp. 158-169, 2013.
[http://dx.doi.org/10.1016/j.cviu.2012.10.002]

[7]   A. Assadi, and A. Behrad, "A new method for human face recognition using texture and depth information", In: *10th Symposium on Neural Network Applications in Electrical Engineering (NEUREL2010).* IEEE, 2010, pp. 201-205.
[http://dx.doi.org/10.1109/NEUREL.2010.5644065]

[8]   W. Burgin, C. Pantofaru, and W.D. Smart, "Using depth information to improve face detection", In: *Proceedings of the 6th international conference on Human-robot interaction.* ACM, 2011, pp. 119-120.
[http://dx.doi.org/10.1145/1957656.1957690]

[9]   D. Huang, M. Ardabilian, Y. Wang, and L. Chen, "Oriented gradient maps based automatic asymmetric 3d-2d face recognition", *5th IAPR International Conference on Biometrics (ICB). IEEE,* 2012 pp. 125-131
[http://dx.doi.org/10.1109/ICB.2012.6199769]

[10]   J.G. Franca, M.A. Gazziro, A.N. Ide, and J.H. Saito, "A 3d scanning system based on laser triangulation and variable field of view", In: *IEEE International Conference on Image Processing (ICIP 2005)*. IEEE, 2005, pp. 425-428.
[http://dx.doi.org/10.1109/ICIP.2005.1529778]

[11]   E. Trucco, and A. Verri, *Introductory techniques for 3-D computer vision.* Prentice Hall Englewood Cliffs, 1998.

[12]   V.R. Ayyagari, F. Boughorbel, A. Koschan, and M.A. Abidi, "A new method for automatic 3d face registration", In: *IEEE Computer Society Conference on Computer Vision and Pattern Recognition-Workshops(CVPR Workshops)*. IEEE, 2005, pp. 119-119.
[http://dx.doi.org/10.1109/CVPR.2005.392]

[13]   W. Qin, Y. Hu, Y. Sun, and B. Yin, "An automatic multi-sample 3d face registration method based on thin plate spline and deformable model", In: *2012 IEEE International Conference on Multimedia and Expo Workshops (ICMEW)*. IEEE, 2012, pp. 453-458.
[http://dx.doi.org/10.1109/ICMEW.2012.85]

[14]   G.C. Sharp, S.W. Lee, and D.K. Wehe, "Icp registration using invariant features", *IEEE Trans. Pattern Anal. Mach. Intell.,* vol. 24, no. 1, pp. 90-102, 2002.
[http://dx.doi.org/10.1109/34.982886]

[15]   N. Ansari, M. Abdel-Mottaleb, and M.H. Mahoor, "3d face mesh modeling from range images for 3d face recognition", In: *IEEE International Conference on Image Processing(ICIP 2007),* vol. 4. IEEE: Washington, DC, USA, 2007, pp. IV-509.

[16]   N. Werghi, M. Rahayem, and J. Kjellander, "An ordered topological representation of 3d triangular mesh facial surface: concept and applications", *EURASIP J. Adv. Signal Process.,* vol. 2012, no. 1, pp. 1-20, 2012.
[http://dx.doi.org/10.1186/1687-6180-2012-144]

[17]   C. Xu, Y. Wang, T. Tan, and L. Quan, "Face recognition based on 3d mesh model", In: *SPIE defense and security symposium, Intelligent Recognition and Digital Security Group.* Citeseer: China, 2004.

[18]   S.M. Kim, J.C. Park, and K.H. Lee, "Natural-textured mesh stream modeling from depth image-based representation", In: *Computational Science and Its Applications(ICCSA 2006)*. Springer, 2006, pp. 480-489.
[http://dx.doi.org/10.1007/11751540_51]

[19]   N. Werghi, H. Bhaskar, M.K. Naqbi, Y. Meguebli, and H. Boukadida, "The spiral facets: A compact 3d facial mesh surface representation and its applications", In: *Computer Vision, Imaging and Computer Graphics. Theory and Applications.* Springer, 2013, pp. 203-224.
[http://dx.doi.org/10.1007/978-3-642-32350-8_13]

[20]   Y. Lei, M. Bennamoun, M. Hayat, and Y. Guo, "An efficient 3d face recognition approach using local geometrical signatures", *Pattern Recognit,* vol. 47, no. 2, pp. 509-524, 2014.
[http://dx.doi.org/10.1016/j.patcog.2013.07.018]

[21]   K.I. Chang, K.W. Bowyer, and P.J. Flynn, "Multiple nose region matching for 3D face recognition under varying facial expression", *IEEE Trans. Pattern Anal. Mach. Intell,* vol. 28, no. 10, pp. 1695-1700, 2006.

[http://dx.doi.org/10.1109/TPAMI.2006.210] [PMID: 16986549]

[22]   C. Xu, T. Tan, Y. Wang, and L. Quan, "Combining local features for robust nose location in 3d facial data", *Pattern Recognit. Lett,* vol. 27, no. 13, pp. 1487-1494, 2006.
[http://dx.doi.org/10.1016/j.patrec.2006.02.015]

[23]   X. Peng, M. Bennamoun, and A.S. Mian, "A training-free nose tip detection method from face range images", *Pattern Recognit,* vol. 44, no. 3, pp. 544-558, 2011.
[http://dx.doi.org/10.1016/j.patcog.2010.09.015]

[24]   T. Russ, C. Boehnen, and T. Peters, "3d face recognition using 3d alignment for pca", In: *2006 IEEE Computer Society Conference on Computer Vision and Pattern Recognition,* vol. 2. IEEE: Washington, DC, USA, 2006, pp. 1391-1398.

[25]   D. Li, and W. Pedrycz, "A central profile-based 3d face pose estimation", *Pattern Recognit,* vol. 47, no. 2, pp. 525-534, 2014.
[http://dx.doi.org/10.1016/j.patcog.2013.07.019]

[26]   Y. Wang, J. Liu, and X. Tang, "Robust 3D face recognition by local shape difference boosting", *IEEE Trans. Pattern Anal. Mach. Intell,* vol. 32, no. 10, pp. 1858-1870, 2010.
[http://dx.doi.org/10.1109/TPAMI.2009.200] [PMID: 20724762]

[27]   T. Heseltine, N. Pears, and J. Austin, "Three-dimensional face recognition: An eigensurface approach", In: *2004 International Conference on Image Processing(ICIP'04),* vol. 2. IEEE: Washington, DC, USA, 2004, pp. 1421-1424.

[28]   X-M. Bai, B-C. Yin, Q. Shi, and Y-F. Sun, "Face recognition using extended fisherface with 3d morphable model", In: *Proceedings of 2005 International Conference onMachine Learning and Cybernetics,* vol. 7. IEEE: Washington, DC, USA, 2005, pp. 4481-4486.

[29]   X. Zhou, H. Seibert, C. Busch, and W. Funk, "A 3d face recognition algorithm using histogram-based features", In: *Proceedings of the 1st Eurographics conference on 3D Object Retrieval.* Eurographics Association, 2008, pp. 65-71.

[30]   A.B. Moreno, A. Sánchez, J.F. Vélez, and F.J. Díaz, "Face recognition using 3d surface-extracted descriptors", In: *Irish Machine Vision and Image Processing Conference,* vol. 2003. Citeseer, 2003.

[31]   A. Colombo, C. Cusano, and R. Schettini, "3d face detection using curvature analysis", *Pattern Recognit,* vol. 39, no. 3, pp. 444-455, 2006.
[http://dx.doi.org/10.1016/j.patcog.2005.09.009]

[32]   G. Pan, Y. Wu, Z. Wu, and W. Liu, "3d face recognition by profile and surface matching", In: *Proceedings of the 2003 International Joint Conference on Neural Networks,* vol. 3. IEEE: Washington, DC, USA, 2003, pp. 2169-2174.
[http://dx.doi.org/10.1109/IJCNN.2003.1223744]

[33]   H. Drira, B. Ben Amor, A. Srivastava, M. Daoudi, and R. Slama, "3D face recognition under expressions, occlusions, and pose variations", *IEEE Trans. Pattern Anal. Mach. Intell,* vol. 35, no. 9, pp. 2270-2283, 2013.
[http://dx.doi.org/10.1109/TPAMI.2013.48] [PMID: 23868784]

[34]   G. Pan, and Z. Wu, "3d face recognition from range data", *Int. J. Image Graph.,* vol. 5, no. 03, pp. 573-593, 2005.

[http://dx.doi.org/10.1142/S0219467805001884]

[35] S. Elaiwat, M. Bennamoun, F. Boussaid, and A. El-Sallam, "3-d face recognition using curvelet local features", *IEEE Signal Process. Lett,* vol. 21, no. 2, pp. 172-175, 2014.
[http://dx.doi.org/10.1109/LSP.2013.2295119]

[36] E. Candes, L. Demanet, D. Donoho, and L. Ying, "Fast discrete curvelet transforms", *Multiscale Model. Simul.,* vol. 5, no. 3, pp. 861-899, 2006.
[http://dx.doi.org/10.1137/05064182X]

CHAPTER 7

Model-Less 3D Face Pose Estimation

Fawzi Khattar[1], Fadi Dornaika[2,3], Ammar Assoum[1,*]

[1] *LaMA Laboratory, Lebanese University, Tripoli, Lebanon*

[2] *University of the Basque Country, San Sebastian, Spain*

[3] *IKERBASQUE, Basque Foundation for Science, Bilbao, Spain*

Abstract: Automatic head pose estimation consists of using a computer to predict the pose of a person based on a given facial image. Fast and reliable algorithms for estimating the head pose are essential for many applications and higher-level face analysis tasks. Many of machine learning-based techniques used for face detection and recognition can also be used for pose estimation. In this chapter, we present a new dimensionality reduction algorithm based on a sparse representation that takes into account pose similarities. Experimental results conducted on three benchmarks face databases are presented.

Keywords: Age classification, Age estimation, Age prediction, Dimensionality reduction, Facial feature extraction, Gabor filter, K-nearest neighbors, Label-sensitive, Local binary pattern, Local regression, Locality preserving projections, Machine learning, Marginal fisher analysis, Mean absolute error, Partial least square regression, Preprocessing, Recognition rate, Support vector regression.

INTRODUCTION

In the domain of computer vision, the identification of specific objects within an image is a well-known and typical task. The aim of the identification is to determine the objects' position and orientation with respect to a given coordinate system. The obtained information may then be used for several purposes, for example to manipulate an object by a robot or to prevent this latter from hitting obstacles. In the related terminology, the pose of an object refers to the combination of its position and orientation, even though it is sometimes used in line with the orientation by itself.

* **Address to Corresponding author Ammar Assoum:** LaMA Laboratory, Lebanese University, Faculty of Science, Section III, Tripoli, Lebanon; Tel: +9613069591; Fax: +9616386365; E-mail: a.assoum@ul.edu.lb

Particularly, human's facial pose is considered as an important cue of non-verbal communication. Indeed, humans can discover and understand other people's intentions easily by interpreting their head pose. However, in order to make a machine capable of interacting with human's head movements and expressions, huge effort has to be done to estimate the pose from the pixel representation of a facial image in a robust and efficient way. The estimation process requires a series of processing steps to transform a pixel-based representation of a head into a high-level concept of direction.

STATE OF THE ART

The head pose estimation refers to the specific task consisting of determining the position and/or the orientation of the head in an image (*e.g.* facial one). This task is a challenging problem because there are many degrees of freedom that should be estimated. During the past years many techniques and approaches have been proposed to solve this problem [1, 2]. Appearance template methods use similarity algorithms and compare a given image to a set of exemplars in order to discover which labelled image (template) is the most similar to the one the pose of which is to be estimated [3, 4]. Nevertheless, even if these methods have the advantage of not requiring a features extraction step, they may suffer from noise caused by illumination and expression changes in addition to the need of high computational power since the matching process they use is based on pair-wise similarities. Classification-based methods [5] operate by training head pose classifiers through the distribution of the training images into a a set of discretized poses. However, both the appearance template and classification-based methods can only return discrete poses and are sensitive to non-uniform sampling in the learn data. Regression-based methods [6] allow to obtain continuous pose estimates. Indeed, they use regression techniques [7, 8] in order to find the relationship between the face image and its corresponding pose and to earn continuous mapping functions between the face image and the pose space. The high dimensionality of the data represents an important challenge in this kind of methods because of the well-known "curse of dimensionality problem" [9]. Many researchers use a dimensionality reduction step before the regression [10, 11]. The main disadvantage of these methods is that their performance deteriorates with bad head localization. The manifold embedding methods [12] consider face images as samples of a low-dimensional manifold embedded in the high-dimensional observation space (the space of all possible images). They try to find a low dimensional representation that is linked to the pose. After that, classification or regression techniques are applied to discover the pose. The main weakness of manifold embedding methods is that appearance variation is not only affected by pose changes but also by other factors such as lighting changes and identity. Geometric methods [13, 14] rely heavily on the estimation of facial features, such as eyes, mouth corners, nose tip, etc. and use their relative position to estimate the pose using projective geometry. For example, if the eyes and the mouth form an isosceles triangle, then the image corresponds to a frontal view. The major disadvantage of these methods is to locate the features needed for estimation in a very precise and accurate way. They also need to handle missing facial features in some poses. The tracking methods track the head and use the relative movement of the face with temporal continuity and smooth motion constraint to estimate the pose. These methods require an initialization step for the 3D head pose parameters [15]. The detector array methods train different detectors for different head poses. These detectors try to detect the face in a new image. It is supposed that only the detector trained for the same exact pose will be able to detect the face in the image. The detector that succeeds to detect the face assigns its pose to the image [16].

THE MACHINE LEARNING METHODOLOGY

The machine learning pipeline used in our work is summarized in Fig. (**1**). It is divided into the following steps:

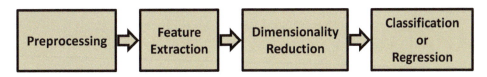

Fig. 1. The proposed machine learning pipeline.

Preprocessing: In this step, image processing techniques are used to prepare the images and put them in a sort of normalized way. The RGB images are converted to grayscale because colors may not bring pertinent information about the pose. During this step we may perform a face alignment and cropping in order to eliminate from the input image, as much as possible, the information that is irrelevant to the pose problem (background). This operation aims at making the pose estimation more robust. After that, the image is normalized and eventually reshaped as a vector that contains its pixels. Thus, at the end of the preprocessing step, face images are represented by high dimensional normalized vectors.

Feature Extraction: Feature extraction is a special form of dimensionality reduction. When the image has high dimensions and is suspected to contain notoriously redundant data, it must be converted into another representation (possibly with lower dimension) that eliminates the redundancy and helps making the estimation more robust to noise. In the pose estimation problem, it is likely that the most variance that exists in the data is due to pose variation. Based on this, principal component analysis (PCA) [17] was used in our work to find the appropriate space that keeps the information related to the pose and eliminates the redundant information.

Dimensionality Reduction: Dimensionality reduction (DR) is the process of reducing the dimensionality of the data in order to make classification or regression techniques that will follow more robust. There are two main reasons for estimating a low-dimensional representation of high-dimensional data: reducing measurement cost of further data analysis and beating the problem knows as the "curse of dimensionality" [18]. In other words, it is less computationally demanding to work with smaller representation of the data than to work with the original high dimensional data and we are less prone to fall in the overfitting trap when we work with smaller dimensions. For high dimensional datasets (principally image-related problems), it is a crucial step that must be taken into consideration. The DR algorithms used in our work are: LPP [19], SLPP [20] and lsLPP [21]. We propose in this chapter a novel method (sparse lsLPP) in order to reduce the number of the lsLPP parameters that demands some tuning and to enhance the result of the estimation.

Regression or Classification: The final step in the approach will be either a regression or a classification. Regression techniques model the dependency or the relationship between a scalar dependent variable (*e.g.*, the yaw angle) and one or more explanatory variables (in our case these variables will be those generated after the Dimensionality Reduction step). In our case, Partial Least Square Regression (PLSR) [8] and Support Vector Regression (SVR) [7] are used to perform regression. Local regression techniques [22] like kNN-SVR and kNN-PLSR are also used. Although the target variables (angles) are continuous, we also intend to see the efficiency of some classification techniques that are famous for their robustness like Support Vectors Machines (SVM) [23] and k-Nearest Neighbors (kNN) [24].

Locality Preserving Projections

Locality preserving projections (LPP) is an unsupervised dimensionality reduction algorithm that tends to preserve the local structure of the high dimensional data. LPP projections are linear projective maps that arise by solving a problem that optimally preserves the neighborhood structure of the data set. It first constructs a graph between the training samples that model the relationship between them in the high-dimensional space and tend to preserve this relationship in the embedded space. In other words LPP tends to map closer samples in the high dimensional space into closer projections and thus preserve the local structure of the data. If there is a reason to believe that the Euclidean distance is meaningful only if it is small (local), then the LPP algorithm finds a projection that respects such a belief [25].

LPP Algorithm

1. ***Constructing the adjacency graph:*** Let G denote a graph that models the relationship between the samples. The graph is formed by nodes and edges. The nodes are the vectors that represent the original images after the distance metric adjustment step. An edge connects nodes i and j if x_i and x_j are "close". There are two variations to determine the structure of the graph:

   ○ ε-neighborhoods: nodes i and j are connected by an edge if $||x_i - x_j||^2 < \varepsilon$, where the norm is the usual Euclidean norm in $\mathbb{R}^n$.

   ○ k-nearest neighbors: nodes i and j are connected by an edge if j is among the k nearest neighbors of i or if i is among the k nearest neighbors of j .

2. ***Choosing the weights:*** If W_{ij} denotes the weight of the edge between nodes i and j, then we can use several possibilities for computing it, for example we can mention the following two cases:

○ Heat kernel: if nodes i and j are connected, put $W_{ij} = e - \frac{\|x_i - x_j\|^2}{t}$.

○ Simple-minded: if nodes i and j are connected, put $W_{ij} = 1$.

This graph can be then represented by a matrix W where the element W_{ij} corresponds to the weight of the edge that connects the samples i and j .

3. ***Eigenmaps:*** Compute the eigenvectors and eigenvalues for the generalized eigenvector problem

$$XLX^T a = \lambda XDX^T a \tag{1}$$

Where D is a diagonal matrix whose entries are column (or row, since W is symmetric) sums of W .

$$D_{ii} = \sum_j W_{ij}$$

L is the Laplacian matrix given by $L = D - W$. Let x_i be the ith column of matrix X and $a_1, a_2, \ldots, a_n$ be the solutions of the equation 1 ordered according to their eigenvalues $\lambda_1, \lambda_2, \ldots, \lambda_n$. Thus the embedding $x_i \to y_i$ is as follows: $y_i = A^T x_i$ where $A = (a_1 a_2 \ldots a_m)$ is a matrix whose columns are formed by m eigenvectors a_i that correspond to the smallest m eigenvalues λ_i . The generalized eigenvector problem is due to the minimization of the criterion:

$$\sum_{i,j} \|y_i - y_j\|^2 W_{ij}$$

where y_i and y_j are the new m-dimensional vectors ($m < n$) that represent the ith and j^{th} sample (image). W_{ij} is the weight of the edge that connects the two samples i and j in the original n-dimensional space. From this criterion we can see that if the weight W_{ij} is high, the algorithm will tend to minimize the difference between y_i and y_j and thus maps the samples in a way that preserves the local structure of the data.

Supervised Locality Preserving Projections

Supervised locality preserving projections SLPP is a modified version of the classic locality preserving projections algorithm described above. Although the LPP method can effectively preserve the manifold structure of the input data, its discriminability is limited because the class (pose) information is neglected during the graph construction phase. Therefore this modified version (SLPP) was proposed in order to enhance the discriminability by using the pose information. In this algorithm the similarity matrix W is computed with the constraint that each point's k nearest neighbors must be chosen from among samples belonging to the same class. The other steps of the algorithm remain the same.

LABEL-SENSITIVE LOCALITY PRESERVING PROJECTION

The label-sensitive locality preserving projection (lsLPP) is a dimensionality reduction algorithm that aims to reduce the dimensionality of the data while preserving the relationship that relates the data in the high dimensional space. The relationship preserved by the lsLPP algorithm can be divided into two types:

- A spatial relationship which consists of the Euclidean distance between the data points in the high dimensional feature space.
- A label relationship which consists of the Euclidean distance between the labels (pose) of the data points.

Similar neighbors are defined by a threshold ε, and the weights of the edges are computed in a way that takes into account the pose similarity. The label-sensitive locality preserving projection (lsLPP) algorithm can be summarized as follows [26].

Presetting:

- Training set: $X = \{x^{\{n\}}_{\{adjust\}} \in \mathbb{R}^d\}^N_{n=1}$, $Y = \{y^{(n)} \in L\}^N_{n=1}$ (X is represented as a $d \times N$ matrix, L represents all the possible values of the classes (angles)).
- Define the similar-label set $N^+(i)$ for each sample $x^{(i)}_{adjust}$: $N^+(i) = \{x^{(j)}_{adjust}$, $\|y^{(i)} - y^{(j)}\| \leq \varepsilon$ and $j \neq i\}$
  where ε is the label-sensitive threshold that defines the range of similar labels.`
- Create an $N \times N$ sample similarity matrix $B^+ = \{b^+_{ij} = 0\}_{(1 \leq i,j \leq N)}$

Algorithm:

- For each sample $x^{(i)}_{adjust}$ find k_1-nearest samples in $N^+(i)$, and denote these samples as $KNN^+(i)$. The parameter k_1 defines the number of neighboring samples.

- For each sample pair $\{x^{(i)}_{adjust}, x^{(j)}_{adjust}\}$, if $x^{(j)}_{adjust} \in KNN^+(i)$ or $x^{(i)}_{adjust} \in KNN^+(j)$

  set: $b^+_{ij} = \exp\left(-\frac{\|x^{(i)}_{adjust} - x^{(j)}_{adjust}\|^2}{t}\right) \exp\left(-\frac{(y^{(i)} - y^{(j)})^2}{v}\right)$

- Compute $L^+ = D^+ - B^+$, where D^+ is a diagonal matrix whose elements d^+ are computed by: $d^+_{ii} = \Sigma_j b^+_{ii}$

- Solve the generalized eigen decomposition problem:

  $(XL^+X^T)v^{(i)} = \lambda^{(i)}(XD^+X^T)v^{(i)} \rightarrow (XL^+X^T)V = (XD^+X^T)V\Lambda$

  where Λ is a diagonal matrix formed by the eigenvalues $\lambda^{(i)}$ arranged in descending order and V is a matrix whose columns are the eigenvectors ordered in descending order of the corresponding eigenvalues.

- Output:

$$\begin{cases} W_{LPP} = [v^{(N-p+1)}, v^{(N-p+2)}, \ldots, v^{(N)}] \in \mathbb{R}^{d \times p} \\ z = W_{LPP}^T x_{adjust} \in \mathbb{R}^p \end{cases}$$

The lsLPP algorithm has four parameters $(k_1, \sigma, t, \varepsilon)$ that need to be tuned in order to obtain the most accurate estimation possible.

PROPOSED APPROACH: SPARSE GRAPH BASED LSLPP

In order to reduce the number of parameters that need to be tuned in the lsLPP algorithm and in order to be able to model the relationship between the samples in the high dimensional space in a better way, we propose a new method which consists in a sparse coding of the lsLPP algorithm. The main difference of our proposed approach with the classic lsLPP is that the construction of the graph similarity matrix B^+ will be carried out *via* a weighted sparse coding that integrates label-sensitivity concept. Sparse representation is, in general, a representation of signals that is the most compact possible in terms of linear combination of atoms taken form an overcomplete dictionary [27]. A dictionary is formed by many signals. Every new signal will be written in terms of the signals available in the dictionary in the most compact way. In other words, it chooses only the most descriptive signals in the dictionary and decomposes the signal in terms of them. Sparse representation means that only some signals will participate in the reconstruction process while the rest of the signals have zero contribution.

This coding of signals is done by minimizing the following objective function:

$$\min(\|y - Ax\|_2^2 + \lambda\|x\|_1)$$

where y is the signal to be decomposed, A carries in its columns the signals forming the dictionary and $x = (x_1, x_2, \ldots, x_n)$ is a column vector formed by the reconstruction coefficients. $\|x\|_1$ denotes the l_1-norm of x.

λ is a scalar regularization parameter that balances the tradeoff between reconstruction error and sparsity. This regularization problem produces a sparse representation because it is regularized on the l_1-norm. In other words the components of the vector x will be all zeros except for some of them that describe the signal the most in terms of linear combination. In the proposed method, this concept was used to construct the modelling graph. Each training sample is constructed by the above criterion from the remaining training samples. The absolute value of the reconstruction coefficients represent the weights on the edges of the graph since they give an indication of the relationship that exists between the samples. This reconstruction is done in a way that respects the label-sensitive concept. The algorithm is summarized as follows:

- Suppose we have N training samples.
- For each sample x_i :
    - Compute $Diag\ (j, j) = 1 - exp\ (-(\frac{class(i) - class(j)}{\sigma})^2\ )$

    $Diag$ is a diagonal similarity matrix that takes into account the label-sensitive concept.
    - We solve for b using the following optimization problem:

$$\min_b(\|Xb - x_i\|^2 + \lambda\sum_j Diag(i,j)|b_j|) \tag{2}$$

where X is a matrix that carries in its columns the remaining $N-1$ training samples. Note that equation 2 is a classic sparse coding problem if we use the auxiliary vector $a = Diag\ b$:

$$\min_a(\|X\,Diag^{-1}\,a - x_i\|^2 + \lambda\|a\|_1)$$

 – We construct the matrix that represents the graph B row by row in the following way:

$B(i,:) = Diag^{-1}a$

- End For
- $B += |B|^+ |B|^T$
- Compute

$L^+ = D^+ - B^+$

where D^+ is a diagonal matrix with $d_{ii}^+ = \sum_j b_{ij}^+$

- After calculating the graph matrix we solve for the following generalized eigenvector problem:

$(XL^+X^T)v^{(i)} = \lambda v^{(i)}(XD^+X^T)v^{(i)} \rightarrow (XL^+X^T)V = (XD^+X^T)V\Lambda$

- The generalized eigenvector problem is due, like in the case of LPP, to the minimization of the criterion:

$$\sum_{i,j} \|y_i - y_j\|^2 B_{ij}$$

Where y_i and y_j are the projections of the ith and j^{th} samples. B_{ij} is the weight of the edge that connects the two samples. This method has the benefit that it needs only 2 parameters that are very easy to tune, λ and σ. λ is the sparsity parameter and must be chosen small to prevent the B matrix to contain a lot of zeros which does not describe well the relationship between the samples.

EXPERIMENTAL RESULTS

In order to test the efficiency of the proposed sparse approach, several experiments are performed on different datasets using different regression and classification algorithms. Two kinds of regression were tested: the global regression and the local regression. The global regression techniques are the commonly known regression algorithms that take all the data available in the training set into account when training and calculating the parameters of the regression model. On the other hand, local regression techniques look for the k-nearest neighbors and train the regression model on these neighbors. Partial Least Square Regression (PLSR) is among the regression techniques tested in the experiments. It consists in regression tool that models the relationship between the observed variables by means of latent variables or hidden variables [8]. PLSR is based on the assumption that the observed variables are generated by means of a small number of hidden variables.

The experiments are performed on three different benchmark datasets in which only the yaw angle vary. The first dataset is the Facepix database[1] which contains images of 30 persons taken at a 1-degree step. The second dataset is the Taiwan dataset[2] which contains images of 90 persons taken at a 5-degree step. The final dataset is the Columbia database[3] which contains images of 56 persons taken at a 15-degree step from −30 to +30 degrees.

Figs. (**2-4**) show samples of each of the tested databases.

Fig. 2. A subset of pictures belonging to seven persons available in the Facepix database. The images are chosen at a step of 10 degree interval for visualization

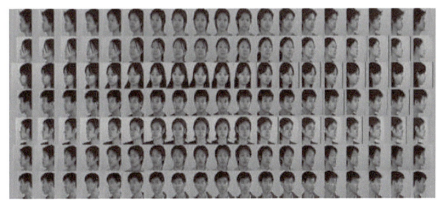

Fig. 3. Face images that belong to seven persons available in the Taiwan database. The images are chosen at a step of 10 degree interval for visualization

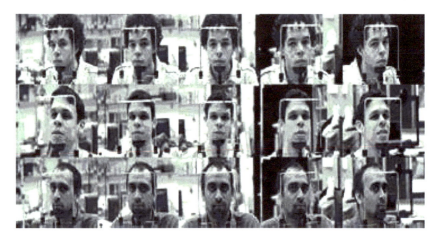

Fig. 4. Pictures that belong to three persons available in the Columbia database

In order to discover the suitable values of the ε and k parameters of the lsLPP algorithm, a first experiment is made on a set of the Facepix database and aims to tune these parameters. Fig. (**5**) shows that the best value of ε is zero, which means that the label-sensitive version of LPP appear to give larger mean absolute error (MAE) than the supervised version. This is due to the fact that the high dimensional patterns of each person are located away from each other due to inter-person differences. Fig. (**6**) shows the pattern distribution after applying lsLPP with a 20-degree interval as a similarity threshold. It is clear that the patterns are organized in the form of curves, each curve corresponding to a person. Fig. (**7**) shows the pattern distribution after applying PCA and SLPP. The previous curves are now mapped closer together, reducing the inter-person differences and giving less error estimation. The proposed sparse representation does not rely on the neighborhood to build the relationship map to preserve. It relies rather on minimizing the reconstruction error of one data sample from the rest of the database which gives it robustness and efficiency. Fig. (**8**) shows that the proposed sparse representation is able to produce a suitable space for classification or regression with only two parameters to tune. Finally, Fig. (**9**) depicts, for Facepix database, the MAE corresponding to each angle from $-90°$ to $+90°$ using PCA for feature extraction, sparse lsLPP for dimensionality reduction and linear PLSR for regression.

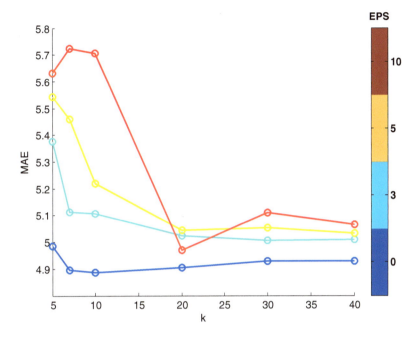

Fig. 5. MAE as a function of k and ε when using lsLPP for dimensionality reduction

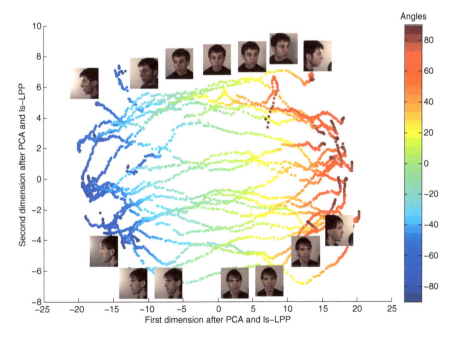

Fig. 6. Patterns Distribution after PCA and lsLPP - ε = 10, k = 7 and σ² = 22.22

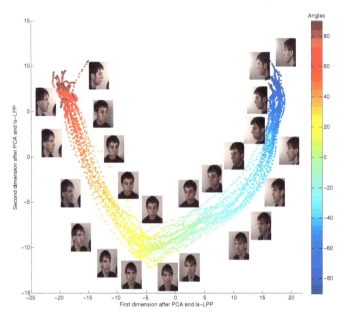

Fig. 7. Patterns Distribution after PCA and lsLPP - ε = 0 and k = 7

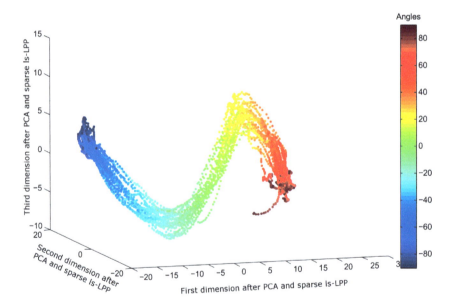

Fig. 8. 3D Patterns Distribution after applying PCA and sparse lsLPP

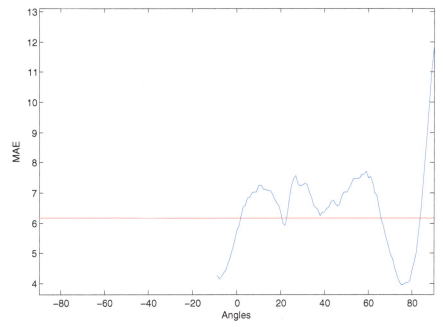

Fig. 9. MAE of each angle using PCA for feature extraction, sparse lsLPP for dimensionality reduction and linear PLSR for regression

Tables **1-4** summarize the experimental results obtained for each combination of processing blocs. The numerical values therein arise from averaging results over five random splits (train/test) of the target databases. Table **1** shows, for Facepix dataset, and for each combination, the mean absolute error (MAE) in degrees as well as the related standard deviation (STD). Two cases are considered and correspond to choosing 10 and 25 persons during the training process respectively. On the other hand, the results corresponding to the five splits of Facepix database with train and test sizes of 25 and 5 samples per pose respectively are give in Table **2**. Also, Table **3** exhibits, for Taiwan dataset, the mean absolute error (MAE) and the related standard deviation (STD) for two percentages of the training set (30% and 80% respectively). Finally, Table **4** shows the results corresponding to the pose estimation process (last bloc of the processing chain) performed by a classifier (SVM). Notice that the results given in the previous three tables are gathered according to the method used for dimensionality reduction: raw (no reduction), LPP, lsLPP and sparse lsLPP.

Table 1. The MAE (degrees) and the standard deviation associated with the yaw angle using 10 and 25 training persons. The results correspond to 5 random splits of Facepix database

	10 pers. Train		25 pers. Train	
Combination	**MAE**	**STD**	**MAE**	**STD**
1. Linear PLSR	7.90	6.48	5.37	4.63
2. Kernel PLSR	5.86	4.80	4.28	3.74
3. PCA-LPP-kNN (kNN=1)	7.03	6.20	6.10	5.15
4. PCA-LPP-kNN (kNN=30)	10.47	8.12	7.94	6.36
5. PCA-LPP-kNN-PLSR-kernel	6.12	4.96	5.44	4.36
6. PCA-LPP-kNN-PLSR-linear	6.18	5.14	5.27	4.38
7. PCA-LPP-PLSR-kernelGlobal	6.30	5.23	4.62	4.00
8. PCA-LPP-PLSR-linearGlobal	7.58	6.04	6.33	4.98
9. PCA-LPP-SVM (Kernel)	5.34	4.58	4.17	3.59
10. PCA-LPP-kNN-SVR (Kernel)	6.25	5.04	5.40	4.37
11. PCA-LPP-SVR (Kernel)	6.19	5.07	4.40	3.90
12. PCA-lsLPP-kNN (kNN=1)	6.09	5.14	5.17	4.07
13. PCA-lsLPP-kNN (kNN=30)	8.43	6.72	6.54	4.97
14. PCA-lsLPP-kNN-PLSR-kernel	5.38	4.25	4.40	3.36
15. PCA-lsLPP-kNN-PLSR-linear	5.36	4.36	4.31	3.40
16. PCA-lsLPP-PLSR-kernelGlobal	6.08	4.74	4.33	3.32
17. PCA-lsLPP-PLSR-linearGlobal	7.70	6.11	6.16	4.78
18. PCA-lsLPP-SVM (Kernel)	5.26	4.45	4.02	3.36
19. PCA-lsLPP-kNN-SVR (Kernel)	5.46	4.36	4.45	3.44
20. PCA-lsLPP-SVR (Kernel)	5.98	4.70	3.86	3.31
21. PCA-sparse-lsLPP-kNN (kNN=1)	6.15	5.23	5.16	3.99
22. PCA-sparse-lsLPP-kNN (kNN=30)	8.41	6.77	6.62	5.03
23. PCA-sparse-lsLPP-kNN-PLSR-kernel	5.39	4.26	4.35	3.30
24. PCA-sparse-lsLPP-kNN-PLSR-linear	5.40	4.39	4.26	3.32
25. PCA-sparse-lsLPP-PLSR-kernelGlobal	6.05	4.73	4.28	3.34
26. PCA-sparse-lsLPP-PLSR-linearGlobal	7.64	6.11	6.16	4.84
27. PCA-sparse-lsLPP-SVM (Kernel)	5.31	4.50	3.99	3.39
28. PCA-sparse-lsLPP-kNN-SVR (Kernel)	5.48	4.38	4.40	3.35
29. PCA-sparse-lsLPP-SVR (Kernel)	5.95	4.66	3.84	3.15

Table 2. The MAE (degrees) corresponding to the five splits of Facepix database with train and test sizes of 25 and 5 samples per pose respectively

Combination	Set 1	Set 2	Set 3	Set 4	Set 5	Mean MAE
1. Linear PLSR	4.12	4.67	6.10	5.26	6.70	5.37
2. Kernel PLSR	3.13	3.90	4.99	3.95	5.43	4.28
3. PCA-LPP-kNN (kNN=1)	5.59	5.41	7.65	5.37	6.49	6.10
4. PCA-LPP-kNN (kNN=30)	6.51	8.38	9.38	9.40	6.02	7.94
5. PCA-LPP-kNN-PLSR-kernel	4.93	4.80	6.80	4.87	5.82	5.44
6. PCA-LPP-kNN-PLSR-linear	4.78	4.59	6.78	4.72	5.51	5.27
7. PCA-LPP-PLSR-kernelGlobal	3.33	3.76	5.06	4.56	6.38	4.62
8. PCA-LPP-PLSR-linearGlobal	5.15	5.90	6.30	6.78	7.52	6.33
9. PCA-LPP-SVM (Kernel)	3.30	4.05	5.20	3.63	4.66	4.17
10. PCA-LPP-kNN-SVR (Kernel)	5.00	4.74	7.20	4.73	5.32	5.40
11. PCA-LPP-SVR (Kernel)	2.96	3.79	5.03	4.01	6.23	4.40
12. PCA-ls-LPP-kNN (kNN=1)	4.70	5.57	6.24	4.36	4.97	5.17
13. PCA-ls-LPP-kNN (kNN=30)	5.00	7.88	6.97	7.71	5.13	6.54
14. PCA-ls-LPP-kNN-PLSR-kernel	3.69	4.74	5.51	3.56	4.18	4.40
15. PCA-ls-LPP-kNN-PLSR-linear	3.69	4.41	5.72	3.56	4.15	4.31
16. PCA-ls-LPP-PLSR-kernelGlobal	3.39	3.69	4.96	4.22	5.41	4.33
17. PCA-ls-LPP-PLSR-linearGlobal	4.89	5.56	6.55	6.55	7.25	6.16
18. PCA-ls-LPP-SVM (Kernel)	3.03	4.03	5.26	3.56	4.23	4.02
19. PCA-ls-LPP-kNN-SVR (Kernel)	3.95	4.65	5.84	3.65	4.14	4.45
20. PCA-ls-LPP-SVR (Kernel)	4.76	3.39	4.59	3.59	4.71	3.86
21. PCA-sparse-ls-LPP-kNN (kNN=1)	5.28	5.59	6.28	4.30	4.88	5.16
22. PCA-sparse-ls-LPP-kNN (kNN=30)	5.28	7.68	7.08	7.86	5.19	6.62
23. PCA-sparse-ls-LPP-kNN-PLSR-kernel	3.83	4.59	5.57	3.59	4.20	5.35
24. PCA-sparse-ls-LPP-kNN-PLSR-linear	3.58	4.29	5.69	3.55	4.21	4.26
25. PCA-sparse-ls-LPP-PLSR-kernelGlobal	3.2	3.65	4.99	4.27	5.29	4.28
26. PCA-sparse-ls-LPP-PLSR-linearGlobal	5.00	5.59	6.45	6.46	7.27	6.16
27. PCA-sparse-ls-LPP-SVM (Kernel)	3.04	4.00	5.12	3.47	4.33	3.99
28. PCA-sparse-ls-LPP-kNN-SVR (Kernel)	3.84	4.52	5.89	3.64	4.12	4.40
29. PCA-sparse-ls-LPP-SVR (Kernel)	3.02	3.34	4.53	3.59	4.73	3.84

Table 3. The MAE (degrees) and the standard deviation associated with the yaw angle using 30% and 80% of the persons for training. The results correspond to 5 random splits of Taiwan database

	30% Train		80% Train	
Combination	**MAE**	**STD**	**MAE**	**STD**
1. Linear PLSR	7.47	5.83	6.94	5.40
2. Kernel PLSR	6.00	4.92	5.44	4.36
3. PCA-LPP-kNN (kNN=1)	7.54	7.06	7.16	6.53
4. PCA-LPP-kNN (kNN=30)	10.96	9.72	9.47	8.68
5. PCA-LPP-kNN-PLSR-kernel	6.85	5.35	6.29	4.98
6. PCA-LPP-kNN-PLSR-linear	5.91	4.95	5.66	4.69
7. PCA-LPP-PLSR-kernelGlobal	6.48	5.14	5.82	4.51
8. PCA-LPP-PLSR-linearGlobal	7.57	5.84	7.45	5.84
9. PCA-LPP-SVM (Kernel)	5.83	5.55	4.96	4.79
10. PCA-LPP-kNN-SVR (Kernel)	6.75	5.31	6.21	4.97
11. PCA-LPP-SVR (Kernel)	6.15	4.86	5.39	4.26
12. PCA-lsLPP-kNN (kNN=1)	6.90	6.31	6.50	5.81
13. PCA-lsLPP-kNN (kNN=30)	9.73	8.31	8.22	7.30
14. PCA-lsLPP-kNN-PLSR-kernel	5.96	4.74	5.51	4.33
15. PCA-lsLPP-kNN-PLSR-linear	5.53	4.57	5.19	4.24
16. PCA-lsLPP-PLSR-kernelGlobal	6.49	5.14	5.86	4.57
17. PCA-lsLPP-PLSR-linearGlobal	7.49	5.81	7.08	5.48
18. PCA-lsLPP-SVM (Kernel)	5.83	5.50	4.92	4.66
19. PCA-lsLPP-kNN-SVR (Kernel)	5.89	4.71	5.43	4.31
20. PCA-lsLPP-SVR (Kernel)	6.16	4.89	5.44	4.23
21. PCA-sparse-lsLPP-kNN (kNN=1)	6.93	6.30	6.38	5.59
22. PCA-sparse-lsLPP-kNN (kNN=30)	9.68	8.31	8.13	7.06
23. PCA-sparse-lsLPP-kNN-PLSR-kernel	5.93	4.74	5.36	4.26
24. PCA-sparse-lsLPP-kNN-PLSR-linear	5.55	4.58	5.23	4.20
25. PCA-sparse-lsLPP-PLSR-kernelGlobal	6.42	5.08	5.76	4.42
26. PCA-sparse-lsLPP-PLSR-linearGlobal	7.42	5.79	7.07	5.50
27. PCA-sparse-lsLPP-SVM (Kernel)	5.84	5.53	4.99	4.76
28. PCA-sparse-lsLPP-kNN-SVR (Kernel)	7.47	5.83	6.94	5.40
29. PCA-sparse-lsLPP-SVR (Kernel)	6.00	4.92	5.44	4.36

Table 4. Percentage of success (recognition rate) for different combinations. The sets were constructed from the Columbia database by using 90% of the subjects for training. The results correspond to 5 random splits

Combination	Average percentage of success
1. PCA-LPP-kNN (k=1)	92.0
2. PCA-LPP-kNN (k=30)	64.0
3. PCA-LPP-SVM (Kernel)	92.8
4. PCA-lsLPP-kNN (k=1)	84.8
5. PCA-lsLPP-kNN (k=30)	54.4
6. PCA-lsLPP-SVM (Kernel)	94.4
7. PCA-sparse-lsLPP-kNN (k=1)	85.6
8. PCA-sparse-lsLPP-kNN (k=30)	48.0
9. PCA-sparse-lsLPP-SVM (Kernel)	94.4

By comparing the performance of some combinations of algorithms which only differ by their dimensionality reduction step, *e.g.* combinations 6, 15 and 24, we can observe that lsLPP (working like SLPP when $\varepsilon = 0$) and our proposed sparse lsLPP give similar results and outperform the classic LPP. However, the proposed sparse representation needs less parameter tuning and can adapt easily to different datasets. PLSR is also found to be very robust in estimating the head pose even when used alone with the raw normalized images without any feature extraction or dimensionality reduction step.

CONCLUSION

In this work, the machine learning approach was used to estimate the pose of human's faces. A new dimensionality reduction algorithm based on a sparse representation was proposed. The obtained results show that the sparse representation with label similarity is an efficient method for dimensionality reduction that outperforms state-of-the-art dimensionality reduction algorithms, that is easy to adapt to different datasets and that only needs two parameters to tune.

NOTES

[1]https://cubic.asu.edu/content/facepix-database

[2]http://bml.ym.edu.tw/bmlab/
[3]http://www.cs.columbia.edu/CAVE/databases/columbia_gaze/

CONFLICT OF INTEREST

The author confirms that author has no conflict of interest to declare for this publication.

ACKNOWLEDGEMENTS

Declared none.

REFERENCES

[1]   E. Murphy-Chutorian, and M.M. Trivedi, "Head pose estimation in computer vision: a survey", *IEEE Trans. Pattern Anal. Mach. Intell.,* vol. 31, no. 4, pp. 607-626, 2009.
[http://dx.doi.org/10.1109/TPAMI.2008.106] [PMID: 19229078]

[2]   C. Wholer, "Three-dimensional pose estimation and segmentation methods", In: *3D Computer Vision.* ser. X.media.publishing: Springer London, 2013, pp. 87-137.

[3]   D.J. Beymer, *Face recognition under varying pose, Massachusetts Institute of Technology Cambridge.* Tech. Rep: Cambridge, MA, USA, 1993.

[4]   S. Niyogi, and W. Freeman, "Example-based head tracking, in Automatic Face and Gesture Recognition, 1996", *Proceedings of the Second International Conference on,* pp. 374-378

[5]   J. Huang, X. Shao, and H. Wechsler, "Face pose discrimination using support vector machines (svm), in Pattern Recognition, 1998", *Fourteenth International Conference on,* vol. 1, pp. 154-156
[http://dx.doi.org/10.1109/ICPR.1998.711102]

[6]   Y. Ma, Y. Konishi, K. Kinoshita, S. Lao, and M. Kawade, "Sparse bayesian regression for head pose estimation, in Pattern Recognition, 2006", *ICPR 2006. 18th International Conference on,* 2006 *Pattern Recognition,* 2006 *ICPR,* 2006.

[7]   H. Drucker, C.J. Burges, L. Kaufman, A.J. Smola, and V. Vapnik, "Support Vector Regression Machines", *Neural Information Processing Systems,* pp. 155-161, 1996.

[8]   V.E. Vinzi, W.W. Chin, J. Henseler, and H. Wang, *Handbook of Partial Least Squares: Concepts, Methods and Applications in Marketing and Related Fields.* European Planning Studies, 2008.

[9]   C.M. Bishop, *Pattern Recognition and Machine Learning (Information Science and Statistics).* Springer-Verlag New York, Inc.: Secaucus, NJ, USA, 2006.

[10]   H. Chun, and S. Keles, *Sparse Partial Least Squares Regression for Simultaneous Dimension Reduction and Variable Selection,* 2007.

[11]   J. Nilsson, F. Sha, and M.I. Jordan, "Regression on manifolds using kernel dimension reduction", In: *Proceedings of the 24th International Conference on Machine Learning.* ACM: New York, NY, USA, 2007, pp. 697-704.

[http://dx.doi.org/10.1145/1273496.1273584]

[12] V. Balasubramanian, J. Ye, and S. Panchanathan, "Biased manifold embedding: A framework for person-independent head pose estimation", In: *Computer Vision and Pattern Recognition CVPR '07. IEEE Conference*, 2007, pp. 1-7.

[13] T. Horprasert, Y. Yacoob, and L.S. Davis, "Computing 3-d head orientation from a monocular image sequence", In: *Proceedings of the 2nd International Conference on Automatic Face and Gesture Recognition (FG'96)*. IEEE Computer Society: Washington, DC, USA, 1996, pp. 242-247. [http://dx.doi.org/10.1109/AFGR.1996.557271]

[14] J-G. Wang, and E. Sung, "Em enhancement of 3d head pose estimated by point at infinity", *Image Vis. Comput.*, vol. 25, no. 12, pp. 1864-1874, 2007. [http://dx.doi.org/10.1016/j.imavis.2005.12.017]

[15] A.H. Gee, and R. Cipolla, "Fast visual tracking by temporal consensus", *Image Vis. Comput.*, vol. 14, no. 2, pp. 105-114, 1996. [http://dx.doi.org/10.1016/0262-8856(95)01044-0]

[16] H. Rowley, S. Baluja, and T. Kanade, "Rotation invariant neural network-based face detection", In: *IEEE Computer Society Conference on Computer Vision and Pattern Recognition*, 1998, pp. 38-44.

[17] M. Turk, and A. Pentland, "Eigenfaces for recognition", *J. Cogn. Neurosci.*, vol. 3, no. 1, pp. 71-86, 1991. [http://dx.doi.org/10.1162/jocn.1991.3.1.71] [PMID: 23964806]

[18] R.E. Bellman, *Dynamic Programming*. Dover Publications, Incorporated, 2003.

[19] X. He, and P. Niyogi, "Locality Preserving Projections", In: *Advances in Neural Information Processing Systems*. 2003.

[20] Z. Zheng, J. Zhao, and J. Yang, "Gabor feature based face recognition using supervised locality preserving projection", In: *Advanced Concepts for Intelligent Vision Systems, ser. Lecture Notes in Computer Science*, vol. 4179. Springer Berlin Heidelberg, 2006, pp. 644-653. [http://dx.doi.org/10.1007/11864349_59]

[21] W-L. Chao, J-Z. Liu, and J-J. Ding, "Facial age estimation based on label-sensitive learning and age-oriented regression", *Pattern Recognit.*, vol. 46, no. 3, pp. 628-641, 2013. [http://dx.doi.org/10.1016/j.patcog.2012.09.011]

[22] J. Fox, and S. Weisberg, *An R Companion to Applied Regression*. SAGE Publications, 2010.

[23] C.J. Burges, "A Tutorial on Support Vector Machines for Pattern Recognition", *Data Min. Knowl. Discov.*, vol. 2, pp. 121-167, 1998. [http://dx.doi.org/10.1023/A:1009715923555]

[24] E. Fix, and J. Hodges, "Discriminatory analysis, nonparametric discrimination: Consistency properties", *USAF School of Aviation Medicine, Randolph Field, Texas, Technical Report 4*, 1951.

[25] X. He, and P. Niyogi, "Locality preserving projections", In: *Advances in Neural Information Processing Systems*. 2003.

[26] W-L. Chao, J-Z. Liu, and J-J. Ding, "Facial age estimation based on label-sensitive learning and age-oriented regression", *Pattern Recognit.*, vol. 46, no. 3, pp. 628-641, 2013.

[http://dx.doi.org/10.1016/j.patcog.2012.09.011]

[27]   K. Huang, and S. Aviyente, "Sparse representation for signal classification", B. Schölkopf, J. C. Platt, T. Hoffman, Eds., In: *Proceedings of the Twentieth Annual Conference on Neural Information Processing Systems.*. MIT Press: Vancouver, British Columbia, Canada, 2006, pp. 609-616.

CHAPTER 8

Efficient Deformable 3D Face Model Fitting to Monocular Images

Luis Unzueta[1,*], Waldir Pimenta[2], Jon Goenetxea[1], Luís Paulo Santos[2], Fadi Dornaika[3,4]

[1] *Vicomtech-IK4, Paseo Mikeletegi, 57, Parque Tecnológico, 20009, Donostia, Spain*

[2] *Departamento de Informática, University of Minho. Campus de Gualtar, 4710-057, Braga, Portugal*

[3] *Computer Engineering Faculty, University of the Basque Country EHU/UPV, Manuel de Lardizabal, 1, 20018, Donostia, Spain*

[4] *Ikerbasque, Basque Foundation for Science, Alameda Urquijo, 36-5, Plaza Bizkaia, 48011, Bilbao, Spain*

Abstract: In this work, we present a robust and lightweight approach for the automatic fitting of deformable 3D face models to facial pictures. Well known fitting methods, for example those taking into account statistical models of shape and appearance, need a training stage based on a set of facial landmarks, manually tagged on facial pictures. In this manner, new pictures in which to fit the model cannot differ excessively in shape and appearance (including illumination changes, facial hair, wrinkles, and so on) from those utilized for training. By contrast, our methodology can fit a generic face model in two stages: (1) the localization of facial features based on local image gradient analysis; and (2) the backprojection of a deformable 3D face model through the optimization of its deformation parameters. The proposed methodology preserves the advantages of both learning-free and learning-based methodologies. Subsequently, we can estimate the position, orientation, shape and actions of faces, and initialize user-specific face tracking approaches, such as Online Appearance Models (OAMs), which have demonstrated to be more robust than generic user tracking methodologies. Experimental results demonstrate that our strategy outperforms other fitting methods under challenging illumination conditions and with a computational footprint that permits its execution in gadgets with reduced computational power, such as cell phones and tablets. Our proposed methodology fits well with numerous systems addressing semantic inference in face images and videos.

---

* **Address to Corresponding Author Luis Unzueta:** Vicomtech-IK4, Paseo Mikeletegi, 57, Parque Tecnológico, 20009, Donostia, Spain; Tel: +[34] 943 30 92 30; Fax: +[34] 943 30 93 93; E-mail:lunzueta@vicomtech.org

Keywords: 2D shape landmarks, 3D face model, Deformable model back projection, facial actions, Facial expression recognition, Facial feature extraction, facial parts, Face gesture analysis, Face model fitting, Face recognition, Face tracking, Gradient maps, Head pose estimation, Learning-free, Levenberg-Marquardt, Monocular image, Online appearance model, Shape variations, Sigmoidal filter, Weak perspective.

INTRODUCTION

Generic face model fitting has been a hot research topic during the last decade. It can be seen as an essential part in numerous Human-Computer Interaction applications since it allows face tracking, head pose estimation, identification, and face gesture analysis. In general terms, two types of methods have been proposed: (i) learning-free and (ii) learning-based. The latter require a training stage with many pictures to construct the model, and therefore rely on the choice of pictures for a good fitting in unseen pictures. Learning-free methodologies depend intensely on some radiometric and geometric properties present in face pictures. These methodologies rely on generic knowledge about faces, which usually incorporates the position, symmetry, and edge profile of facial organs. They can place facial features using low-level methods (*e.g.* filtering, gradients), typically relying on recognizing individual face features (lips, nose, irises, ...) [1 - 4]. A large portion of the learning-free methodologies do not produce a full collection of extracted face features, contrary to learning-based strategies.

For example, in [5], the authors exploit a range facial scan in order to automatically distinguish the nose tip for both frontal and non frontal poses. In [7], an incremental certainty methodology regarding the extraction of facial features over real video frames is explained. The proposed procedure adapts to large varieties of subject appearances, including frame-to-frame changes within video sequences. The framework identifies the zones of the face that are measurably exceptional and assembles an initial set of regions that are expected to incorporate data about the features of interest. In this methodology, core facial features, for example the eyes and the mouth, are in effect reliably identified. In [6], the authors try to recognize the eyes and mouth utilizing the separation vector field that is structured by attributing a vector to every pixel indicating its nearest edge. Separation vector fields are based on geometrical structure, and consequently can help in evading illumination issues in the location of the eyes and mouth areas. In [9], the authors demonstrated that the eyes and mouth in facial pictures can be robustly identified. They used their locations to normalize the pictures, assuming affine transformation, which can make up for different viewpoints. In [10], real-time face detection algorithm for searching faces, eyes and lips in pictures and videos is explained. The calculation builds upon the extraction of skin pixels based on rules derived from a straightforward quadratic polynomial model in a normalized color space. In [8], the authors separated the facial feature extraction into three core steps. The initial step is preprocessing. The objective of this step is to get rid of high intensity noise and to binarize the input picture. The second step incorporates a labeling procedure and an aggregation procedure. This step tries to create facial feature candidates block by block. Finally, a geometrical face model is utilized to detect the face position.

As can be seen, learning-free methodologies have appealing characteristics. Nonetheless, they present a few deficiencies. Firstly, the majority of them makes the assumption that a few conditions are met (for instance, that face pictures are taken in controlled conditions and in an upright orientation). Furthermore, they usually depend on the discovery of few facial features (primarily the eyes and the mouth). Almost no consideration is given to the assembly of an extensive collection of facial features. Thirdly, accurate localization of the detected face features is still faulty.

Learning-based methodologies, on the other hand, aim to overcome these deficiencies. Three subcategories can be identified: parameterized appearance models, part-based deformable models and discriminative methodologies.

Parameterized appearance models generate a statistical model of shape and appearance from a collection of manually marked data [11 - 15]. In the 2D data domain, Active Shape Models (ASM) [11, 16], Active Appearance Models (AAM) [13, 14] and more recently, Active Orientation Models (AOM) [15] have been proposed. The ASM methodology generates 2D shape models and relies on motion constraints in conjunction with some image data from the regions near the 2D shape landmarks to find features on new pictures. The AAM uses both the shape and the texture [13, 14]. The AOM approach [15] takes is similar to AAM, differing in the utilization of gradient orientations rather than the texture and an enhanced cost function, which generalizes better to unknown faces. In the 3D data domain, 3D morphable models (3DMMs) have been proposed [12, 17], which incorporate the 3D shape and texture models, assembled from 3D scans.

Part-based deformable models maximize the posterior likelihood of part areas given a picture, so as to adjust the learned model [23 - 26]. Recently, the Constrained Local Model (CLM) methodology has attracted interest since it bypasses a large number of the disadvantages of AAM, for example, demonstrating robustness to lighting changes. CLM utilizes a set of several local detectors combined with a statistical shape model, amplifying the ASM approach. It achieves remarkable fitting results with unseen images [24]. In [25] a part based ASM and a semi-automatic refinement calculation are proposed, which results in more adaptability for facial pictures with large variation. In [26], a globally optimized tree shape model was introduced, which discovers facial points of interest as well as estimates the pose and the face image region, unlike the mentioned approaches, which all depend on a preparatory face localization stage [27] and do not assess the head posture from 2D picture information. In [28], a hybrid discriminative and part-based methodology is proposed enhancing the outcomes achieved by [24, 26] in the location of feature points.

Finally, discriminative methodologies build a correspondence between image features and motion parameters or feature point positions [18 - 21]. Facial landmark detectors usually apply a sliding window-based scanning throughout various regions in facial images [18]. Nonetheless, this is a time-consuming procedure, as the scanning time increases proportionally with the size of the search zone. In recent times, various methodologies have been proposed that aim at alleviating this, by utilizing local image information and regression-based techniques applied to the ASM approach [19 - 21], obtaining state-of-the-art performance in the field of 2D facial feature detection. In [22] discriminative techniques and parameterized appearance models are bound together through the proposed Supervised Descent Method (SDM) for solving Non-direct Least Squares problems, obtaining significantly quick and precise fitting results.

On the other hand, Online Appearance Models (OAM) [35, 36] permit a more effective person-specific face tracking without the need for an earlier training stage. They compute a quick 3D head posture estimation and facial action extraction with sufficient precision for an extensive variety of uses – for example, live facial puppetry, facial expression recognition, and face recognition. Nonetheless, this methodology demands an initial head posture estimation in the first frame so that the person-specific texture can be learned and subsequently updated. In [32], a holistic technique for the simultaneous estimation of two sorts of parameters (3D head pose and person-specific shape parameters that are consistent for a given subject) from a single picture is proposed, utilizing just a statistical facial texture model and a generic deformable 3D model. One advantage of the proposed fitting methodology is that it does not require a precise parameter initialization. Nevertheless, this methodology needs a training stage, with the same disadvantages as in the case of statistical shape and appearance models.

In this work, we propose a learning-free approach for identifying facial features, which can overcome the majority of the inadequacies specified previously. The proposed system can preserve the positive aspects of both learning-free and learning-based methodologies. Specifically, the advantages of learning-based methodologies (*i.e.*, rich sets of facial features, accurate and real-time estimation) are preserved in our proposed methodology. Additionally, the proposed methodology will have the two advantages that are connected with learning-free approaches[1]. To start with, there is no learning stage. Second, unlike numerous learning methodologies whose execution can degrade if imaging conditions change, our proposed methodology is training free and subsequently free from the influence of training conditions. Our proposed methodology has two primary parts. The initial step is the recognition of fiducial facial features using smoothed gradient maps and some prior knowledge about face geometry. The second part is the 3D fitting of a deformable 3D model to the detected feature points. In this step, a 3D fitting method is designed for extracting the 3D pose and its deformable parameters (facial actions and shape variations) at the same time. A result of this fitting is that additional facial features can be acquired by basically projecting the 3D vertices of the adjusted 3D model onto the picture. The deformable model used is a generic model with a set of parameters permitting a 3D fitting to different people and to diverse facial actions. In this way, we can estimate the position, orientation, shape and facial actions, and initialize person-specific face tracking procedures, such as OAM, with higher accuracy than state-of-the-art approaches, under difficult illumination conditions, and sufficiently low processing power requirements as to permit its execution in gadgets with lesser capabilities, such as cell phones and tablets. The use of a generic 3D deformable model is vital for having a efficient and adaptable fitting system.

This chapter is organized as follows. Section 2 explains the proposed learning-free approach for detecting facial features from an image. Section 3 describes the proposed approach to fit the deformable 3D facial shape to the detected 2D features. Section 4 presents the obtained experimental results compared to state-of-the-art techniques. Finally, in section 5, these results and future work are discussed. In addition, appendix A explains the 3D deformable face model used in this work.

LIGHTWEIGHT FACIAL FEATURE DETECTION

Our methodology for fitting 3D generic face models comprises two stages: facial features on the picture and (2) adjust the deformable 3D face model such that the projection of a set of key vertices onto the 2D plane of the picture matches the positions of the corresponding facial features. In this work we consider perspectives in which both eyes can be seen, regardless of the possibility that they are occluded, for instance, by eyeglasses. The proposed methodology requires an initial step of face detection, which, depending on the methodology taken, may require a facial training stage, for example, [38, 39]. We can likewise apply the same detection methods (*i.e.*, [38, 39]) for locating facial parts, for example, the eyes, nose and mouth, although we do not consider their identification as a *strict* prerequisite because we also include low resolution facial pictures or partially occluded ones, which would prevent the detectors to discover the features appropriately.

The entire fitting methodology, step by step, is shown in Fig. (**1**) and algorithm 1, where the term *ROI* alludes to a *region of interest* (the sought region) and *SROI* to

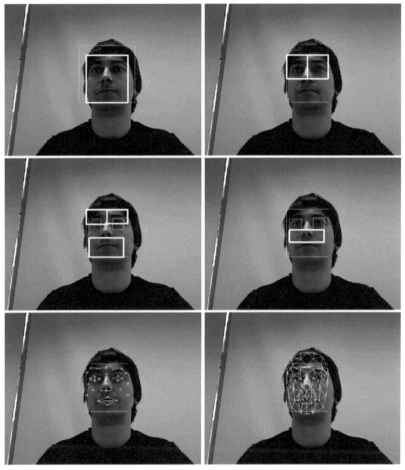

Fig. (1). Proposed fitting approach. From left to right and top to bottom: (1) The detected face region and the *faceROI* derived from it (thicker line), (2) *faceROI* and the *eyeSROIs* derived from it (thicker line), (3) *faceROI*, the estimated eyeROIs and the *eyebrowSROIs* and *mouthSROI* derived from them (thicker lines), (4) *faceROI*, the estimated eyeROIs and the noseSROI derived from them (thicker line), (5) the detected facial features and (6) the fitted 3D face model projection.

a *search ROI*. Depending on whether they have already been detected by the corresponding object detector or not, the input data related to the eyes, nose and mouth can be either *ROI* or *SROI*, as specified previously. Algorithm 1 attempts to identify 32 facial features in the input monocular image (Fig. **2**). These 32 features correspond to a subset of vertices in the Candide-3m model (index A). Their 2D positions are settled inside their corresponding regions considering the size of the areas and the in-plane face rotation (sideways head tilt, or roll angle).

This way, by finding the *ROI* of a face part and the roll angle, the 2D points of that face part will be quickly and automatically located. This methodology is adequate to initialize an OAM tracker, for example [36], to fit the 3D model frame-by-frame with the correlation between the model and the face pictures. This is particularly the case of contour points, which help in the initialization despite not matching with real landmarks, and thus cannot be located with high confidence on a face picture even by expert observers. When a face region has been found on a picture (*e.g.*, utilizing [38, 39]), each of the 32 point positions are calculated, even if some are occluded.

The search regions are estimated from the detected face and eye regions (Fig. **1**). In case external detectors were not used to find the *eyeROIs* (*i.e.*, they have not been input to algorithm 1), we apply algorithms 2, 3 and 4 to estimate their boundaries[2]. Next, the eye point positions and the face projection *roll* angle θ are set, derived in a proportional and fixed way from the geometry of those *ROIs*. Particularly, the *eyeROI* centers correspond to eye center positions, the eye widths and heights are the same in both sides relying on the mean *ROI* sizes, where θ is measured, and the remaining eye points are located around the centers. Using face detectors, there is a limited *roll* angle range, and subsequently the eyes have well-defined search regions.

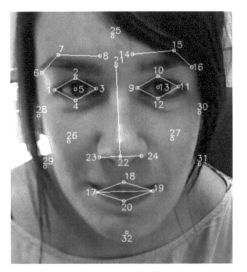

DETECTED FACIAL POINTS

1. Left eye left corner	17. Mouth left corner
2. Left eye upper corner	18. Mouth upper corner
3. Left eye right corner	19. Mouth right corner
4. Left eye lower corner	20. Mouth lower corner
5. Left eye center	21. Nose top
6. Left eyebrow left corner	22. Nose base
7. Left eyebrow upper corner	23. Left nostril
8. Left eyebrow right corner	24. Right nostril
9. Right eye left corner	25. Forehead center
10. Right eye upper corner	26. Left cheek
11. Right eye right corner	27. Right cheek
12. Right eye lower corner	28. Left facial upper corner
13. Right eye center	29. Left facial lower corner
14. Right eyebrow left corner	30. Right facial upper corner
15. Right eyebrow upper corner	31. Right facial lower corner
16. Right eyebrow right corner	32. Chin bottom

Fig. (2). The 32 detected facial points. Note that the words *left* and *right* are relative to the observer rather than the subject.

Algorithm 1 Lightweight facial feature detection algorithm

1: **procedure** FACIALPOINTDETECTION(*faceROI, lEye(S)ROI, rEye(S)ROI, nose(S)ROI, mouth(S)ROI, peakValX, peakValY, binThresh*)
2:     **for** each eye **do**
3:         **if** ¬ *eyeROI* **then**
4:             *eyeROI* ← ROIBOUNDDETECTION(*eyeSROI, peakValX, peakValY*)
5:         **end if**
6:     **end for**
7:     θ ← Estimate *roll* rotation angle derived from *eyeROIs*
8:     *eyePoints* ← Estimate eye point positions in a fixed way derived from (*eyeROIs* and θ)
9:     **for** each eyebrow **do**
10:        *rotEyebrowSROI* ← Get the eyebrow search region derived from (*faceROI* and *eyeROI*) and rotate it $(-\theta)$
11:        *rotEyebrowROI* ← ROIBOUNDDETECTION(*rotEyebrowSROI*, NOT_USED, *peakValY*)
12:        *eyebrowPoints* ← Estimate eyebrow point positions in a fixed way derived from *rotEyebrowROI* and apply θ rotation and transform to global image coordinates
13:     **end for**
14:     **for** mouth and nose **do**
15:        **if** ¬ *partROI* **then**
16:            *rotPartSROI* ← Rotate *partSROI* $(-\theta)$
17:            *rotPartROI* ← ROIBOUNDDETECTION(*rotPartSROI, peakValX, peakValY*)
18:        **else**
19:            *rotPartROI* ← Rotate *partROI* $(-\theta)$
20:        **end if**
21:        *partPoints* ← Estimate part point positions in a fixed way derived from *rotPartROI* and apply θ rotation and transform to global image coordinates
22:     **end for**
23:     *contourPoints* ← CONTOURPOINTDETECTION(*faceROI, eyeCenters, lEyeLCorner, rEyeRCorner, mouth-Corners, binThresh*)
24:     **return** (*eyePoints* and *eyebrowPoints* and *mouthPoints* and *nosePoints* and *contourPoints*)
25: **end procedure**

The corresponding ROI boundaries of eyebrows, mouth and nose are used as a reference, also in a fixed way, for the estimation of their corresponding facial features. Algorithms 2, 3 and 4 are also used to obtain these boundaries, taking into account the influence of the *roll* angle θ. In the specific case of eyebrows, we do not calculate the boundaries in the X direction, but fix them according to the search region width and the expected eyebrow geometry in the 3D model, as some people have bangs occluding them, or even lack eyebrows altogether. The parameters *peakValX* and *peakValY* are thresholds for detecting the horizontal and vertical boundaries in the normalized gradient maps. In our experiments we use *peakValX* = 20 and *peakValY* = 50 in all cases.

We can reduce the influence of directional illumination by applying the double sigmoidal filtering applied to the search regions (algorithm 2), while the candidate edges are accentuated through the squared sigmoidal gradient calculation, which considers only the edge strength and neglects the edge direction information [40]. The contour point positions are estimated in a fixed way too, relying on the eye and mouth positions. Algorithm 5 returns 8 contour points: the forehead center, the left and right cheeks, the 4 facial corners and the chin bottom point. Although none of them are fiducial points, they are useful for 3D model fitting and tracking. In the case of the facial side corner estimation, we analyze the image region that goes from the facial region boundary to its corresponding mouth corner, assuming that in that region a noticeable X gradient appears only in one of the sides, when the subject exhibits a non-frontal pose, corresponding to the face side boundary. The squared sigmoidal gradient in X is calculated, assuming that those side points lie on it. Then, these side points allow us to better estimate the *pitch* angle of the face. Nonetheless, it can occur that both sides have a noticeable gradient in X, such as in the case of the existence of other features such as local shadows or a beard. In order to circumvent these conditions, we assume that the side that should have the gradient applied to estimate the X positions is the one in which the mean positions are closer to the face region boundary, while for the other side the X positions correspond to those of the boundary itself. The parameter *binThresh* is the binarization threshold for the normalized gradient map in X. In our experiments we use *binThresh* = 150.

Algorithm 2 ROI boundary detection algorithm

1: **procedure** ROIBOUNDDETECTION(*SROI, peakValX, peakValY*)
2:    *dsSROI* ← Apply double sigmoidal filter to *SROI*
3:    *ssySROI* ← Apply squared sigmoidal Y gradient to *dsSROI*
4:    (*bottomY* and *topY*) ← YBOUNDDETECTION(*ssySROI, peakValY*)   ▷ (ALGORITHM 3)
5:    (*leftX* and *rightX*) ← XBOUNDDETECTION(*ssySROI, peakValX, bottomY, topY*)   ▷ (ALGORITHM 4)
6:    **return** (*leftX* and *rightX* and *bottomY* and *topY*)
7: **end procedure**

Algorithm 3 ROI Y boundary detection algorithm

1: **procedure** YBOUNDDETECTION($ssySROI, peakValY$)
2: **for each** row in $ssySROI$ **do**
3:      $w \leftarrow (ssySROI_{height}/2 - |ssySROI_{height}/2 - y|) \cdot peakValY$
4:      $wVertProj_{row} \leftarrow (w \cdot \sum_{x=1}^{width} ssySROI_x)$
5: **end for**
6: Normalize $wVertProj$ values from 0 to 100
7: $maxLowY \leftarrow$ Locate the local maximum above $peakValY$ with the lowest position in $wVertProj$
8: $topY \leftarrow (maxLowY + ssySROI_{height}/4)$
9: $bottomY \leftarrow (maxLowY - ssySROI_{height}/4)$
10: **return** ($bottomY$ and $topY$)
11: **end procedure**

Algorithm 4 ROI X boundary detection algorithm

1: **procedure** XBOUNDDETECTION($ssySROI, bottomY, topY, peakValX$)
2: **for each** col in $ssySROI$ **do**
3:      $w \leftarrow (ssySROI_{width}/2 - |ssySROI_{width}/2 - x|) \cdot peakValX$
4:      $wHorProj_{col} \leftarrow (w \cdot \sum_{y=bottomY}^{topY} ssySROI_y)$
5: **end for**
6: Normalize $wHorProj$ values from 0 to 100
7: ($leftX$ and $rightX$) $\leftarrow$ Locate the first value above $peakValX$ starting from the left and right sides in $wHorProj$
8: **return** ($leftX$ and $rightX$)
9: **end procedure**

Algorithm 5 Contour feature detection algorithm

1: **procedure** CONTOURPOINTDETECTION(*faceROI, eyeCenters, lEyeLCorner, rEyeRCorner, mouthCorners, binThresh*)
2: $faceVector \leftarrow (lEyeCenter + rEyeCenter - mouthLCorner - mouthRCorner)/2$
3: $foreheadCenter \leftarrow (lEyeCenter + rEyeCenter + faceVector)/2$
4: $lCheek \leftarrow (lEyeLCorner + lEyeCenter - faceVector)/2$
5: $rCheek \leftarrow (rEyeRCorner + rEyeCenter - faceVector)/2$
6: $ssxFaceROI \leftarrow$ Apply squared sigmoidal X gradient to $faceROI$ and normalize between 0 and 255
7: **for each** facial side **do**
8:      $ssxFacialCornerROI \leftarrow$ Get region between $mouthCorner$ and $faceROI$ outer boundary
9:      $binFacialCornerROI \leftarrow$ Binarize $ssxFacialCornerROI$ with $binThresh$ and remove clusters (obtained through [41]) with $area < 0.8 \cdot ssxFacialCornerROI_{height}$
10:     $facialUCorner_y \leftarrow 0.75 \cdot ssxFacialCornerROI_{height}$
11:     $facialUCorner_x \leftarrow$ Get X centroid of white pixels at $facialUCorner_y$ in $binFacialCornerROI$
12:     $facialLCorner_y \leftarrow 0.25 \cdot ssxFacialCornerROI_{height}$
13:     $facialUCorner_x \leftarrow$ Get X centroid of white pixels at $facialUCorner_y$ in $binFacialCornerROI$
14:     $facialCorners \leftarrow$ Transform to global image coordinates
15: **end for**
16: $facialCorners \leftarrow$ Check which side from $facialCorners$ mean X position is further from its corresponding face region boundary, and then set their X positions in the boundary
17: $chinBottom \leftarrow$ Calculate the intersection between the bottom of $faceROI$ and the line traced by $faceVector$
18: **return** ($foreheadCenter$ and $lCheek$ and $rCheek$ and $facialCorners$ and $chinBottom$)
19: **end procedure**

DEFORMABLE MODEL BACKPROJECTION

The next stage is to determine the position, orientation, shape units (SUs) and animation units (AUs) (appendix A) which best fit the 32 detected facial features. In order to make the face model fitting more efficient, we use the existing correspondence between the 2D facial features and the 3D model points. The 3D generic model is given by the 3D coordinates of its vertices $\mathbf{P}i$, $i = 1, ..., n$, where n is the number of vertices. This way, the shape, up to a global scale, can be fully described by a $3n$-vector $\mathbf{g}$, the concatenation of the 3D coordinates of all vertices (Eq. 1), where $\mathbf{g}$ is the standard shape of the model, the columns of $\mathbf{S}$ and $\mathbf{A}$ are the shape and animation units, and $\tau_s \in \mathbf{R}^m$ and $\tau_a \in \mathbf{R}^k$, are the shape and animation control vectors, respectively.

The 3D generic model configuration is given by the 3D face pose parameters (rotations and translations in the three axes) and the shape and animation control vectors, τ_s and τ_a. These define the parameter vector $\mathbf{b}$ (Eq. 2).

$$\mathbf{g} = \bar{\mathbf{g}} + \mathbf{S}\tau_s + \mathbf{A}\tau_a \tag{1}$$

$$\mathbf{b} = [\theta_x, \theta_y, \theta_z, t_x, t_y, t_z, \tau_s, \tau_a]^T \tag{2}$$

Inter-person parameters, such as the eye width and the eye separation distance, can be controlled through shape units (see appendix A). The term $\mathbf{S}\,\tau_s$ accounts for the shape or inter-person variability, while the term $\mathbf{A}\,\tau_a$ accounts for the facial or intra-person animation. Thus, in theory, the shape units would remain constant for face tracking, while the animation units could vary. Nevertheless, as they are meant to fit any kind of human face, it is challenging to perfectly separate both kinds of parameters, because the neutral facial expression can be significantly different from person to person. Hence, we have to take into account both the shape and animation units in our initialization process, without an explicit distinction between them. After the initialization we can assume that the shape units remain constant. Moreover, in order to reduce the computational burden we consider a subset of the animation units [36].

The 3D shape in Eq. 1 is expressed in a local coordinate system, but this should be related to the 2D image coordinate system. Thus, we adopt the *weak perspective* projection model. The perspective effects can be neglected since the depth variation of the face is small, when compared to its absolute depth from the camera viewpoint. The mapping between the image and the 3D face model is given by a 2×4 matrix $\mathbf{M}$, encapsulating both the camera parameters and the 3D face pose. Therefore, as defined in Eq. 3, a 3D vertex $\mathbf{P}_i = [X_i, Y_i, Z_i]^T \subset \mathbf{g}$ will be projected onto the image point $\mathbf{p}_i = [u_i, v_i]^T \subset \mathbf{I}$ (where $\mathbf{I}$ refers to the image).

$$\mathbf{p}_i = [u_i, v_i]^T = \mathbf{M}[X_i, Y_i, Z_i, 1]^T \tag{3}$$

The projection matrix $\mathbf{M}$ is given by Eq. 4, where αu and αv are the camera focal length expressed in vertical and horizontal pixels, respectively. (uc, vc) represent the principal point 2D coordinates, s is a global scale and $\mathbf{r}^T_1$ and $\mathbf{r}^T_2$ are the first two rows of the 3D rotation matrix.

$$\mathbf{M} = \begin{bmatrix} \frac{\alpha_u}{t_z} s \, \mathbf{r_1^T} & \alpha_u \frac{t_x}{t_z} + u_c \\ \frac{\alpha_v}{t_z} s \, \mathbf{r_2^T} & \alpha_v \frac{t_y}{t_z} + v_c \end{bmatrix} \tag{4}$$

The core idea of our approach is to estimate the 3D model parameters by minimizing the distances between the detected facial points ($\mathbf{d}_j = [x_j, y_j]^T \subset \mathbf{I}$, where $j = 1, ..., q$ and $q \leq n$) and their corresponding projected vertices from the 3D model. Algorithm 6 shows the procedure, called *deformable model backprojection*. The more points are detected on the image (32 with the proposed learning-free method), the more shape and animation units can vary in the model. The minimal requirement is that the points to be matched must not be coplanar. This way, the objective is to minimize Eq. 5, where $\mathbf{p}_j$ is the 2D projection of the 3D point $\mathbf{P}_j$. Its 2D coordinates rely on the model parameters (encapsulated in $\mathbf{b}$). These coordinates are obtained *via* equations 1 and 3. The weight elements w_j refer to confidence values ($0 \leq w_j \leq 1$) for their corresponding $\mathbf{d}_j$, and depend on the approach used for facial point detection. For our method (section 2), higher weights (*e.g*, 1) should correspond to eye points, mouth points, nose top and base points, and the forehead center point; in a second level (*e.g.*, 0.8) the eyebrow points and the rest of contour points; and finally in a third level (*e.g.*, 0.2) the left and right nostrils. In order to get an initial guess of the position and orientation of the face object, before the optimization procedure starts, the POS algorithm[3] is applied.

$$\mathbf{b}^* = arg \min_{\mathbf{b}} \sum_{j=1}^{q} w_j \cdot [(\{\mathbf{d}_j\}_x - \{\mathbf{p}_j(\mathbf{b})\}_x)^2 + (\{\mathbf{d}_j\}_y - \{\mathbf{p}_j(\mathbf{b})\}_y)^2] \qquad (5)$$

The degrees of freedom of the Candide model (to be optimized) are initially normalized, so that their values are not biased towards any of them in particular. Empirically, we observed that it was recommendable to keep the translation estimated by POS constant because of the high sensitivity of the Levenberg-Marquardt (LM) algorithm to these global parameters. Therefore, we keep the position from POS constant, and optimize the rest of parameters.

EXPERIMENTAL RESULTS AND DISCUSSION

We have used the CMU Pose, Illumination, and Expression (PIE) database [44], in order to evaluate the suitability of our approach for the initialization of an OAM-based 3D face tracking. We have used the images where the flash system was activated, in order to get challenging illumination conditions while subjects maintained a neutral facial expression. In our context, in which we expect to fit the face model for a posterior OAM-based tracking, we can assume that in the first frame the person will have the mouth closed, which is valid for many applications. For this experiment we have selected the images where the subject has frontal or near-frontal views. In total, we have used 7134 images for the test (68 subjects × 5 cameras × 21 flashlights − 6 missing images in the database). We created the ground truth by manually configuring the Candide-3m model on each of the faces, then applied the automatic fitting approach (described in sections 2 and 3) and measured the fitting error with respect to the ground truth as a percentage, in the same way as [18, 19]. This is described by Eq. 6, where $\mathbf{p}^{\text{fit}}$ and $\mathbf{p}^{\text{gt}}$ correspond to the fitted and ground truth projections of point i respectively, and $\mathbf{l}^{\text{gt}}$ and $\mathbf{r}^{\text{gt}}$ to the ground truth left and right eye center projections. If no face region was detected, or one was incorrectly detected, we excluded that image from the evaluation. All vertices of Candide-3m are used for computing the fitting error.

$$e = \frac{\sum_{i=1}^{n} \|\mathbf{p}_i^{\text{fit}} - \mathbf{p}_i^{\text{gt}}\| / n}{\|\mathbf{l}^{\text{gt}} - \mathbf{r}^{\text{gt}}\|} \cdot 100 \qquad (6)$$

Algorithm 6 Deformable model backprojection algorithm

1: **procedure** MODELBACKPROJECTION($\bar{\mathbf{g}}$, $\mathbf{w}$, $\mathbf{S}$, $\mathbf{A}$, $\mathbf{d}$)

2: (θ_x^0 and θ_y^0 and θ_z^0 and t_x^0 and t_y^0 and t_z^0) $\leftarrow$ Apply POS algorithm [42] to $\bar{\mathbf{g}}$ with $\mathbf{d}$

3: $\mathbf{b}$ $\leftarrow$ Starting from (θ_x^0 and θ_y^0 and θ_z^0 and t_x^0 and t_y^0 and t_z^0 and τ_s = 0 and τ_a = 0) minimize Eq. 5 through the Levenberg-Marquardt algorithm [43], taking into account equations 1 and 3 for the update in the iterative optimization process. The position is kept constant ($t_x = t_x^0, t_y = t_y^0, t_z = t_z^0$).

4: **return b**

5: **end procedure**

Six alternatives are compared in the test: (1) *HA* (Holistic Approach) [32], *CLM* (Constrained Local Model) [24] with head orientation obtained by [29], (3) *SDM* (Supervised Descent Method) [22] with head orientation obtained by [42], (4) *FFBP* (Facial Feature Backprojection), our approach combining both the proposed facial feature detector and the backprojection, (5) *CLMBP*, the CLM approach but replacing its estimated orientation by our full backprojection approach and (6) *SDMBP* the SDM approach but with our full backprojection approach.

We used all the Candide-3m points in order to measure the fitting error, for all approaches. The used weights for the partial backprojection in *CLM* and *SDM* and the full backprojection in *CLMBP* and *SDMBP* are all equal to 1, except for the eyebrows and contours, which have 0.8. This challenging illumination test is unfavorable for the *HA* approach (fully appearance-based approach), as it relies on a PCA model obtained from a training stage. Hence, we train user-specific PCA models from the images in which we want to fit the face model, in order to obtain the best possible results from this approach. For the optimization a differential evolution strategy is adopted with an exponential crossover, a random-to-best vector to be perturbed, one difference vector for perturbation and the following parameter values: maximum number of iterations = 10, population size = 300, F = 0.85, and CR = 1. The random numbers are set to the range [−0.5, 0.5].

We solve the same number of shape and animation units (12 SUs and 3 AUs) in all the methods, maintaining the rest of Candide-3m parameters to a value of 0. The considered SUs correspond to *Eyebrows Vertical Position, Eyes Vertical Position, Eyes Width, Eyes Height, Eyes Separation Distance, NoseVertical Position, Mouth Vertical Position, Mouth Width, Eyebrow Width, Eyebrow Separation, Nose Width* and *Lip Thickness*, while the selected AUs correspond to *Brow Lowerer, Outer Left Brow Raiser* and *Outer Right Brow Raiser*. This way, the LM minimization in algorithm 6 attempts to simultaneously approximate 21 unknowns (3D pose and facial deformations).

Table 1. Fitting error comparison obtained in the CMU PIE database illumination variation images.

	C05		C07		C09		C27		C29		GLOBAL	
	Mean	StDev	Mean	StDev	Mean	StDev	Mean	StDev	Mean	StDev	Mean	StDev
FFBP	16.02	7.28	12.48	5.84	16.83	7.52	13.57	6.34	15.93	8.58	14.93	7.35
CLMBP	11.55	9.74	8.52	5.12	10.96	7.18	8.73	6.07	11.49	9.72	10.23	7.87
SDMB	9.13	3.76	8.24	3.05	9.06	4.87	8.23	2.83	9.24	3.63	8.78	3.72
CLM	18.29	8.97	13.44	5.11	12.27	6.82	11.32	5.80	12.11	9.57	13.44	7.82
SDM	9.79	4.10	10.18	3.44	8.03	4.99	7.25	2.67	10.05	4.24	9.05	4.14
HA	37.60	20.20	31.06	16.40	30.26	15.80	32.06	16.54	31.39	15.67	32.42	17.16

The obtained results for the six considered alternatives are shown in Table **1** This comparison allows us to evaluate the not only the relative performance of our full approach (*i.e., FFBP*, which combines the feature detection and the deformable backprojection), but also the deformable backprojection itself (*i.e.*, the approaches that include the suffix *BP*), with respect to other alternatives. The results we obtain with the full approach (*FFBP*) have less error than *HA* and have similar values to those of *CLM*, with the advantage of not being dependent on the quality of a trained model for the fitting. Moreover, this comparison also shows that our deformable backprojection approach improves the fitting quality (*CLMBP vs. CLM* and *SDMBP vs. SDM*). Next we will show that under a face tracking setting *FFBP* (with OAM) behaves better than *CLM* and is computationally less intensive, allowing its utilization in gadgets with lower computational capabilities.

Table **2** shows the fitting errors obtained with *FFBP* for the points corresponding to each facial part separately. It can be observed that the lowest errors correspond to the eyes. This was expected, since eye regions can be found in a specific area which usually presents significant gradient levels with similar patterns from face to face. This is in contrast to other facial regions such as the mouth.

Table 2. Fitting errors of facial parts obtained with FFBP in the CMU PIE database illumination variation images.

	C05		C07		C09		C27		C29		GLOBAL	
	Mean	StDev	Mean	StDev	Mean	StDev	Mean	StDev	Mean	StDev	Mean	StDev
Eyes	8.62	6.65	7.56	5.46	8.85	6.91	7.14	5.52	8.06	8.67	8.03	6.75
Eyebrows	12.54	6.65	11.53	6.02	13.69	6.41	10.98	5.39	12.40	9.22	12.21	6.91
Nose	12.42	7.42	9.28	6.29	11.00	8.14	8.84	6.21	10.88	8.58	10.46	7.48
Mouth	12.75	10.19	9.97	8.02	11.93	9.40	10.10	9.11	11.02	10.58	11.13	9.54

We have also evaluated our approach in combination with OAM (*FFBP-OAM*) in a tracking scenario using the camera of the iPad 2. We have only integrated in the device *FFBP-OAM* and *CLM* in its original form (*i.e.*, with its own model, without transferring its tracked points and orientations to Candide-3m). The computation power required by *HA* was too high compared to the others and the code of *SDM* was implemented exclusively for desktop computers, which prevented us to integrate it in the device. In this test, the faces have severe occlusions at certain times, and they adopt different positions, orientations and expressions. We evaluate how the full system (initialization + tracking) behaves in these circumstances, where it has to (1) detect and fit the 3D model when a new face appears, (2) track the face while it is visible and (3) detect when the tracking is lost and reinitialize the tracking when a face becomes visible again. Fig. (**3**) shows how both approaches behave under severe occlusion. In this case, *CLM* does not detect the occlusion correctly, does not restart the face detection process until the face is visible again, and repeatedly fits the graphical model to neighboring regions not corresponding to the face. On the contrary, *FFBP-OAM* properly detects the occlusion time and stops tracking, and then restarts the tracking once the face is visible again. The metrics inherently available in model-based tracking approaches, such as OAM, to better evaluate the current observation's divergence from the reference model, present a clear advantage over other alternatives for this kind of situations.

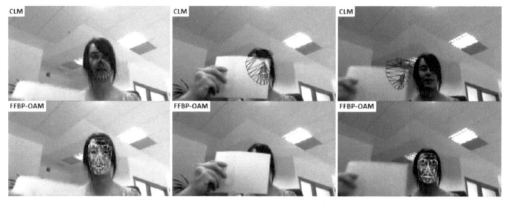

Fig. (3). Comparison between *CLM* and *FFBP-OAM* on an iPad 2 under a severe occlusion.

Table **3** shows the computation times obtained in this test. *CLM* needs an average time of 250 ms for the initial fitting with a detected face region of about 200 × 200, whereas our approach needs an average time of about 60 ms. During the tracking stage, *CLM* needs an average of 88 ms whereas the OAM tracking [36] requires only about 42 ms to fit the model. Table **4** shows the computation times obtained for the proposed facial feature detection and model backprojection separately, on the iPad 2. Fig. (**4**) shows images of our full system running on an iPhone 5. These results demonstrate the better suitability of our approach when compared to other state-of-the-art alternatives for 3D deformable face model fitting.

Fig. (4). The full system running on an iPhone 5 at 24 FPS.

Table 3. Average computation times (in ms) obtained with *FFBP-OAM* and *CLM* [24] on iPad 2.

	Initialization	Frame-to-Frame Tracking
FFBP-OAM	60	42
CLM [24]	250	88

Table 4. Average computation times (in ms) obtained with *FFBP* in the facial feature detection and model backprojection stages on iPad 2.

	Facial Feature Detection	Model Backprojection
FFBP	22	38

Finally, we analyze the suitability of our approach for the estimation of facial actions (intra-person variability) in a video sequence in which a face exaggerated facial expressions. In this experiment, the observed face starts with a neutral face, which allows our full approach combined with OAM (*FFBP-OAM*) to be used. It is compared to other two alternatives that involve the use of our backprojection, applied to every frame of the sequence, and that can infer facial actions in the lower face region by estimating the positions of sufficient mouth contour points, *i.e.*, *CLMBP* and *SDMBP*. We estimate 26 variables (6 pose parameters, 12 SUs and 8 AUs) in the Candide- 3m mode with these three approaches. The considered SUs are those used in the test with the CMU database, while the AUs correspond to *Jaw Drop, Lip Stretcher, Brow Lowerer, Lip Corner Depressor, Outer Left Brow Raiser, Outer Right Brow Raiser, Left Eye Closed* and *Right Eye Closed*.

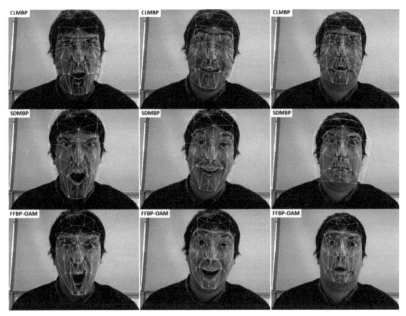

Fig. (5). Comparison between *CLMBP, SDMBP* and *FFBP-OAM* in a video sequence with exaggerated facial expressions

Some samples of this comparison are shown in Fig. (**5**), while Fig. (**6**) shows the *Jaw Drop* AU and upper/lower lip distance variations. In the three cases, images with a resolution of 320×240 are used for processing, and the results are visualized in images of size 640×480. It can be seen how exaggerated AUs can be estimated from the sequence by the three alternatives. The trained CLM in *CLMBP* includes contour facial points, while the trained SDM from *SDMBP* does not, and therefore, when those contour points are well adjusted, the Candide-3m model adjusts better to the real contour of the person in the former. Nevertheless, the CLM was trained with limited mouth variations, and therefore, especially when the mouth is fully open, the point adjustment is not accurate around the mouth. Nevertheless, the AU variation is distinguishable with the three alternatives and therefore action activation moments can be detected with appropriate thresholds. The frame-to-frame transition in the case of *FFBP-OAM* is better suited for video sequences as it is much smoother than in the other two cases.

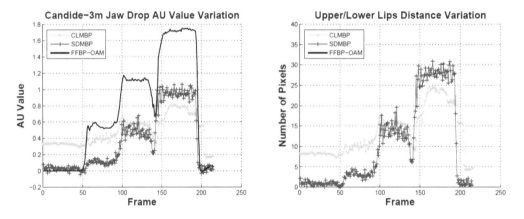

Fig. (6). The *Jaw Drop* AU and upper/lower lip distance variations with *CLMBP, SDMBP* and *FFBP-OAM*.

CONCLUSION

In this work, we proposed a robust and lightweight procedure for the automatic fitting of 3D face models on facial pictures. Our approach is divided in two stages: (1) the detection of facial features on the picture and (2) the adjustment of the deformable 3D face model. The adjustment is performed by projecting its vertices into the 2D plane of the picture, and assessing the matching accuracy between the projected locations and the points of the detected facial features. For the first step, we propose a gradient analysis using filtered local image regions instead of popular techniques such as those based on statistical models of shape and appearance. This approach has the following benefits: (1) lower computational cost (2) non-reliance on a preliminary training stage, which avoidis the biased result provided by pre-trained statistical databases, (3) efficient matching as the 32 detection points are directly related to a subset of the generic 3D face model and (4) robust handling of challenging illumination. For the second step, we propose to use the detected facial points to estimate the 3D model configuration by minimizing the distances between the paired points across both point sets: those in the detected facial point set and their counterparts in the projected model. This approach assumes a camera with weak perspective, and uses a lightweight iterative approach to estimate the considered face model variations.

We have demonstrated the capability of our learning-free facial point detection and of our deformable backprojection approaches, by contrasting their performance with respect to state-of-the-art approaches. The challenging CMU PIE database was used for testing due to its illumination variation images. Similarly, videos captured with the camera of an iPad2 were used to test tracking scenarios. Furthermore, we also have tested the integration of our method in low hardware capacity devices such as smartphones and tablets, with similar accuracy than in state-of-the-art methods but with an improved performance when compared to other recent alternatives.

Our proposed approach only needs an input snapshot image combined with the detected face features. Accordingly, it gets rid of tedious learning processes and also of the dependency on the related learning conditions. The current limitations of the proposed strategy are only related to the face pose. Although the method does not need a frontal face, the 3D orientation of the face should not be arbitrary. We estimate that the working ranges of the proposed method are around $(-20\circ, +20\circ)$ for the roll angle and around $(-30\circ, +30\circ)$ for the out-of-plane rotations.

Future work may concentrate on increasing the head orientation angle ranges, using lower image resolutions, and also the inclusion of other types of deformable objects apart from human faces. The management of the partial occlusions is another possible improovement for this method.

APPENDIX A: MODIFICATIONS TO CANDIDE-3

Our fundamental interest for this work is to fit a 3D generic face model on a facial picture under uncontrolled light conditions utilizing a computationally lightweight system, and avoiding previous learning phases. The objective of a computationally light processing is to permit the last application to run in gadgets with low computational capacities, for example, smartphones and tablets. We are using an adaptation of Candide-3 [34] as a 3D generic face model. We call to this modification Candide-3m. This new Candide version is more simple is streamlined model so as to improve the fitting and tracking abilities of the original one.

The Candide-3m model has the following modifications with respect to Candide-3:

• Some vertices were removed from the geometry around the eyes to simplify the shape of the eyelids.
• The mesh around the eyes and mouth is more uniform. This is made tweaking the triangulation in those areas.
• The SUs have been changed to adapt them for the proposed initialization procedure:(1) *Cheeks Z*, *Chin Width* and *Eyes Vertical Difference* SUs have been removed, and (2) three more have been added, called *Eyebrow Width*, *Eyebrow Separation* and *Nose Width*.
• The AUs have been changed to increase the expressiveness of the tracking through an OAM approach such as [36]: (1) All MPEG-4 FAPs have been deleted, (2) the *Upper Lip Raiser*, *Lid Tightener*, *Nose Wrinkler*, *Lip Presser* and *Upper Lid Raiser* animation unit vectors (AUVs) have been deleted, and (3) the *Outer Brow Raiser* AUV has been split two different AUs (one for each eyebrow), and (4) the *Eyes Closed* AUV has been split in two different AUVs (one for each eye).

NOTES
[1]These are clearly favorable features if the framework is to be utilized on portable equipment, for example PDAs and tablets.

[2]Note that the ROI boundaries of the eyebrows, nose and mouth are also estimated through algorithms 2, 3 and 4. Algorithm 2 invokes both algorithms 3 and 4.

[3]POS is a pose solver based on a linearization of the perspective projection equations, which corresponds to a single iteration of POSIT [42].

[4]The implementations of CLM (https://github.com/kylemcdonald/FaceTracker) and SDM (http://www.humansensing.cs.cmu.edu/intraface) also provide the head orientation, obtained through [29] for CLM and [42] for SDM. In these two methods, given the 2D points and the head orientation, we apply the rest of our backprojection approach to place the 3D object, *i.e.* we only adjust the head position and the facial deformations to the 2D detections, not the orientation. The orientation would be that of [29] and [42], respectively.

CONFLICT OF INTEREST

The author confirms that author has no conflict of interest to declare for this publication.

ACKNOWLEDGMENTS

We want to thank Nerea Aranjuelo and Victor Goni from Vicomtech-IK4 for their aid in the experimental work. We want to thank also Jason Saragih and Fernando De la Torre for their explanations about the implementations of their methods CLM and SDM for the experimental setup. Luís Paulo Santos is partially funded by the FCT (Portuguese Foundation for Science and Technology) within Project Scope UID/CEC/00319/2013. This work is partially supported by the Basque Government under the project S-PR13UN007. Finally, we want to thank Elsevier for allowing us to reuse material for this chapter from our following paper: Unzueta, L., Pimenta, W., Goenetxea, J., Santos, L.P. and Dornaika, F., "Efficient Generic Face Model Fitting to Images and Videos." Image and Vision Computing, 32(5), 321-334, 2014, doi:10.1016/j.imavis.2014.02.006.

REFERENCES

[1]   H. Kalbkhani, M. Shayesteh, and S. Mousavi, "Efficient algorithms for detection of face, eye and eye state", *IET Computer Vision,* vol. 7, no. 3, pp. 184-200, 2013.
       [http://dx.doi.org/10.1049/iet-cvi.2011.0091]

[2]   M. Perreira, V. Courboulay, A. Prigent, and P. Estraillier, "Fast, low resource, head detection and tracking for interactive applications", *PsychNology J.,* vol. 7, no. 3, pp. 243-264, 2009.

[3]   T. Hamada, K. Kato, and K. Kawakami, "Extracting facial features as in infants", *Pattern Recognit. Lett.,* vol. 21, no. 5, pp. 407-412, 2000.
[http://dx.doi.org/10.1016/S0167-8655(00)00009-X]

[4]   K-W. Wong, K-M. Lam, and W-C. Siu, "An efficient algorithm for human face detection and facial feature extraction under different conditions", *Pattern Recognit.,* vol. 34, no. 10, pp. 1993-2004, 2001.
[http://dx.doi.org/10.1016/S0031-3203(00)00134-5]

[5]   X. Peng, M. Bennamoun, and A. Mian, "A training-free nose tip detection method from face range images", *Pattern Recognit.,* vol. 44, no. 3, pp. 544-558, 2011.
[http://dx.doi.org/10.1016/j.patcog.2010.09.015]

[6]   S. Asteriadis, N. Nikolaidis, and I. Pitas, "Facial feature detection using distance vector fields", *Pattern Recognit,* vol. 42, no. 7, pp. 1388-1398, 2009.

[7]   G. Votsis, A. Drosopoulos, and S. Kollias, "A modular approach to facial feature segmentation on real sequences", *Signal Process. Image Commun.,* vol. 18, pp. 67-89, 2003.
[http://dx.doi.org/10.1016/S0923-5965(02)00103-0]

[8]   S. Jeng, H. Liao, C. Han, M. Chern, and Y. Liu, "Facial feature detection using geometrical face model: an efficient approach", *Pattern Recognit.,* vol. 31, no. 3, pp. 273-282, 1998.
[http://dx.doi.org/10.1016/S0031-3203(97)00048-4]

[9]   D. Reisfeld, and Y. Yeshurun, "Preprocessing of face images: detection of features and pose normalization", *Comput. Vis. Image Underst.,* vol. 71, no. 3, pp. 413-430, 1998.
[http://dx.doi.org/10.1006/cviu.1997.0640]

[10]   C. Chiang, W. Tai, M. Yang, Y. Huang, and C. Huang, "A novel method for detecting lips, eyes and faces in real time", *Real-Time Imaging,* vol. 9, pp. 277-287, 2003.
[http://dx.doi.org/10.1016/j.rti.2003.08.003]

[11]   T. Cootes, C. Taylor, D. Cooper, and J. Graham, "Active shape models - their training and application", *Comput. Vis. Image Underst.,* vol. 61, pp. 38-59, 1995.
[http://dx.doi.org/10.1006/cviu.1995.1004]

[12]   V. Blanz, P. Grother, P. Phillips, and T. Vetter, "Face recognition based on frontal views generated from non-frontal images", *Proceedings of the IEEE International Conference on Computer Vision and Pattern Recognition,* vol. vol. 2, 2004pp. 454-461

[13]   T. Cootes, G. Wheeler, K. Walker, and C. Taylor, "View-based active appearance models", *Image Vis. Comput.,* vol. 20, no. 9-10, pp. 657-664, 2002.
[http://dx.doi.org/10.1016/S0262-8856(02)00055-0]

[14]   I. Matthews, and S. Baker, "Active appearance models revisited", *Int. J. Comput. Vis.,* vol. 60, pp. 135-164, 2004.
[http://dx.doi.org/10.1023/B:VISI.0000029666.37597.d3]

[15]   G. Tzimiropoulos, J. Alabort-i Medina, S. Zafeiriou, and M. Pantic, "Generic active appearance models revisited", In: *Proceedings of the Asian Conference on Computer Vision*, 2013, pp. 650-663.

[16]   T. Cootes, and C. Taylor, "Active shape models - smart snakes", In: *Proceedings of the British Machine Vision Conference*, 1992, pp. 266-275.

[17] V. Blanz, and T. Vetter, "Face recognition based on fitting a 3D morphable model", *IEEE Trans. Pattern Anal. Mach. Intell.,* vol. 25, pp. 1-12, 2003.
[http://dx.doi.org/10.1109/TPAMI.2003.1227983]

[18] D. Vukadinovic, and M. Pantic, "Fully automatic facial feature point detection using Gabor feature based boosted classifiers", *Proceedings of the IEEE International Conference on Systems, Man and Cybernetics,* vol. 2, 2005
[http://dx.doi.org/10.1109/ICSMC.2005.1571392]

[19] M. Valstar, B. Martinez, X. Binefa, and M. Pantic, "Facial point detection using boosted regression and graph models", In: *Proceedings of IEEE International Conference on Computer Vision and Pattern Recognition,* 2010, pp. 2729-2736.
[http://dx.doi.org/10.1109/CVPR.2010.5539996]

[20] X. Cao, Y. Wei, F. Wen, and J. Sun, "Face alignment by explicit shape regression", In: *Proceedings of the IEEE Conference on Computer Vision and Pattern Recognition,* 2012, pp. 2887-2894.

[21] B. Martinez, M.F. Valstar, X. Binefa, and M. Pantic, "Local evidence aggregation for regression-based facial point detection", *IEEE Trans. Pattern Anal. Mach. Intell.,* vol. 35, no. 5, pp. 1149-1163, 2013.
[http://dx.doi.org/10.1109/TPAMI.2012.205] [PMID: 23520256]

[22] X. Xiong, and F. De la Torre, "Supervised descent method and its application to face alignment", In: *Proceedings of the IEEE Conference on Computer Vision and Pattern Recognition,* 2013.

[23] D. Cristinacce, and T. Cootes, "Feature detection and tracking with constrained local models", In: *Proceedings of the British Machine Vision Conference,* 2006, pp. 929-938.
[http://dx.doi.org/10.5244/C.20.95]

[24] J. Saragih, S. Lucey, and J. Cohn, "Face alignment through subspace constrained mean-shifts", In: *Proceedings of the International Conference of Computer Vision,* 2009.

[25] V. Le, J. Brandt, Z. Lin, L. Bourdev, and T. Huang, "Interactive facial feature localization", In: *Proceedings of the IEEE European Conference on Computer Vision,* 2012, pp. 679-692.

[26] X. Zhu, and D. Ramanan, "Face detection, pose estimation, and landmark localization in the wild", In: *Proceedings of the IEEE International Conference on Computer Vision and Pattern Recognition,* 2012, pp. 2879-2886.

[27] C. Zhang, and Z. Zhang, *A survey of recent advances in face detection.* 2010.

[28] A. Asthana, S. Zafeiriou, S. Cheng, and M. Pantic, "Robust discriminative response map fitting with constrained local models", In: *Proceedings of the IEEE Conference on Computer Vision and Pattern Recognition,* 2013.

[29] J. Xiao, S. Baker, I. Matthews, and T. Kanade, "Real-time combined 2D+3D active appearance models", In: *Proceedings of the IEEE International Conference on Computer Vision and Pattern Recognition,* 2004, pp. 535-542.

[30] J. Sung, T. Kanade, and D. Kim, "Pose robust face tracking by combining active appearance models and cylinder head models", *Int. J. Comput. Vis.,* vol. 80, pp. 260-274, 2008.
[http://dx.doi.org/10.1007/s11263-007-0125-1]

[31] C. Chen, and C. Wang, "3D active appearance model for aligning faces in 2D images", In:

Proceedings of the IEEE/RSJ International Conference on Intelligent Robots and Systems, 2008, pp. 3133-3139.

[32]   F. Dornaika, and B. Raducanu, "Simultaneous 3D face pose and person- specific shape estimation from a single image using a holistic approach", In: *Proceedings of the Workshop on Applications of Computer Vision*, 2009, pp. 1-6.
[http://dx.doi.org/10.1109/WACV.2009.5403101]

[33]   M. Zhou, Y. Wang, and X. Huang, "Real-time 3D face and facial action tracking using extended 2D+3D AAMs", In: *Proceedings of the IEEE International Conference on Pattern Recognition*, 2010, pp. 3963-3966.

[34]   J. Ahlberg, *Candide-3 - an updated parameterized face.* 2001.

[35]   A. Jepson, D. Fleet, and T. El-Maraghi, "Robust online appearance models for visual tracking", *IEEE Trans. Pattern Anal. Mach. Intell.,* vol. 25, no. 10, pp. 1296-1311, 2003.
[http://dx.doi.org/10.1109/TPAMI.2003.1233903]

[36]   F. Dornaika, and F. Davoine, "On appearance based face and facial action tracking", *IEEE Trans. Circ. Syst. Video Tech.,* vol. 16, no. 9, pp. 1107-1124, 2006.
[http://dx.doi.org/10.1109/TCSVT.2006.881200]

[37]   "Simultaneous facial action tracking and expression recognition in the presence of head motion", *Int. J. Comput. Vis.,* vol. 76, no. 3, pp. 257-281, 2008.
[http://dx.doi.org/10.1007/s11263-007-0059-7]

[38]   P. Viola, and M.J. Jones, "Rapid object detection using a boosted cascade of simple features", In: *Proceedings of the IEEE International Conference on Computer Vision and Pattern Recognition,* vol. 1. IEEE Computer Society: Washington, DC, USA, 2001, pp. 511-518.
[http://dx.doi.org/10.1109/CVPR.2001.990517]

[39]   R. Lienhart, and J. Maydt, "An extended set of Haar-like features for rapid object detection", In: *Proceedings of the IEEE International Conference on Image Processing,* vol. 1. IEEE Computer Society: Washington, DC, USA, 2002, pp. 900-903.
[http://dx.doi.org/10.1109/ICIP.2002.1038171]

[40]   M. Zhou, Y. Wang, X. Feng, and X. Wang, "A robust texture preprocessing for AAM", In: *Proceedings of the International Conference on Computer Science and Software Engineering,* vol. 2. IEEE Computer Society: Washington, DC, USA, 2008, pp. 919-922.

[41]   S. Suzuki, and K. Be, "Topological structural analysis of digitized binary images by border following", *Comput. Vis. Graph. Image Process.,* vol. 30, no. 1, pp. 32-46, 1985.
[http://dx.doi.org/10.1016/0734-189X(85)90016-7]

[42]   D. DeMenthon, and L. Davis, "Model-based object pose in 25 lines of code", *Int. J. Comput. Vis.,* vol. 15, pp. 123-141, 1995.
[http://dx.doi.org/10.1007/BF01450852]

[43]   J. Moré, "The Levenberg-Marquardt algorithm: implementation and theory", In: *in Numerical Analysis, Lecture Notes in Mathematics 630, G. A. Watson, Ed. Springer-Verlag,* vol. 18. 1977, pp. 105-116.

[44]   T. Sim, S. Baker, and M. Bsat, "The CMU pose, illumination, and expression database", *IEEE Trans.*

Pattern Anal. Mach. Intell., vol. 25, no. 12, pp. 1615-1618, 2003.
[http://dx.doi.org/10.1109/TPAMI.2003.1251154]

CHAPTER 9

Face Detection Using the Theory of Evidence

Franck Luthon[*]

Computer Science Lab., University of Pau, 2 allée parc Montaury, 64600, Anglet, France

Abstract: Face detection and tracking by computer vision is widely used for multimedia applications, video surveillance or human computer interaction. Unlike current techniques that are based on huge training datasets and complex algorithms to get generic face models (*e.g.* active appearance models), the proposed approach using evidence theory handles simple contextual knowledge representative of the application background, *via* a quick semi-supervised initialization. The transferable belief model is used to counteract the incompleteness of the prior model due to lack of exhaustiveness in the learning stage.

The method consists of two main successive steps in a loop: detection, then tracking. In the detection phase, an evidential face model is built by merging basic beliefs carried by a Viola-Jones face detector and a skin color detector. The mass functions are assigned to information sources computed from a specific nonlinear color space. In order to deal with color information dependence in the fusion process, a cautious combination rule is used. The pignistic probabilities of the face model guarantee the compatibility between the belief framework and the probabilistic framework. They are the inputs of a bootstrap particle filter which yields face tracking at video rate. The proper tuning of the few evidential model parameters leads to tracking performance in real-time. Quantitative evaluation of the proposed method gives a detection rate reaching 80%, comparable to what can be found in the literature. Nevertheless, the proposed method requires a scanty initialization only (brief training) and allows a fast processing.

Keywords: Belief function, Cautious rule, Classification, Computer vision, Conjunctive rule, Dempster-Shafer, Face tracking, Fusion of information, LUX color space, Mass set, Particle filter, Pattern recognition, Pignistic probability, Region of interest, Skin hue, Source of information, Transferable belief model, Uncertainty management, Viola-Jones detector, Visual servoing.

[*] **Address to Corresponding Author F. Luthon:** IUT de Bayonne Pays Basque, Université de Pau Pays d'Adour, 2 allée du parc Montaury, 64600, Anglet, France; Tel: +33(0)5.59.57.43.44; Fax: +33(0)5.59.57.43.49; E-mail: Franck.Luthon@univ-pau.fr

INTRODUCTION

Real-time face detection and tracking in video sequences has been studied for more than twenty years by the computer vision and pattern recognition community, owing to the multiplicity of applications: teleconferencing, closed-circuit television (CCTV), human machine interface and robotics. Despite the ongoing progress in image processing and the increase in computation speed of digital processors, the design of generic and robust algorithms is still the object of active research. Indeed, face image analysis (either detection, recognition or tracking) is made difficult by the variability of appearance of this deformable moving object due to many factors: individual morphological differences (nose shape, eye color, skin color, beard), presence of visual artifacts (glasses, occlusions, make-up), illumination variations (shadow, highlight) and facial expression changes depending on context (social, cultural, emotional). Those are difficult to model and do not easily cope with real-time implementations. Moreover, the scene background might disturb detection, in case of foreground-background similarity or background clutter.

To handle the face specificity, a semi-supervised learning method is presented here, where the user selects manually a zone of the face in the first image of the video. This rapid initializing step constitutes the learning stage which yields simply a prior model for face class and background class. It is however dependent on the user subjectivity while selecting the face zone and it suffers from incompleteness because of lack of exhaustiveness of this short training. In this context, a probabilistic modeling is not relevant. Therefore, the proposed approach is based on belief functions: indeed the transferable belief model (TBM) is well suited to model partial knowledge in a complex system [1]. It was successfully applied to classification of emotions and facial expressions, or to human activity recognition [2].

The goal of the application is to automatically track the face of a person placed in the field of view of a motorized pan-tilt-zoom camera (or simply a webcam). The tracking technique should be as robust as possible to occlusions, pose, scale, background and illumination changes. It should take control of the camera to perform an automatic centering of the face in the image plane during the whole video sequence. The algorithm consists of two main steps: face detection and then tracking (Fig. **1**). An elliptical region of interest (ROI) including the face is computed by particle filtering, and held at the center of the image by visual servoing. The context of application is indoor environments, typically a laboratory or an office. As regards acquisition conditions, the distance between user and sensor ranges from about 50 cm to a few meters. Ordinary lighting conditions prevail (uncontrolled illumination context), possibly in the presence of additional light sources, like a desk lamp or the influence of outside light entering through a window.

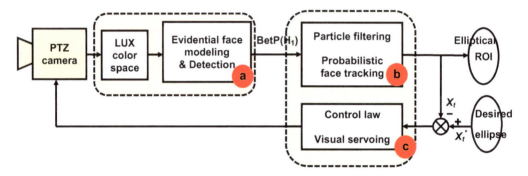

Fig. (1). Overview of the processing with feedback loop: a) face detection by evidential modeling; b) face tracking by particle filtering; c) camera control by visual servoing.

After a state of the art about face detection, the theory of belief functions is briefly exposed. The proposed evidential model for face detection is then detailed in the application section. The tracking with particle filter and visual servoing of the camera are described. Performance analysis, both qualitative and quantitative, is presented. The chapter ends with a discussion.

STATE OF THE ART

Face detection methods may be grouped into two categories differing in the way of processing prior information [3]. It is also worth making a difference between detection methods dedicated to still images, where complex algorithms can be used, and methods dedicated to video sequences where the computation cost is of major concern for real-time processing.

Feature-based methods use as primitives local properties of the face. The so-called low-level analysis (or early vision) handles the information obtained directly from the pixels such as luminance or color, or indirectly after computation of edges, motion or texture from pixels neighborhood. Color is a key feature because of its invariance with respect to translation, rotation or scale. Nevertheless, skin color is made of a great variety of hues depending both on the person and on illumination conditions (shadowy, pale, overexposed skin). Therefore, the design of a robust hue detector requires the choice of a proper colorimetric space [4, 5]. Anyway, the primitives and estimates induced from low level analysis remain ambiguous (ill-posed problem). To validate the detection, additional information is required.

The feature analysis is based both on the knowledge of an adequate prior model (a priori constraints, contextual information) and on measurements of normalized distances and angles derived from the individual description of face parts (eyes, nose, mouth). With this first family of methods, the processing is potentially fast, as few training is necessary. The methods for parameter extraction are often specific to the context at hand, and are designed empirically based on color, edge or motion cues. The parameter tuning relies on heuristics.

Holistic approaches, by contrast, address the detection problem as a global identification problem (high level analysis). The key-point is to compare a test image with a generic face model and to deduce if there is resemblance or not. Priors about geometrical or physiological specificities are discarded to limit the modeling errors due to incomplete and imprecise knowledge of the face. These methods rely on the learning of a generic face model from a database of samples as much complete as possible. Linear methods of subspaces, statistical approaches (Monte-Carlo methods), support vector machines (SVM) or neural networks can be used. An important step forward was made when the first holistic face detector with real-time capability was proposed by Viola and Jones [6]. It is based on an automatic selection of *2D* Haar wavelet filters applied to monochrome images and it uses a cascade of boosted classifiers with increasing complexity. The active shape models (ASM), introduced by Cootes and Taylor [7], are deformable models which depict the highest level of appearance of face features. Once initialized near a facial part, the model modifies its local characteristics (outline, contrast) and evolves gradually in order to take the shape of the target feature. The active appearance models (AAM) are an extension of the ASM by Cootes *et al.* [8]. The use of the third dimension, namely the temporal one, can lead to real-time *3D* deformable face models varying according to morphological parameters. Therefore, this second family of methods provides flexibility with respect to different contexts such as number of faces in the scene or type of lighting. However, these methods are strongly dependent on the choice and quality of the face models: they require a huge training dataset to be sufficiently representative. Whatever the face database used, it is of course rarely exhaustive and its choice remains a full problem. In addition, algorithms are complex and induce heavy computation cost.

Here, two complementary face detection methods will collaborate in a fusion process [9]. One of them refers to induction, the other one refers to deduction, as illustrated in Fig. (**2**), and as explained in the AudioSlides available online [10]. First, among the feature-based methods, a skin color discriminating detector is chosen. Indeed, its properties of invariance with respect to motion allow to track a face whatever its pose during the video sequence. Second, among holistic approaches, the Viola-Jones (VJ) face detector is chosen due to its real-time ability and the availability of an open source implementation. It provides a target container (rectangular bounding box surrounding the face) highly reliable in the case of front-view faces. However as the authors [6] have made their classifier public but not their training, the classifier used here was not trained on our data. We will see that the proposed method, which applies evidence theory, circumvents this point. The key point, then, is the proper fusion of information delivered by the two detectors.

THEORY OF BELIEF FUNCTIONS

Mass Sets

The theory of belief functions, also called Dempster-Shafer theory or evidence theory, dates back to the 1970s. Inspired by the upper and lower probabilities first studied by Dempster [11], then by Shafer [12], it may be interpreted as a formal quantitative model of degrees of belief. This theory increases modeling flexibility and allows to solve complex problems since: (i) it does not require complete prior knowledge about the problem at hand, and (ii) it offers the possibility to distribute the belief in compound hypotheses (and not only on singletons as is the case in the probability modeling). It was successfully applied to image fusion for medical application in magnetic resonance imaging [13].

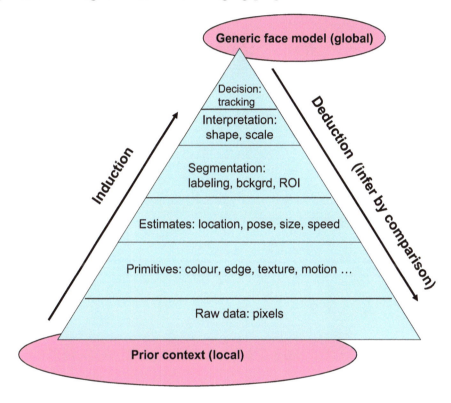

Fig. (2). Image processing pyramidal framework.

The basic concept of the evidence theory is the mass function which characterizes the opinion of an agent about a question or the state of a system. The frame of discernment Ω is the finite set of answers (called focal elements) to this question (typ. $\Omega = \{H_1, H_2\}$ in the simple binary case with two hypotheses only). A mass function $m(.)$ is an application of the set 2^Ω (typ. $2^\Omega = \{\varnothing, H_1, H_2, \Omega\}$) towards the real interval [0,1] which satisfies:

$$\sum_{A \subseteq \Omega} m(A) = 1.$$

(1)

This constraint guarantees a commensurability between several mass sets. The mass $m(A)$ is the part of belief placed strictly in A.

Belief $Bel(.)$, plausibility $Pl(.)$ and commonality $q(.)$ are three common measures derived from the mass function. They are defined, $\forall A \subseteq \Omega, A \neq \varnothing$:

$$Bel(A) = \sum_{B \subseteq A, B \neq \varnothing} m(B) \; ; \quad Pl(A) = \sum_{B \cap A \neq \varnothing} m(B) \quad \text{and} \quad q(A) = \sum_{B \supseteq A} m(B) \qquad \textbf{(2)}$$

For the empty set: $Bel(\varnothing) = Pl(\varnothing) = 0$ and $q(\varnothing) = 1$. The interval $[Bel(A), Pl(A)]$ is the confidence interval that represents the lower and upper bounds of the likelihood of the subset A. The maximum of plausibility is often used as decision criterion.

A simple mass set, or elementary state of belief, is defined by a mass function m so that $A \subset \Omega$ is set along with a weight $w \in [0,1]$:

$$\begin{aligned} m(A) &= 1 - w, \\ m(\Omega) &= w, \\ m(B) &= 0, \quad \forall B, B \neq A, B \neq \Omega. \end{aligned} \qquad \textbf{(3)}$$

Denoted as shortcut $m = A^w$, it represents the belief put in Ω instead of A. For any A, A^1 ($w = 1$) is the vacuous simple mass function ($m(A) = 0$), whereas A^0 ($w = 0$) is the categorical simple mass function ($m(A) = 1$).

A complex state of belief may be modeled with a set of independently weighted hypotheses. This is called canonical decomposition: any non categorical mass function m (*i.e.* when Ω is one of the a focal elements, that is when $m(\Omega) \neq 0$) may be expressed as the conjunctive combination (defined in Eq. 5) of simple mass sets: $m = \bigcirc_{A \subset \Omega} A^{w(A)}$, where the weights are computed from commonalities: $\log w(A) = - \sum_{B \supseteq A} (-1)^{|B| - |A|} \log q(B)$.

Modeling of Mass Functions

The mass function modeling is a non trivial problem. Difficulty grows if one wants to assign beliefs to compound hypotheses (*e.g.,* $H_1 \cup H_2 \cup H3$).

One may distinguish models based on distance computations, stemming from pattern recognition [14] where mass functions are built from available learning vectors, and models using likelihood computations, stemming form Bayesian probabilistic approach. These last ones decompose into global [15] and separable methods.

Separable methods build a belief function for each hypothesis H_i of the frame of discernment. They rely on an initial learning for estimating conditional probabilities $P(s_j|H_i)$ where s_j represents an observation of the source j and H_i is one of the hypotheses. This approach was first proposed by Smets [16] then used by Appriou for multisensor signal fusion [17]. Appriou's model #1 is derived from the generalized Bayesian theorem:

$$
\begin{cases}
m_{ij}(H_i) &= 0, \\
m_{ij}(\overline{H_i}) &= d_{ij}[1 - R_j.P(s_j|H_i)], \\
m_{ij}(\Omega) &= 1 - m_{ij}(\overline{H_i}).
\end{cases}
\tag{4}
$$

where $\overline{H_i}$ is the hypothesis opposite of H_i . The discounting coefficient d_{ij} characterizes the *a priori* degree of confidence in the knowledge of the distribution $P(s_j|H_i)$. It stands for the metaknowledge about the representativeness of the learning of each class H_i with each source j. This parameter tends to 1 when the learning is perfectly representative of the actual distribution, whereas $d_{ij} \rightarrow 0$ when the distribution of probabilities is poorly estimated (*e.g.* in case of a too small training dataset). R_j is a coefficient weighting the probabilities. It acts as a normalization factor bounding the dynamic range: $R_j \in [0; 1/\max\{P(s_j|H_i)\}]$. For $R_j = 0$, only the *a priori* reliability of the source is taken into account, otherwise the actual data are also considered.

The two types of approaches (distance *i.e.,* model-based, and likelihood *i.e.,* case-based) yield similar performances when applied to classification problems [18]. Here, a separable likelihood approach is chosen. Indeed, as our method uses a simple and hence incomplete learning stage, it is safer to estimate conditional probabilities and to fix a priori reliability degrees, rather than mass sets directly.

Furthermore, Appriou's model #1 turns out to be well suited for facial analysis as one learns easily the face class against all the other classes (here the background class only), since a specific detector may be tuned on this class.

Combination of Beliefs

The belief combination, also called revision, is involved when one has new information, coded in the form of a belief function, to merge with existing mass functions, in order to make up a synthesis of knowledge in a multi-source environment. Two constraints must be fulfilled: every source of information belongs to the same frame of discernment Ω, and all sources are independent. Conjunctive and disjunctive rules are the two basic operators for combination. For J independent and totally reliable information sources, whose hypotheses are defined in Ω, the result of the conjunctive combination, denoted by $m_{\bigcirc}$, is:

$$m_{\bigcirc}(A) = \bigcirc_{A \subset \Omega} m_j(A) = \sum_{A_1 \cap \ldots \cap A_J = A} \left(\prod_{j=1}^{J} m_j(A_j) \right), \quad \forall A \subseteq \Omega. \tag{5}$$

This rule is commutative, associative, with the total ignorance as neutral element and the total certainty as absorbing element. It is however not idempotent. This rule leads generally to an unnormalized mass of conflict ($m_{\bigcirc}(\emptyset) \neq 0$). Dempster proposed a normalization version of this law better known as the Dempster combination rule, or orthogonal sum [11]:

$$\begin{aligned} m_{\oplus}(A) &= \frac{m_{\bigcirc}(A)}{1 - K}, \quad \forall A \subseteq \Omega, A \neq \emptyset, \\ m_{\oplus}(\emptyset) &= 0, \end{aligned} \tag{6}$$

where $K = m_{\bigcirc}(\emptyset)$ reflects the conflicting mass that belongs to [0, 1].

The disjunctive rule [16] replaces the intersection by the union in Eq. 5 and yields a mass denoted $m_{\bigcirc}(A)$. The disjunctive rule is used when at least one source of information is unreliable. This rule does not generate conflict but yields less precise fusion as the focal elements of the resulting mass function are widened. On the contrary, the conjunctive rule is used when all information sources are reliable. It yields a more precise fusion but might generate conflict.

Management of Conflict

When using the conjunctive combination, some information sources might be discordant and give incompatible propositions. The mass value $m(\emptyset)$ assigned to the empty set quantifies this conflict. Numerous combination rules are proposed to solve this problem [19]. For example, Florea advocates an intermediate solution between conjunction and disjunction, yielding a family of robust adaptive rules [20].

Combination Rules for Dependent Sources

Conjunctive and disjunctive rules rely on the assumption that the combined mass functions come from independent sources. In real-world situations however, this is not always true. To address this problem, Denœux *et al.* introduced two new rules: the cautious conjunctive rule and the bold disjunctive rule [21, 22].

The cautious conjunctive rule relies on the least commitment principle which states that, when several belief functions are compatible with a set of constraints, one should choose the least informative one. This principle means that one should not give more belief than required to an information source. It is similar to the maximum entropy principle in the theory of probabilities.

Under the constraint that the combined mass be richer than m_1 and m_2, the least informative mass exists, is unique and is defined with the minimum (denoted by $\wedge$) of the weight functions associated with m_1 and m_2. If A^{w_1} and A^{w_2} are two simple mass sets, their combination by the cautious rule is the simple mass function denoted by $A^{w_1 \wedge w_2}$:

$$
\begin{aligned}
w_{min}(A) &= w_1(A) \wedge w_2(A), \quad \forall A \subset \Omega, \\
m_{1 \wedge 2} &= \bigcirc_{A \subset \Omega} A^{w_{min}(A)}.
\end{aligned}
\tag{7}
$$

The normalized version of this cautious rule denoted by $\oslash$ is defined by replacing the conjunctive rule $\bigcirc$ by the Dempster rule $\oplus$ in Eq.7 so that:

$$m_{1\oslash 2}(A) = \frac{m_{1\wedge 2}(A)}{1 - m_{1\wedge 2}(\varnothing)}, \quad \forall A \subseteq \Omega, A \neq \varnothing,$$

$$m_{1\oslash 2}(\varnothing) = 0$$

(8)

The bold disjunctive rule, denoted by $\oslash$, is the operator opposite of the cautious rule: it takes the maximum of weights instead of their minimum. In [23], these new rules were extended to become adaptive. The properties of the cautious and bold rules result from those of the minimum and maximum: commutative, associative and idempotent.

Table **1** illustrates the computation of the three combination rules $\oslash$, $\oplus$, and $\oslash$ in the case of two non separable sources, given by their respective mass sets m_1 and m_2. Note that one obtains here generalized simple mass functions yielding weights $w(\varnothing) > 1$. Indeed, weights w are no longer constrained to belong to the interval $[0,1]$ for generalized simple mass sets.

Table 1. Combination of 2 masses m_1, m_2: conjunction $\oslash$, Dempster-Shafer $\oplus$, cautious $\oslash$.

A	m_1	m_2	$m_\oslash$	$m\oplus$	q_1	q_2	w_1	w_2	w_{min}	$m_{1\wedge 2}$	$m^\oslash$
$\varnothing$	0	0	0.19	0	1	1	1.333	1.35	1.333	0.081	0
H_1	0.5	0.7	0.66	0.815	0.8	0.9	0.375	0.222	0.222	0.622	0.677
H_2	0.2	0.1	0.09	0.111	0.5	0.3	0.6	0.667	0.6	0.119	0.129
Ω	0.3	0.2	0.06	0.074	0.3	0.2				0.178	0.194

Decision with Transferable Belief Model

The TBM is a subjectivist interpretation of a mass function that models the partial knowledge of the value of a variable [24]. The TBM is a mental model with two levels: the credal level and the pignistic one. The credal level includes the static part of the model representing the knowledge in the form of mass functions, plus the dynamic part of the model which corresponds to the combination of beliefs. Decision is done at the pignistic level that transforms the masses into probabilities by equally sharing the conflict among every normalized mass function. For all $A \in 2^\Omega$ with $A \neq \varnothing$, the pignistic probability *BetP* is defined as:

$$BetP(A) = \sum_{B \in 2^\Omega \,;\, B \neq \varnothing} \frac{|A \cap B|}{|B|} \frac{m(B)}{1 - m(\varnothing)}, \quad \text{with } m(\varnothing) \neq 1. \tag{9}$$

where $|B|$ denotes the cardinal of set B. Typically, in the binary case of two disjoint hypotheses without conflict ($m(\varnothing) = 0$), one gets: $BetP(A) = m(A) + m(\Omega)/2$, since $|\Omega| = 2$ and $|A| = 1$. Note that the computation of the pignistic probability implies a loss of information, since the degree of ignorance $m(\Omega)$ is dispatched among all the various hypotheses. The decision consists simply in choosing the hypothesis that gives the maximum of $BetP$, which is similar to the maximum plausibility criterion [17].

APPLICATION TO EVIDENTIAL FACE MODEL

The face modeling strategy consists of an evidential fusion process using two complementary information sources: a VJ face shape detector (Fig. **3a**) and a skin color detector (Fig. **3b**). In order to account for the dependence between color sources, the fusion process uses the cautious rule to merge color mass sets. The fusion of color mass sets and VJ mass sets (Fig. **3c**) gives a robust face model (applied here to indoor environment). For skin hue modeling, the learning stage consists of a quick initialization (Fig. **3i**). This learning step is interesting for its simplicity, but it is obviously not exhaustive since it suffers from incompleteness as only the first video frame is taken into account. A classic Bayesian probabilistic approach is inefficient in this case. Therefore, the TBM framework (Fig. **3d**) is used instead, since it is adequate to model partial knowledge of prior models that are incomplete, ambiguous, imprecise or unreliable. It is efficient for uncertainty management.

To each pixel p, a frame of discernment is associated with two mutually exclusive classes: $\Omega_p = \{\{H_{1p}\}, \{H_{2p}\}\}$, where $\{H_{1p}\}$ represents the face hypothesis and $\{H_{2p}\}$ represents the complementary set called the background. Dealing with only two hypotheses limits the complexity and thus the processing time, which is important for real-time tracking. Moreover, it is enough for the face/non-face binary decision. To simplify the notations in the following, we will skip the index p, and only write Ω, $\{H_1\}$ and $\{H_2\}$ for all those quantities that relate to pixel p.

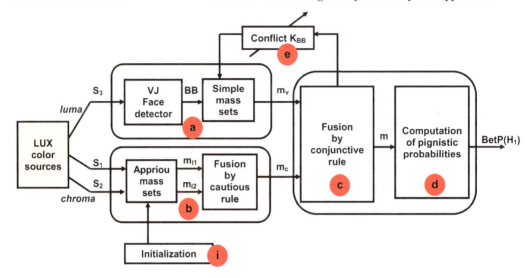

Fig. (3). Block-diagram of the evidential face model: a) mass sets of the VJ face detector; b) color mass sets; c) fusion of VJ and color mass sets; d) computation of pignistic probabilities in the TBM; e) conflict management feedback; i) initialization.

Information Sources

Skin color is a relevant information since it allows to implement fast algorithms that are invariant to orientation and scale. However, skin color distribution strongly depends on lighting conditions and on the color space chosen [5]. To improve robustness to light changes, the logarithmic LUX color space [25] may be used instead of linear color spaces like RGB, YUV or other nonlinear spaces like HSV which is sensitive to noise. The three components of LUX space are computed from RGB components (with $M = 256$):

$$L = (R+1)^{0.3}(G+1)^{0.6}(B+1)^{0.1} - 1$$
$$U = \begin{cases} \frac{M}{2}\left(\frac{R+1}{L+1}\right) & \text{for } R < L \\ M - \frac{M}{2}\left(\frac{L+1}{R+1}\right) & \text{otherwise} \end{cases}$$
$$X = \begin{cases} \frac{M}{2}\left(\frac{B+1}{L+1}\right) & \text{for } B < L \\ M - \frac{M}{2}\left(\frac{L+1}{B+1}\right) & \text{otherwise.} \end{cases}$$

$$(10)$$

L stands for the logarithmic luminance, whereas U and X are the two logarithmic chrominances (resp. red and blue). This nonlinear color space based on logarithmic image processing is known for rendering good contrast in low luminance. Besides, since it is inspired by biology (logarithmic response of retina cells), it ensures an efficient description of hues, it is little sensitive to noise and has proved its efficiency in color segmentation, compression or rendering [26]. Fig. (**4**) illustrates the adaptive property of LUX in bright or dark context.

Hereafter, the three information sources s_j (j = 1, 2, 3) used for face modeling are: ($s_1 = U$, $s_2 = X$) for the skin hue detector, and $s_3 = L$ for the VJ detector respectively.

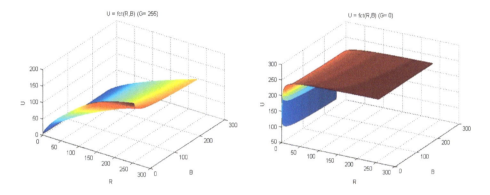

Fig. (4). Variation of U as a function of (R,B) in two contexts: a) G = 255 (bright); b) G = 0 (dark).

Mass Sets for VJ Face Detector

This section explains how to obtain the mass m_v from the luma component L (Fig. **3a**). The VJ face detector works on gray levels (source $s_3 = L$). It gives a target container (rectangular bounding box around the face denoted by BB) highly reliable when the face is in front-view or slightly from profile (Fig. **5a**, **5b**, **5c**). However it fails in case of important rotation or occlusion or when it recognizes a shape-like face-artifact in the cluttered background (Fig. **5d**).

In order to model the VJ detector by a belief function, a simple mass set $m_v(.)$ is assigned to each pixel p, according to its position with respect to BB. The mass is defined by a weight parameter (reliability) $v \in [0, 1]$:

$$m_v = \{H_1\}^{1-v}, \forall p \in BB,$$
$$m_v = \{H_2\}^{1-v}, \forall p \notin BB. \tag{11}$$

The value $1 - v$ stands for the uncertainty in the belief about $\{H_1\}$ inside BB (resp. $\{H_2\}$ outside BB). For $v = 0$, the information source is not reliable at all, and the maximal belief is put on the tautology $\Omega = H_1 \cup H_2$. For $v = 1$, the source is reliable, the mass is maximal for the face class $\{H_1\}$ inside BB, and for the background class $\{H_2\}$ outside of BB.

    a) sequence #1   b) sequence #2   c) sequence #3   d) sequence #4

Fig. (5). Rectanguler bounding box BB produced by the VJ face detector in various sequences: a), b), c) correct detections; d) false detection.

Color Mass Functions

This section explains how the color masses m_c are computed from the chroma components (Fig. **3b**). For the current image, let use the following notations:

- S is the set of source vectors of size $Z \times J$, where Z is the image size (typically 400×400), and J is the dimension of the color space. Here, $J = 2$ since only two chromatic information sources s_1 and s_2 are used to build the color masses. s_j represents the color plane j of S,
- s_{jp} is one elementary observation data. It is the jth component of the color vector associated with pixel p,
- c_p is the class of pixel p (hidden primitive corresponding to one of the two hypotheses: face H_1 or non-face $H_2 = \overline{H_1}$).

Given a pixel p with known observation s_{jp} but of unknown class c_p , the classification problem consists in producing a belief about the current value of its class c_p without using any learning dataset apart from a quick initialization on the first image.

Appriou's model #1 (Eq. 4) requires the conditional likelihoods of the classes, that characterize the relationship between color components s_j and hypotheses H_1 or H_2. These priors are obtained during a semi-supervised learning step when the user selects manually in the first image of the video a free-shape zone of the face including mainly skin (Fig **6a**). Hair should be discarded. This selection exhibits both: (i) a prior model of the face zone including mainly skin hue (Fig. **6b**), (ii) a prior model of the background by considering all pixels outside of the selected zone (Fig. **6c**). Histograms are built by considering all the color observations s_{jp} inside the face zone, resp. outside (background). Then, four conditional probabilities $P(s_j|H_i)$ (for source $j = 1$ or 2, and hypothesis $i = 1$ or 2) are deduced by simple normalization of the histograms as exemplified in Fig. (**6d**, **6e**).

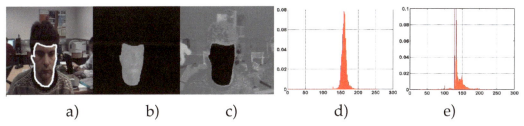

a)   b)   c)   d)   e)

Fig. (6). Initialization on sequence #2: a) selected area of the face on the first image of the video; b) source s_1 : face zone; c) source s_1 : background; d) distribution $P(s_1|H_1)$; e) distribution $P(s_1|H_2)$.

Four Appriou mass sets $m_{ij}(H_i)$ are assigned to each pixel p having color value s_{jp} (one for each source $s_j, j \in \{1; 2\}$ and for each class H_i, $i \in \{1; 2\}$):

$$\begin{aligned} m_{ij}(H_i) &= 0, \\ m_{ij}(\overline{H_i}) &= d_{ij}[1 - R_j.P(s_{jp}|H_i)], \\ m_{ij}(\Omega) &= 1 - m_{ij}(\overline{H_i}). \end{aligned} \qquad (12)$$

Given a pixel p, its probability $P(s_{jp}|H_i)$ is quickly retrieved from the tabulated histograms by a look-up table (L.U.T.) addressing operation. Parameter R_j, that weights the conditional likelihoods, is set to its maximal value. For simplicity, all parameters d_{ij} are initialized to the same value $d_0 = 0.9$ (we mention in the conclusion some hints to implement a more sophisticated model). One takes $d_0 < 1$ in order to force non categorical mass sets (*i.e.* $m_{ij}(\Omega) \neq 0$). This Appriou model gives two complementary mass functions, one for each color source $s_j, j \in \{1; 2\}$ (Eq. 3 with weights denoted by w_{ij}) so that for any hypothesis $A = \{H_i\}$ and any observation s_{jp}, one can compute the weight:

$$w_{ij}(\overline{A}) = 1 - m_{ij}(\overline{A}) \text{ computed from the prior model } P(s_{jp}|A). \tag{13}$$

Altogether, this yields four simple mass sets per pixel (two sources j, two hypotheses i).

Color Fusion by Cautious Rule

The concept of independence means that two pieces of evidence are obtained by different ways. Color sources s_1 and s_2 (the two logarithmic hues in LUX space), and hence their mass functions m_{ij} are obviously not independent as they are computed from the same raw data R, G, B (Eq. 10). Indeed, when red component R varies, both values of U and X change. To deal with the fusion of information from dependent sources, a conservative combination rule like the Denœux cautious conjunctive rule is well suited. Because of its conjunctive property, it strengthens the certainty in the information fusion. Nevertheless it ensures that the recursive combination of information with itself always gives the same result (idempotence). In that case, independence of information sources is not mandatory: idempotence authorizes dependence. So, it offers a compromise between reinforcement and idempotence. Here, this fusion operator with idempotence property is preferred.

For two distinct weights belonging to the interval $[0,1]$, the cautious rule is defined by Eq. 7. Here, we have: $w_1 = w_{i1}$ (for red chrominance U), $w_2 = w_{i2}$ (for blue chrominance X), and $A \in 2^{\Omega} = \{\varnothing, \{H_1\}, \{H_2\}, \Omega\}$. The combined weights w are computed as: $w(A) = \min\{w_{ij}(A)\}$. Finally, the color masses $m_{i1 \wedge i2}$ (A) assigned to each pixel p are computed by Eq. 7, and then normalized by Eq. 8, giving the final masses $m_c(A)$ that yield, for each pixel, the belief in each class H_i (Table **2**).

Table 2. Fusion by cautious rule: computation of color mass sets for pixel *p*.

A	$w(.)$	$m_{i1 \wedge i2}(.)$	$m_c(.)$
$\varnothing$		$[1 - w(H_1)][1 - w(H_2)]$	0
$\{H_1\}$	$\min\{w_{ij}(H_1)\}$	$[1 - w(H_1)]w(H_2)$	$m_c(H_1)$
$\{H_2\}$	$\min\{w_{ij}(H_2)\}$	$w(H_1)[1 - w(H_2)]$	$m_c(H_2)$
Ω		$w(H_1)w(H_2)$	$m_c(\Omega)$

Typical results of this color fusion are shown in Fig. (**7**). The evidential model classifies correctly the image regions whose color corresponds to skin hue (face, arms). The red tee-shirt in seq. #4 is correctly detected as background by the cautious rule. The model fails however in certain background areas whose color is too close to skin hue.

Fig. (7). Fusion results of color sources s_1 and s_2 by the cautious rule (display of pignistic probability $BetP(H_1)$) for the four sequences of Fig. 5, with $R_j = R_{max}$ and $d_{ij} = d_0 = 0.9$.

Illustrative Example

Let us illustrate the processing with a sample case study. Table **3** shows the weights w_{ij} obtained from the following conditional probabilities: $P(s_1|H_1) = 0.05$, $P(s_1|H_2) = 0.04$, $P(s_2|H_1) = 0.07$ and $P(s_2|H_2) = 0.01$.

Table 3. Example of cautious color fusion: weights w_{ij}, combined weights w and masses m_c.

A	red source U		blue source X		combination		
	w_{11}	w_{21}	w_{12}	w_{22}	$w(.)$	$m_{i1 \wedge i2}(.)$	$m_c(.)$
$\varnothing$						0.3645	0
$\{H_1\}$		0.46		0.19	0.19	0.4455	0.701
$\{H_2\}$	0.55		0.73		0.55	0.0855	0.1345
Ω						0.1045	0.1644

The discounting coefficient is set to $d_0 = 0.9$ and R_j is set to its maximal value: $R_1 = R_2 = 1/0.1 = 10$ (by taking as reference the sample histograms in (Fig. **6**)). The combined weights $w(A)$ are simply the minimal values among the w_{ij} (A). The color mass set m_c resulting from the combination of weight function w is given in Table **3**. The decision is cleary for H_1 (heaviest mass).

Let us compare with the classic Bayesian approach. The a posteriori probability is given by:

$$P(H_1|s_1, s_2) = \frac{P(H_1) \prod_j P(s_j|H_1)}{\sum_i P(H_i) \prod_j P(s_j|H_i)}. \tag{14}$$

First, let us suppose equiprobability: $P(H_1) = P(H_2) = 0.5$; then one obtains: $P(H_1|s_1, s_2) = 0.897$. The decision is clearly for H_1.

Then, if one takes: $P(H_1) = 0.2$, $P(H_2) = 0.8$, by supposing that the face size is kept to about 20% of the image surface thanks to the proper action of visual servoing, then: $P(H_1|s_1, s_2) = \frac{0.2(0.05 \times 0.07)}{0.2(0.05 \times 0.07) + 0.8(0.04 \times 0.01)} = 0.686$.   Decision is still for H_1.

In contrary, if one has: $P(H_1) = 0.1$, $P(H_2) = 0.9$ (*i.e.* when the face size decreases), then one gets stuck in indecision since $P(H_1|s_1, s_2) \approx 0.5$. Similarly to the maximum *a posteriori* criterion, the evidential decision consists in choosing the hypothesis H_i that has the maximum mass, and thus the maximum plausibility Pl or the maximum pignistic probability $BetP$. In this case, we get: $Pl(H_1) = m_c(H_1) + m_c(\Omega) = 0.8655$, and $Pl(H_2) = 0.299$, or equivalently: $BetP(H_1) = 0.783$, and $BetP(H_2) = 0.217$; the decision is still easy to take. So, the proposed method outperforms the Bayesian approach when the prior probability decreases (*i.e.* when $P(H_1) << 0.5$).

Global Fusion of Color and VJ Mass Sets by Conjunctive Rule

In this section, we describe the fusion of color masses m_c with VJ masses m_v (Fig. **3c**). On one hand, the color model faithfully shows the skin hue but is not able to differentiate the face color from that of an arm or a hand. On the other hand, the VJ face detector detects a front-view face with a high reliability as it validates the presence of eyes, nose and mouth in the bounding box, but it might fail in case of rotated faces or background artifacts. As the information of these two sources is complementary, it is interesting to make them collaborate in order to synthetize a more robust face model.

Since these two pieces of information are elaborated from the same image raw data, the question to address before implementing a proper fusion is to know whether they are dependent or not. For that purpose, a simple test is presented here: the merging of these two sources is compared using resp. the cautious rule (Fig. **8a**) and the classic conjunctive rule (Fig. **8b**).

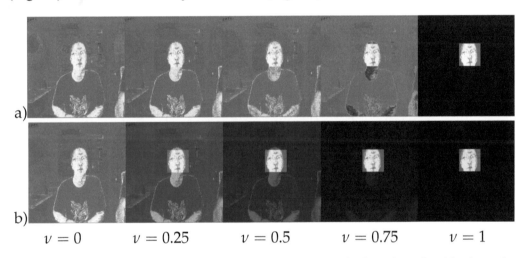

$$v = 0 \qquad v = 0.25 \qquad v = 0.5 \qquad v = 0.75 \qquad v = 1$$

Fig. (8). Fusion results of color and VJ mass functions on sequence #4 for five values of v: a) by the cautious conjunctive rule; b) by the classic conjunctive rule.

For $v < 0.75$ the cautious rule favours the color masses as their weights are lower (hence the masses are heavier) than the VJ ones. The VJ information has little influence for low values of v, and the fusion process is inefficient in that case. On the contrary, using the classic conjunctive rule, the VJ information is taken into account as soon as $v > 0$. The background is toned down proportionally to parameter v, and the effect of the bounding box is more visible. The certainty on the face class is more strengthened with the classic conjunctive rule. One can induce from this simplistic test that VJ information is relatively independent from the color sources (even if this is not a formal proof of independence). This seems coherent as the VJ bounding box is computed using *2D* Haar filters applied on the

L component, whereas color cues are computed from U and X components. Therefore, color and VJ mass functions are combined using the classic conjunctive rule (Eq.5):

$$m(A) = m_c(A) \textcircled{\bigcirc} m_v(A). \tag{15}$$

A problem occurs when the VJ detector recognizes a face-like artifact in the background (Fig. **5d**) with a high reliability ($v \geq 0.5$). In this case, skin color ($m_c(H_1) < 0.5$) and VJ mass functions disagree. This yields an important conflict inside the bounding box BB. In order to limit false detection, we dynamically discount the initial value v_0 of parameter v by considering the global conflict inside BB (cf. feedback loop, Fig. **3e**):

$$
\begin{aligned}
v_t &= v_0 && \text{for } t = 0, \\
v_t &= v_0(1 - K_{BB}) && \text{for } t > 0, \text{ with } K_{BB} = \frac{1}{N_{BB}} \sum_{p \in BB} K_p
\end{aligned}
\tag{16}
$$

Table 4. Fusion of m_c and m_v by the conjunctive rule, depending on pixel position.

A	$m(.)$ for $p \in BB$	$m(.)$ for $p \notin BB$
$\emptyset$	$m_c(H_2) \cdot v_t$	$m_c(H_1) \cdot v_t$
$\{H_1\}$	$m_c(H_1) + m_c(\Omega) \cdot v_t$	$m_c(H_1) \cdot (1 - v_t)$
$\{H_2\}$	$m_c(H_2) \cdot (1 - v_t)$	$m_c(H_2) + m_c(\Omega) \cdot v_t$
Ω	$m_c(\Omega) \cdot (1 - v_t)$	$m_c(\Omega) \cdot (1 - v_t)$

N_{BB} is the number of pixels inside the bounding box, and $\forall p \in BB$, $K_p = m_c(H_2) \times v_t$ is the conflict $m(\emptyset)$ between color and VJ masses at pixel level, thus K_{BB} denotes the average conflict. The mass m resulting from the conjunctive combination of m_c and m_v with the implementation of this discounting strategy on v is detailed in (Table **4**).

Computation of Pignistic Probabilities

This section describes the final step of the face modeling to get pignistic probabilities (Fig. **3d**). The transformation of the mass functions $m(.)$ into the probabilistic framework is necessary for taking the decision and for the tracking operated by particle filter described in next section. The pignistic probability attributed to the face class $\{H_1\}$ is, for each pixel p:

$$BetP(H_1) = [m(H_1) + m(\Omega)/2]/[1 - m(\varnothing)], \qquad (17)$$

Since *BetP* belongs to [0,1], it is multiplied by 255 in order to display legible gray level images of this probability (like in Fig. **7**).

Table **5** summarizes the behaviour of the evidential face model when the pixel hue is either close to face hue ($m_c(H_1) \rightarrow 1$), really different ($m_c(H_2) \rightarrow 1$) or in between ($m_c(H_2) \rightarrow 0.5$), and according to VJ detector reliability parameter v. Note that color uncertainty is of course: $m_c(\Omega) = 1 - m_c(H_1) - m_c(H_2)$. The performance of the evidential model depends both on color masses and on the VJ face detector reliability (Fig. **8**). Face is correctly detected if both $v \geq 0.5$ and $m_c(H_1) + m_c(\Omega) \geq 0.5$. A too low value of v ($v < 0.5$) limits the influence of the VJ face detector and finally reduces the evidential model to a simple skin color detector.

A too high value of v ($v > 0.9$) can be counter-productive when the VJ detector fails and focuses on an artifact with color close to skin hue. Therefore we recommend to initialize the v value such as $0.7 \leq v_0 \leq 0.9$. When the VJ face detector fails, *i.e.* when it does not deliver any bounding box, v is temporarily set to zero.

PROBABILISTIC FACE TRACKING

This section describes the second part of the processing, namely the face tracking procedure (Fig. **1b**). The goal is to obtain in real-time the trajectory of the target (tracked object) in the video stream [27]. Tracking techniques can be grouped into three categories: (i) low level methods achieve tracking by performing color segmentation, background subtraction (in case of stationary background), or optical flow estimation; (ii) active contours, snakes or AAM track the face by template matching; (iii) filtering methods perform temporal tracking by predicting the future state (localization) of a dynamic system (the target) using past measurements. Kalman filtering is used for Gaussian uni-modal models, whereas particle filtering is widely used for nonlinear models, non-Gaussian processes

[28]. An extension of Bayesian particle filters to Dempster-Shafer theory is proposed in [29] for multi-camera people tracking in indoor environments. Evidential particle filtering is also used in [30] for robust multiple-source object tracking.

Table 5. Output of evidential model: decision depending on color masses m_c and VJ detector reliability v.

$m_c(.)$		VJ v	$m_c(\Omega)$	$BetP(H_1)$		decision	
$\{H_1\}$	$\{H_2\}$			$p \in BB$	$p \notin BB$	$p \in BB$	$p \notin BB$
0	1	0	0	0	0	$\{H_2\}$	$\{H_2\}$
		0.5					
		1					
0.5	0.5	0	0	0.5	0.5	indecisive	indecisive
		0.5		0.67	0.33	$\{H_1\}$	$\{H_2\}$
		1		1	0	$\{H_1\}$	$\{H_2\}$
1	0	0	0	1	1	$\{H_1\}$	$\{H_1\}$
		0.5			1		$\{H_1\}$
		1			0		$\{H_2\}$
0	0	0	1	0.5	0.5	indecisive	indecisive
		0.5		0.75	0.25	$\{H_1\}$	$\{H_2\}$
		1		1	0	$\{H_1\}$	$\{H_2\}$
0	0.5	0	0.5	0.25	0.25	$\{H_2\}$	$\{H_2\}$
		0.5		0.5	0.125	indecisive	
		1		1	0	$\{H_1\}$	
0.5	0	0	0.5	0.75	0.75	$\{H_1\}$	$\{H_1\}$
		0.5		0.875	0.5		indecisive
		1		1	0		$\{H_2\}$

In the application context here, the face is a deformable object moving close to the camera, whose egomotion is unpredictable with frequent direction changes. The scene is a priori cluttered, with changes in background due to camera motion. Therefore a probabilistic tracking method based on a bootstrap particle filter is chosen, as this technique is efficient for objects with nonlinear trajectory and as it takes the temporal redundancy between frames into account. The goal is to estimate the parameters of a state vector which represents the cinematics of the target, *i.e.* the face at time t. The outer contour of the face is approximated by an ellipse with center (x_{ct}, y_{ct}), main axis h_t, minor axis l_t and orientation θ_t. These parameters are grouped into the state vector $X_t = [x_{ct}, y_{ct}, h_t, l_t, \theta_t]$ to be estimated. The particle filtering technique applies a recursive Bayesian filter to several hypothetical face locations, and merges these hypotheses according to their likelihood, conditionally to the predicted state.

The observation used as input for the particle filter is $Y_t = BetP(H_1)$, *i.e.*, an image whose high-valued pixels indicate the presence of the face at time t (cf. Fig. **8**). The knowledge of these observations Y_t allows to recover the *a posteriori* probabilities: the particle filter estimates the posterior conditional probability distribution $P(X_t|Y_{1:t})$ under the form of a linear combination of weighted Dirac masses called particles:

$$P(X_t|Y_{1:t}) = \sum_{n=1}^{N} \omega_t^{(n)} \delta_{\lambda_t^{(n)}}. \tag{18}$$

A particle $\Lambda_t^{(n)} = \{\lambda_t^{(n)}, \omega_t^{(n)}\}$ represents an hypothesis on the state of the target. $\lambda_t^{(n)}$ denotes position and $\omega_t^{(n)}$ denotes weight assigned to the nth particle at time t.

The tracking algorithm begins with an initialization step (Fig. **9i**). The zone of the face selected manually by the user during the learning stage is used to initialize X_t. Then the algorithm consists of two main successive stages: (i) first, the coordinates of the center of the state vector (x_{ct}, y_{ct}) are estimated by particle filtering (Fig. **9f**); (ii) then, the ellipse size and orientation (h_t, l_t, θ_t) are estimated by a second particle filter (Fig. **9g**).

If necessary, a resampling operation [31] is triggered inbetween (Fig. **9h**): it occurs when the informative content associated with the particle estimating the state vector position is lower than a preset threshold value NR_{thresh} (typ. set to 10000 for an image size of 400×400, which is about 5% of image size). In that case, all the weights are equally reset to: $\omega_t^{(n)} = 1/N$, where N is the number of particles (typ. $N = 50$). Then, one draws randomly new positions of the face by generating particles from a uniform law U_X (see Eq. 19). When a particle finds a face zone again, the filter converges after a few iterations, which ensures tracking to resume.

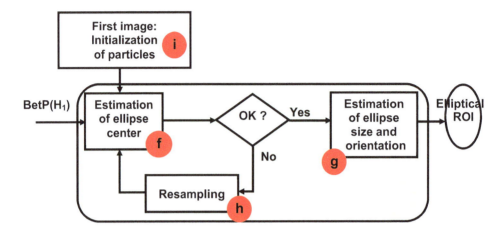

Fig. (9). Block-diagram of the tracking algorithm by particle filtering.

Estimation of Ellipse Center

The state vector reduces here to $X_t = [x_{ct}, y_{ct}]$. A simple dynamic model [32] randomly distributes the centers of the particles in the image:

$$P(\tilde{X}_t|X_{t-1}) = (1-\alpha)\mathcal{N}(\tilde{X}_t|X_{t-1},\Sigma) + \alpha\mathcal{U}_{\tilde{X}}(\tilde{X}_t) \tag{19}$$

where $N(.|\mu, \Sigma)$ is a normal Gaussian law with average μ and covariance Σ. The diagonal matrix $\Sigma = \text{diag}(\sigma_{xct}, \sigma_{yct})$ sets the *a priori* constraints: it imposes the variances to the position components of the state vector (typ. $\Sigma = \text{diag}(5, 5)$). The coefficient α weights the uniform distribution: $0 \leq \alpha \leq 1$. It accounts for the rare erratic face movements acting as jumps in the video sequence. It also helps the algorithm resume tracking after a momentary period of partial or total occlusion. This uniform factor is heuristically set to $\alpha = 0.1$ so that the majority of particles (90%) remains around the center predicted at time $t - 1$. It ensures some inertia in the particle distribution along time. A too high value of α is counter-productive in presence of multiple or erratic blobs in the frame. Indeed the risk of multiple jumps is increased, that can cause filter instability.

In Fig. (**10a**), the influence of the Gaussian distribution is characterized by the concentration of most particles around the center estimated from the previous image. The influence of parameter α can be seen, as a few isolated particles spread over other regions in the image background.

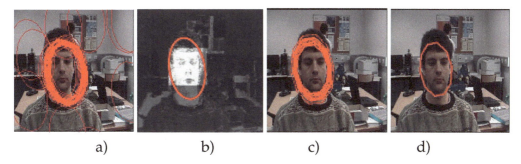

Fig. (10). Sequence #2: a) particles generated for the center estimation stage ($N = 50$); b) best position result; c) particles generated for the size and pose estimation step; d) final best ellipse in size and pose.

After the particle prediction, the filter evaluates the fitting of Y_t measured in the predicted ellipse $\tilde{X}_t^{(n)}$ with the face model data to compute the likelihood $P(Y_t|\tilde{X}_t)$. The fitting criterion is the quadratic sum of pignistic probabilities $BetP(H_1)$ contained inside the ellipse. Hence the estimated weight of each particle is given by:

$$\tilde{\omega}_t^{(n)} = \sum_{p \in \tilde{X}_t^{(n)}} [BetP(H_1)]^2. \tag{20}$$

The fitting criterion is the maximum likelihood, to select the most significant ellipse whose center position gives the state vector (Fig. **10b**).

The nonlinearity (quadratic sum) used to compute the weight $\tilde{\omega}_t^{(n)}$ favours particles containing pignistic probabilities of high values. The transformation of the mass set into pignistic probabilities (Eq. 17) ensures the compatibility with the probabilistic framework of particle filtering (the compound hypothesis Ω does not appear any longer). The mutual exclusion principle, which states that two hypotheses must be antagonist is fulfilled. This justifies the choice of pignistic probabilities as output of the face model.

Estimation of Size and Pose

The size and pose at time t are predicted by running the particle filter again, with a dynamic model similar to Eq. 19, but with a state vector reduced to $X_t = [h_t, l_t, \theta_t]$, as particles are now propagated around the fixed center (x_{ct}, y_{ct}) already estimated, and with a parameter setting $\alpha = 0$. Indeed it is not relevant to take erratic variations of size and pose into account. The covariance matrix $\Sigma = \text{diag}(\sigma_{ht}, \sigma_{lt}, \sigma_{\theta t})$ constrains the model so that particles deviate little from those estimated at time $t - 1$ (typ. $\Sigma = \text{diag}(5, 5, 0.1)$). Fig. (**10c**) illustrates the distribution of the different predicted ellipses around the center x_{ct}, y_{ct}.

For the final correction step, the following observation is used: the pignistic probabilities from the evidential model are filtered (by nonlinear morphological image filling), and then thresholded to exhibit a binary shape whose contour is approximated by least squares fitting to an ellipse (measured ellipse) that serves as new observation Y_t for the second particle filter. The weights are simply the inverse of the MSE between the predicted ellipse and the measured ellipse. At last, the maximum likelihood criterion selects the most significant particle: among all the predicted ellipses around the previously estimated center (Fig. **10c**), the algorithm selects the one Fig. (**10d**) whose size and pose are closest to the observation (*i.e.* measured ellipse).

Visual Servoing

The purpose is to keep the face in the center of the image plane, with an almost constant size (approximately 10% of the image size). The tracking (task of centering) and the zoom control strategy (task of scaling) are done with a classic regulation approach (Fig. **1c**). The visual servoing controls the three degrees of freedom of the PTZ camera (panoramic, tilt, zoom) . In Fig. (**1**), X_t stands for the servoing command (desired ellipse center, size and pose, typ. $X_t = [0, 0, 120, 100, 0]$) and X_t is the state vector measured from the particle filter. Fig. (**11**) shows the visual servoing behavior. On image im_{15} the face is located on the left side of the field of view. The joint action of panoramic motion and zoom focuses the face in the center of the image plane in image im_{18}. From image im_{20} to im_{24}, the user moves backward on his chair (and hence gets smaller). Then, the control of the zoom and the vertical movement of the camera (tilt) allow to refocus the face in the center of the image with the desired size (image 29).

im_{15} im_{18} im_{20} im_{24} im_{26} im_{29}

Fig. (11). Tracking results for sequence #8, with visual servoing of the camera in position (pan and tilt) and control of the zoom.

PERFORMANCE ANALYSIS

Performance evaluation of tracking systems is mandatory. This requires both the definition of quantitative criteria like precision, MSE, robustness, execution time, etc. and the availability of a ground truth (GT), that is, a dataset coding the exact position of the face image by image. However the task of obtaining the GT by a human expertise is tedious and subjective. Here, we consider the face present in the image when a sufficient part of its skin is visible. Hair is not taken into account. Faces can be viewed full frontal but also from aside. During a total occlusion, the face is supposed to be missing.

Qualitative Evaluation

The algorithm behaviour is illustrated with two sequences: (i) sequence #1 registered in our laboratory exhibits partial or total occlusions and pose variations; (ii) benchmark sequence David Indoor from the literature [33] contains pose changes, lighting and background variations, disruptive elements (the user removes his glasses, then puts them on again).

In sequence #1 (Fig. **12**), the Viola-Jones masses increase the informative content in the face zone on images im_{57} and im_{73}: pignistic probabilities are most significant (white pixels in Fig. (**12b**)) on the face zone where color and VJ mass sets are fused, but not on other skin color regions (arms, hands, or neck).

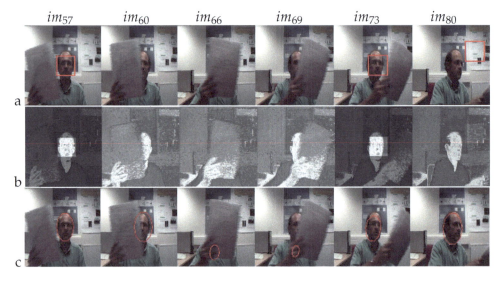

Fig. (12). Face tracking for sequence #1: a) Bounding box supplied by the VJ face detector; b) Pignistic probability of the face model; c) Ellipse resulting from particle filter.

No bounding box is delivered by the VJ detector in images im_{60}, im_{66}, im_{69}, so that $v_t = 0$ is set in the evidential model since only color information is available. Therefore, in the presence of total occlusion (im_{66}), the resulting ellipse lies on the hand of the user. The uniform distribution in the filter dynamics (Eq. 19 with $\alpha = 0.1$) ensures a correct repositioning when a candidate particle locates on the face zone again (im_{73}). The VJ bounding box might degrade the tracking quality when the VJ detector focuses on a face-like artifact (frame im_{80}). An important conflict is measured inside the bounding box ($K_{BB} = 0.7$). Then the adjustment of parameter v_t ($v_t \rightarrow 0.24$ since $v_0 = 0.8$) favours more the color information and the resulting ellipse correctly lies on the face.

In the sequence of Fig. (**13**), the learning stage is set up on an underexposed frame (im_{200}). On frames im_{202} and im_{300}, the pignistic probabilities are most significant in the face zone where color and VJ attributes are fused. As the person leaves the under-exposed hall (frame im_{351}), tracking remains efficient: no updating of the evidential model is necessary even if illumination conditions have changed. As the face is in profile in frame im_{465}, no bounding box is delivered by the VJ detector and only color information is considered ($v_t = 0$). When hands are in contact with the face in frame im_{598}, the center and pose estimations deviate little.

When the hands go away from the face, they are not tracked any longer (frame im_{604}). This shows the robustness of the method: the presence of disruptive elements alters weakly pose and size estimation and only slightly perturbs the tracking in position.

im_{202} im_{300} im_{351} im_{465} im_{598} im_{604}

Fig. (13). Tracking results on David Indoor sequence : a) evidential fusion (pignistic probability $BetP(H_1)$); b) ellipse positioning.

Quantitative Evaluation

In order to quantify the tracking performance in various contexts on statistically significant data, we have manually segmented (*i.e.* cut-out) the face in various video sequences registered in our laboratory to get the ground truth, and in 500 images of the David Indoor benchmark sequence [33]. Pixels located inside the cut-out face represent the ground truth (*GT*). The tracking algorithm delivers an ellipse denoted by *ROI* (region of interest). True positive pixels (*TP*) belong to the intersection: $TP = ROI \cap GT$, whereas false positives (*FP*) lay outside of *GT*: $FP = ROI \cap \overline{GT}$. Two measures are classically used to quantify tracking performance, namely **Precision**=$\frac{|TP|}{|ROI|}$ and **Recall**=$\frac{|TP|}{|GT|}$. Precision is the probability that a pixel detected as a face pixel is actually a face pixel: it is computed as the ratio of the correct measures (*TP*) on all measures taken ($ROI = TP \cup FP$). Recall is the probability that a face pixel is detected: it is computed as the ratio between correct measures and the whole ground truth (as $GT = TP \cup FN$). False negative pixels (*FN*) belong to the intersection: $FN = \overline{ROI} \cap GT$. Precision and Recall are computed individually on every image, then averaged on each sequence (to precisely exhibit the influence of the parameters in every context), and finally on all the data to assess the global performance of the method. From these measurements, the ROC curves (Receiver Operating Characteristics) are built with x-coordinate $x = (1 - \text{Precision})$ and y-coordinate $y = \text{Recall}$, and drawn for various values of the influence parameters. The point of the curves closest to the ideal point $(x = 0; y = 1)$ corresponds to the best tuning of parameter values. The study gives the sensibility of the method to the VJ detector reliability parameter v. The point drawn for the adaptive parameter $v = v_t$ shows the tracking performance obtained when the discounting factor by feedback is implemented (Eq. 16). This dynamic setting of v leads to a performance optimization (Precision and Recall $\approx$ 80%). ROC curves can be found in [9]. Results are comparable to those of standard classifiers whose detection rate reaches 80% [34].

Another quantitative evaluation criterion for the assessment of tracking performance is the center location error: $\varepsilon = \sqrt{(x_{GT_t} - x_{c_t})^2 + (y_{GT_t} - y_{c_t})^2}$, where x_{GT_t}, y_{GT_t} are the coordinates of the face center given by the ground truth (GT), whereas x_{ct}, y_{ct} are the center location coordinates of the detected ellipse (ROI). With a location error lower than $\varepsilon_{\max} = 25$ pixels during most of the sequence (Fig. **14a**), the proposed algorithm exceeds the performances of the best algorithm (MILTrack) evaluated in [33] (Fig. **14b**). Our approach fails locally on images 380 to 430, when the algorithm positions on an artifact. A mean location error $\varepsilon_{mean} = 15$ pixels and a standard deviation $\Sigma_{mean} = 11$ pixels on this benchmark sequence are performances similar to or even better than those presented in the literature about particle filter [35].

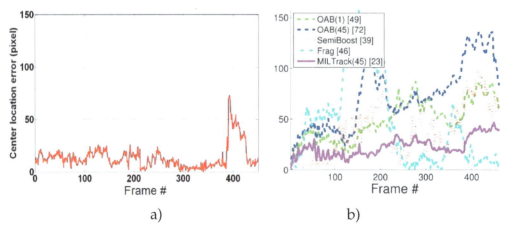

a)   b)

Fig. (14). Tracking results (center location error) on David Indoor sequence, with: a) the proposed method; b) various algorithms according to Babenko [33].

DISCUSSION

This chapter has presented an original method both for face detection based on evidential modeling, and for face tracking with a classic particle filter technique. A strategy is adopted which takes the background class H_2 in addition to face class H_1 into account. Concerning the face tracking performance, Precision and Recall reach 80% with an adequate parameter setting, but noteworthy without having to train on a huge learning dataset, which is the originality of the approach. The computation simplicity makes the method usable in a real-time (tracking at video rate). The results show the robustness of the dynamic fusion thanks to idempotent combination rules which limit the belief contraction. By setting jointly the few adaptive parameters of the evidential model and of the particle filter, we show that it is possible to finely tune the tracking behaviour. It is also more robust with respect to context variation when background or lighting conditions change during the video sequence. The statistical results confirm the qualitative observations reported here.

In the current work, the optimal setting of parameter values is deduced from an averaging of few experimental data. Consequently, this study poorly estimates the setting of the parameters to properly tackle transient variations of context in parts of a video sequence (but it still works). A time-dynamic adjustment of parameters is required to improve the tracking robustness (as done for v in Eq. 16). Therefore, the dynamic setting of the algorithm parameters deserves further investigation: distinct values for parameter v could be chosen, depending on the position with respect to BB ($v_1 \neq v_2$) and also various values for parameters d_{ij}. Indeed, *a priori* knowledge about the acquisition could be used for that purpose: for face tracking purpose, red is maybe more relevant than blue ($\Rightarrow d_{i1} > d_{i2}$). Moreover, the learning of the face class H_1 is certainly more accurate than the learning of the non-face class H_2 ($\Rightarrow d_{1j} > d_{2j}$). The bounding box may be more reliable for the face model than for non-face model ($\Rightarrow v_1 > v_2$). The mass function modeling could also be improved by using a rough learning on the ground truth in the first image at initialisation, to estimate the rates *TP, FP, TN, FN* and then modelize and maximize the beliefs as done in [36].

CONFLICT OF INTEREST

The author confirms that author has no conflict of interest to declare for this publication.

ACKNOWLEDGEMENTS

I am grateful to my former PhD students, Francis Faux and Marc Liévin, for their respective contribution to the evidential face model [37, 38] and to the nonlinear LUX color space.

REFERENCES

[1]   P. Smets, and R. Kennes, "The transferable belief model", *Artif. Intell.*, vol. 66, no. 2, pp. 191-243, 1994.
        [http://dx.doi.org/10.1016/0004-3702(94)90026-4]

[2]   E. Ramasso, C. Panagiotakis, M. Rombaut, and D. Pellerin, "Belief scheduler based on model failure detection in the TBM framework. Application to human activity recognition", *Int. J. Approx. Reason.*, vol. 51, no. 7, pp. 846-865, 2010.
        [http://dx.doi.org/10.1016/j.ijar.2010.04.005]

[3]   M-H. Yang, D. Kriegman, and N. Ahuja, "Detecting faces in images: a survey", *IEEE Trans. Pattern Anal. Mach. Intell.*, vol. 24, no. 1, pp. 35-58, 2002.
        [http://dx.doi.org/10.1109/34.982883]

[4]   J.M. Chaves-Gonzalez, M.A. Vega-Rodriguez, J. Gomez-Pulido, and J.M. Sanchez-Perez, "Detecting skin in face recognition systems: A colour spaces study", *Digit. Signal Process.*, vol. 20, no. 3, pp. 806-823, 2010.
        [http://dx.doi.org/10.1016/j.dsp.2009.10.008]

[5]   P. Kakumanu, S. Makrogiannis, and N. Bourbakis, "A survey of skin-color modeling and detection methods", *Pattern Recognit.*, vol. 40, no. 3, pp. 1106-1122, 2007.
        [http://dx.doi.org/10.1016/j.patcog.2006.06.010]

[6]   P. Viola, and M. Jones, "Robust real-time face detection", *Int. J. Comput. Vis.*, vol. 57, no. 2, pp. 137-154, 2004.
        [http://dx.doi.org/10.1023/B:VISI.0000013087.49260.fb]

[7]   T.F. Cootes, C.J. Taylor, D.H. Cooper, and J. Graham, "Active shape models - Their training and application", *Comput. Vis. Image Underst.*, vol. 61, no. 1, pp. 38-59, 1995.
        [http://dx.doi.org/10.1006/cviu.1995.1004]

[8]   T.F. Cootes, G.J. Edwards, and C.J. Taylor, "Active appearance models", *IEEE Trans. Pattern Anal. Mach. Intell.*, vol. 23, no. 6, pp. 681-685, 2001.
        [http://dx.doi.org/10.1109/34.927467]

[9]   F. Faux, and F. Luthon, "Theory of evidence for face detection and tracking", *Int. J. Approx. Reason.*, vol. 53, no. 5, pp. 728-746, 2012.

[http://dx.doi.org/10.1016/j.ijar.2012.02.002]

[10] F. Luthon, *Audioslide ScienceDirect http://www.youtube.com/watch?v=AaV5IgzIGBU*, 2013.

[11] A.P. Dempster, "Upper and lower probabilities induced by a multivalued mapping", *Ann. Math. Stat.*, vol. 38, pp. 325-339, 1967.
[http://dx.doi.org/10.1214/aoms/1177698950]

[12] G. Shafer, *A Mathematical Theory of Evidence.*. Princeton University Press: New Jersey, 1976.

[13] I. Bloch, "Defining belief functions using mathematical morphology. Application to image fusion under imprecision", *Int. J. Approx. Reason.*, vol. 48, no. 2, pp. 437-465, 2008.
[http://dx.doi.org/10.1016/j.ijar.2007.07.008]

[14] L.M. Zouhal, and T. Denoeux, "An evidence-theoretic k-NN rule parameter optimization", *IEEE Transactions on Systems, Man and Cybernetics - Part C*, vol. 28, no. 2, pp. 263-271, 1998.
[http://dx.doi.org/10.1109/5326.669565]

[15] P. Walley, and S. Moral, "Upper probabilities based only on the likelihood function", *J. R. Stat. Soc., B*, vol. 61, no. Part 4, pp. 831-847, 1999.
[http://dx.doi.org/10.1111/1467-9868.00205]

[16] P. Smets, "Belief functions: the disjunctive rule of combination and the generalized Bayesian theorem", *Int. J. Approx. Reason.*, vol. 9, pp. 1-35, 1993.
[http://dx.doi.org/10.1016/0888-613X(93)90005-X]

[17] A. Appriou, "Multisensor signal processing in the framework of the theory of evidence", *Application of Mathematical Signal Processing Techniques to Mission Systems, Research and Technology Organisation (Lecture Series 216).*, pp. 5.1-5.31, November 1999.

[18] T. Denoeux, and P. Smets, "Classification using belief functions: relationship between case-based and model-based approaches", *IEEE Trans. Syst. Man Cybern. B*, vol. 36, no. 6, pp. 1395-1406, 2006.
[http://dx.doi.org/10.1109/TSMCB.2006.877795] [PMID: 17186815]

[19] A. Martin, C. Osswald, J. Dezert, and F. Smarandache, "General combination rules for qualitative and quantitative beliefs", *Journal of Advances in Information Fusion*, vol. 3, no. 2, pp. 67-82, 2008.

[20] M.C. Florea, A-L. Jousselme, E. Bossé, and D. Grenier, "Robust combination rules for evidence theory", *Inf. Fusion*, vol. 10, pp. 183-197, 2009.
[http://dx.doi.org/10.1016/j.inffus.2008.08.007]

[21] T. Denœux, "Conjunctive and disjunctive combination of belief functions induced by non distinct bodies of evidence", *Artif. Intell.*, vol. 172, pp. 234-264, 2008.
[http://dx.doi.org/10.1016/j.artint.2007.05.008]

[22] B. Quost, M.H. Masson, and T. Denœux, "Classifier fusion in the Dempster-Shafer framework using optimized t-norm based combination rules", *Int. J. Approx. Reason.*, vol. 52, no. 3, pp. 353-374, 2011.
[http://dx.doi.org/10.1016/j.ijar.2010.11.008]

[23] A. Kallel, and S. Le Hégarat-Mascle, "Combination of partially non-distinct beliefs: the cautious-adaptive rule", *Int. J. Approx. Reason.*, vol. 50, no. 7, pp. 1000-1021, 2009.
[http://dx.doi.org/10.1016/j.ijar.2009.03.006]

[24] P. Smets, "Decision making in the TBM: the necessity of the pignistic transformation", *Int. J. Approx.*

Reason., vol. 38, no. 2, pp. 133-147, 2005.
[http://dx.doi.org/10.1016/j.ijar.2004.05.003]

[25]   M. Liévin, and F. Luthon, "Nonlinear color space and spatiotemporal MRF for hierarchical segmentation of face features in video", *IEEE Trans. Image Process.,* vol. 13, no. 1, pp. 63-71, 2004.
[http://dx.doi.org/10.1109/TIP.2003.818013] [PMID: 15376958]

[26]   F. Luthon, B. Beaumesnil, and N. Dubois, "LUX color transform for mosaic image rendering", *17th IEEE Int. Conf. on Automation, Quality and Testing, Robotics (AQTR 2010),* vol. III, pp. 93-98 Cluj-Napoca, Romania
[http://dx.doi.org/10.1109/AQTR.2010.5520671]

[27]   A. Yilmaz, O. Javed, and M. Shah, "Object tracking: a survey", *ACM Comput. Surv.,* vol. 38, no. 4, pp. 1-45, 2006.
[http://dx.doi.org/10.1145/1177352.1177355]

[28]   M.S. Arulampalam, S. Maskell, N. Gordon, and T. Clapp, "A tutorial on particle filters for online nonlinear/non-Gaussian Bayesian tracking", *IEEE Trans. Signal Process.,* vol. 50, no. 2, pp. 174-188, 2002.
[http://dx.doi.org/10.1109/78.978374]

[29]   R. Muñoz-Salinas, R. Medina-Carnicer, F.J. Madrid-Cuevas, and A. Carmona-Poyato, "Multi-camera people tracking using evidential filters", *Int. J. Approx. Reason.,* vol. 50, no. 5, pp. 732-749, 2009.
[http://dx.doi.org/10.1016/j.ijar.2009.02.001]

[30]   J. Klein, C. Lecomte, and P. Miché, "Hierarchical and conditional combination of belief functions induced by visual tracking", *Int. J. Approx. Reason.,* vol. 51, no. 4, pp. 410-428, 2010.
[http://dx.doi.org/10.1016/j.ijar.2009.12.001]

[31]   A. Doucet, S.J. Godsill, and C. Andrieu, "On sequential Monte Carlo sampling methods for Bayesian filtering", *Stat. Comput.,* vol. 10, no. 3, pp. 197-208, 2000.
[http://dx.doi.org/10.1023/A:1008935410038]

[32]   P. Pérez, J. Vermaak, and A. Blake, "Data fusion for visual tracking with particles", *Proc. IEEE,* vol. 92, no. 3, pp. 495-513, 2004.
[http://dx.doi.org/10.1109/JPROC.2003.823147]

[33]   B. Babenko, M.H. Yang, and S. Belongie, "Robust object tracking with online multiple instance learning", *IEEE Trans. Pattern Anal. Mach. Intell.,* vol. 33, no. 8, pp. 1619-1632, 2011.
[http://dx.doi.org/10.1109/TPAMI.2010.226]

[34]   M. Castrillón, O. Déniz, D. Hernández, and J. Lorenzo, "A comparison of face and facial feature detectors based on the Viola-Jones general object detection framework", *Mach. Vis. Appl.,* vol. 22, pp. 481-494, 2011.

[35]   W. Zheng, and S.M. Bhandarkar, "Face detection and tracking using a boosted adaptive particle filter", *J. Vis. Commun. Image Represent.,* vol. 20, pp. 9-27, 2009.
[http://dx.doi.org/10.1016/j.jvcir.2008.09.001]

[36]   M. Shoyaib, M. Abdullah-Al-Wadud, and O. Chae, "A skin detection approach based on the Dempster-Shafer theory of evidence", *Int. J. Approx. Reason,* vol. 53, no. 4, pp. 636-659, 2012.
[http://dx.doi.org/10.1016/j.ijar.2012.01.003]

[37]   F. Faux, and F. Luthon, "Théorie de l'évidence pour suivi de visage", *Traitement du Signal,* vol. 28, no. 5, pp. 515-545, 2011.
[http://dx.doi.org/10.3166/ts.28.515-545]

[38]   F. Faux, Détection et suivi de visage par la théorie de l'évidence, Université de Pau et Pays de l'Adour: Anglet, France, October 2009.Ph.D. dissertation

CHAPTER 10

Fuzzy Discriminant Analysis: Considering the Fuzziness in Facial Age Feature Extraction

Shenglan Ben[*]

School of Electronic Science and Engineering, Nanjing University, Nanjing, 210023, China

Abstract: In traditional age estimation methods which utilize discriminative methods for feature extraction, the biological age labels are adopted as the ground truth for supervision. However, the appearance age, which is indicated by the facial appearance, is intrinsically a fuzzy attribute of human faces which is inadequate to be labeled as a crisp value. To address this issue, this paper firstly introduces a fuzzy representation of age labels and then extends the LDA into fuzzy ones. In the definition of fuzzy labels, both the ongoing property of facial aging and the ambiguity between facial appearance and biological age are considered. By utilizing the fuzzy labels for supervision, the proposed method outperforms the crisp ones in both preserving ordinal information of aging faces and adjusting the inconsistency between the biological age and appearance. Experiments on both FG-NET and MORPH databases confirm the effectiveness of the proposed method.

Keywords: Age information, Aging pattern subspace, Appearance age, Biological age, Conformal embedding analysis, Cumulative score, Facial age estimation, Facial appearance, Facial landmark, Facial shape, Fuzziness in Facial aging, Fuzzy discriminant analysis, Fuzzy LDA, Fuzzy representation of age labels, Intra-class and inter-Class neighbors, Linear discriminant analysis, Marginal Fisher analysis, Mean absolute error, Ordinary preserving LDA, Ordinary preserving MFA.

INTRODUCTION

The objective of facial age estimation is to evaluate a person's age from facial images [1]. It has wide applications in human-computer interactions such as

[*] **Address to Corresponding Author Shenglan Ben:** School of Electronic Science and Engineering, Nanjing University, Nanjing, 210023, China; Tel: +86 25 89686705; Fax: +86 25 84317235; E-mail: benshenglan@mail.njust.edu.cn

internet access control, underage alcohol vending machine and age specific advertising. Attracted by the potential applications, many researchers have devoted to investigate techniques to achieve reliable age estimation. Among the research topics, feature extraction plays a crucial role in determining the performance of the system since facial appearance is an intricate composition of age, identity, pose, expression and illumination.

Early works utilized the ratios of the distance between facial landmarks as the age related features [2, 3]. Obviously, such anthropometric features are sensitive to the accuracy of landmark localization. And, they are only effective in classifying the face images into children and adult because the facial shape does not change too much during adult aging.

To solve such problem, Lanitis [4 - 6] utilized the active appearance model (AAM) [7], which combines both the shape and texture information of a face image, in regression based age estimation methods. Also using AAM based face encoding, Geng *et al.* [8] proposed aging pattern subspace (AGES) method, which learns a subspace from sequences of individual aging images. The AAM based methods utilized PCA to do dimension reduction and thus may omit some useful information such as facial wrinkles. The supervised methods, which benefit from the information of age labels, are also widely adopted to extract the discriminative features for facial age estimation. Fu *et al.* [9, 10] utilized manifold embedding techniques such as Marginal Fisher Analysis (MFA) [11] and Conformal Embedding Analysis (CEA) [12], to learn discriminative subspace. In [13, 14], the biologically- inspired features (BIF) were extended to age estimation and combined with manifold learning to get even lower age estimation errors.

To preserve the ordinal information of age labels, Li [15] formulated feature extraction as an optimization problem which considered the temporally ordinal and continuous characteristic of facial aging in the objective function. Lu [16, 17] constructed an age locality graph for the labels of training samples and proposed ordinary preserving LDA (OPLDA) and ordinary preserving MFA (OPMFA) to project the samples with similar ages closer than those with dissimilar ages.

In the above methods, crisp biological ages/age groups are used as the ground truth for supervision. We notice that the fuzziness is an intrinsic feature of facial aging. Firstly, the fuzziness also exists in continuous age labeling because facial aging is an ongoing process. It is ambiguous to label a face image with an exact value of 'year'. Secondly, the fuzziness exists in the relationship between the biological age and facial appearance since facial aging is a personalized procedure. Some people may look younger or older than their biological age. Thus, it is inadequate to use the biological age as the ground truth of appearance age.

Considering the above observations, we propose methods to solve the fuzziness in extracting the age related features from facial image. In the proposed method, the fuzziness in age labeling is firstly tackled by viewing the age labels as fuzzy sets, and the fuzziness between facial appearance and biological age can then be handled by combining the fuzzy labels of a sample's neighborhoods. Using the fuzzy age labels for supervision, we extend LDA into fuzzy one. Experimental results on FGNET [18] and MORPH [19] database demonstrate that the proposed method can extract age features from face images efficiently and outperforms several state of the art methods.

The remainder of the paper is organized as follows. The fuzzy representation of age labels is firstly illustrated. A fuzzy discriminant analysis approach is then described. Experimental results and comparisons are made and conclusions are given.

CHARACTERIZATION OF THE FUZZINESS IN FACIAL AGING

In traditional age estimation methods, each sample is labeled with a crisp age value which is typically consistent with the biological age. Supervised feature extractions can then be conducted by viewing each age as a class. However, the appearance age, which is indicated by the facial appearance, is intrinsically a fuzzy attribute of human faces, and is inadequate to be labeled as a crisp value.

The fuzziness of facial age is in two folds. Firstly, facial aging is an ongoing process. Each person is in the period of transition from one exact age to another in most of time. It is inadequate to label a face image with an exact age. Secondly, facial aging is an intricate progress depending on various factors, including human gene, health condition, lifestyle, and environments. Some people may look older than their biological age, while some others may look younger. As a result, it is inappropriate to use the biological age as the ground truth.

To tackle the above problems, we introduce a fuzzy representation of age labels. Specifically, the age labels are firstly extended into fuzzy sets to handle the ongoing properties of facial aging. The inconsistency between facial appearance and biological age can then be solved by combining the fuzzy labels of a sample's neighbors.

It can be noticed that one's appearances in adjacent years often look similar. This indicates the face images in adjacent ages can share age labels to some extent. We define a membership function to quantify to what extend the age labels can be shared and convert the age labels into fuzzy ones.

$$\mu_1(x_i, a) = exp\{-\frac{\|age(x_i) - a\|^2}{2\sigma^2}\} \tag{1}$$

where σ is a constant which controls the speed of the decrease of member-ship degrees. In Eq. (1), the ongoing property of facial aging is considered by using the distances to the biological age to define the membership degree. As is shown by the curve in Fig. (1), a sample will be assigned larger membership degree to the neighboring labels of his biological age.

Now the problem is to solve the inconsistency between biological age and facial appearance. To this end, the locality of the facial appearance is considered since the appearance age is intrinsically the age information revealed by facial appearance. We identify the sample's neighborhoods in the appearance space and averaging the membership degrees to quantify the fuzziness in appearance:

$$\mu_2(x_i, a) = \frac{1}{k} \sum_{x_j \in N_k(x_i)} \mu_1(x_j, a) \tag{2}$$

The inconsistency between biological age and facial appearance can then be solved by using μ_2 to adjust the labeling of the sample. Sample x_i's membership degree to age label a can finally be defined as:

$$\mu_a(x_i) = \lambda_1 \mu_1(x_i, a) + \lambda_2 \mu_2(x_i, a) \tag{3}$$

where λ_1 and λ_2 are the weights satisfying $\lambda_1 + \lambda_2 = 1$. We can simply use $\lambda_1 = 0.51$ and $\lambda_2 = 0.49$ to ensure that a sample will have larger membership degrees to his biological age.

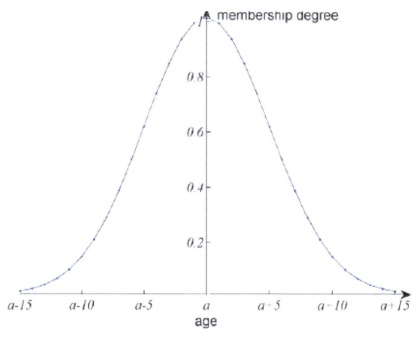

Fig. (1). The curve of membership function.

THE FUZZY DISCRIMINATIVE MANIFOLD ANALYSIS

Traditional Discriminative Manifold Methods

The objective of LDA can be summarized as to find an optimal projection matrix that can maximize the between-class variance while minimize the within-class variance.

$$\min_{W} tr((W^T S_b W)^{-1}(W^T S_w W)) \tag{4}$$

According to [20], the within-class and between-class scatter matrixes (S_w and S_b) can be calculated by Eq. (5) and Eq. (6) respectively:

$$S_w = \frac{1}{2} \sum_{i=1}^{N} \sum_{j=1}^{N} H_w(i,j)(x_i - x_j)(x_i - x_j)^T \tag{5}$$

$$S_b = \frac{1}{2} \sum_{i=1}^{N} \sum_{j=1}^{N} H_b(i,j)(x_i - x_j)(x_i - x_j)^T \tag{6}$$

Where

$$H_w(i, j) = \begin{cases} \dfrac{1}{N_k}, & \text{if } x_i \text{ and } x_j \text{ both belong to the } k\text{th class} \\[2mm] 0, & \text{otherwise} \end{cases} \tag{7}$$

$$H_b(i, j) = \begin{cases} \dfrac{1}{N} - \dfrac{1}{N_k}, & \text{if } x_i \text{ and } x_j \text{ both belong to the } k\text{th class} \\[2mm] \dfrac{1}{N}, & \text{otherwise} \end{cases} \tag{8}$$

In Eq. (7) and Eq. (8), crisp class labels are used to construct the adjacency graphs and thus supervise the learning of the projection matrix. However, as discussed previously, the appearance age is intrinsically a fuzzy attribute of human face. Thus, it is inadequate to use the crisp discriminant method to extract the age related features from facial age image. We also notice that the sample pairs of different age gaps are considered equally in weight matrices of the above methods. For example, the relation of two samples of 20 and 25 years old shares the same weights in H_b and H_w with those of 20 and 50 years old. It is obviously inadequate to fully characterize the relation between samples because people in similar ages have more common than those with larger age gaps.

To solve the above problems, we utilize the fuzzy labels for supervision and extend LDA into fuzzy one in the following subsection.

Fuzzy Discriminative Analysis for Age Estimation

In traditional discriminative methods which use crisp class labels, it is apparently to determine whether the class labels of two samples are the same or not. However, it is not an easy work in fuzzy manifold analysis because there are no distinct boundaries between the fuzzy labels. To solve this problem, we use the min-max closeness degree to characterize to what degree two samples x_i and x_j are belonging to the same class.

Definition 1 (The similarity of age labels) Assume $\{1, 2, \cdots, C\}$ be the set of age labels. Let $\tilde{A}_i = [\mu_1(x_i), \cdots, \mu_C(x_i)]$ and $\tilde{A}_j = [\mu_1(x_j), \cdots, \mu_C(x_j)]$ be x_i and x_j's membership degrees to the age labels respectively. The similarity of x_i and x_j's age labels can be calculated as:

$$S(i,j) = \frac{\sum\limits_{k=1}^{C} \min(\mu_k(x_i), \mu_k(x_j))}{\sum\limits_{k=1}^{C} \max(\mu_k(x_i), \mu_k(x_j))} \tag{9}$$

Obviously, we have $S(i,j) \in [0, 1]$. If the two samples have the same degree to the age labels, *i.e.*, $\tilde{A}_i = \tilde{A}_j$, we have $S(i,j) = 1$.

In facial age estimation, samples also have some contributions to their neighbor ages since facial aging is an ongoing process. Thus, the sample pairs with similar fuzzy labels (*i.e.* larger $S(i, j)$) can be assigned larger weights of H_w, while those with larger dissimilarities (*i.e.* smaller $S(i, j)$) should have larger contributions to the between-class scatters. Following this rule, we reconstruct the similarity graphics based on the value of $S(i, j)$ and obtain the weight matrixes of Fuzzy LDA:

$$H_w^{FLDA}(i,j,k) = \begin{cases} \dfrac{1}{N_k} S(i,j), & \text{if } |age(x_i) - k| < T \\ & \quad \text{and } |age(x_j) - k| < T \\ 0, & \text{otherwise} \end{cases} \tag{10}$$

$$H_b^{FLDA}(i,j,k) = \begin{cases} (\dfrac{1}{N} - \dfrac{1}{N_k}) S(i,j), & \text{if } |age(x_i) - k| < T \\ & \text{and } |age(x_j) - k| < T \\ \dfrac{1}{N}(1 - S(i,j)), & \text{otherwise} \end{cases} \tag{11}$$

And the within-class scatter and the between scatter can then be calculated as:

$$S_w = \frac{1}{2} \sum_{k=1}^{C} \sum_{i=1}^{N} \sum_{j=1}^{N} H_w^{FLDA}(i,j,k)(x_i - x_j)(x_i - x_j)^T \qquad (12)$$

$$S_b = \frac{1}{2} \sum_{k=1}^{C} \sum_{i=1}^{N} \sum_{j=1}^{N} H_b^{FLDA}(i,j,k)(x_i - x_j)(x_i - x_j)^T \qquad (13)$$

Since facial aging is a personalized procedure, some people's appearance age may be quite different from their biological ages. To reduce the influence of such outlier samples, we only use the typical sample whose biological ages are within a range T to calculate the within-class and between-class scatters.

Based on the above descriptions, the proposed Fuzzy LDA algorithm can be summarized as follows:

Step 1 : Convert the age labels into fuzzy ones by calculating the fuzzy membership degree matrix using Eq. (3).
Step 2 : Compute the similarity of the samples' fuzzy labels using Eq. (9). And construct the similarity graphics and calculate the weight matrixes using Eq. (10) and Eq. (11) .
Step 3 : Calculate the within-class and between-class scatter matrixes. The optimal projection matrix of Eq. (4) can be solved by calculating the eigenvectors of $S_w^{-1} S_b v = \lambda v$.
Step 4 : Project all samples onto the obtained optimal projection matrix and do age estimation.

The fuzzy method outperforms the crisp one in several aspects. Firstly, the ordinal information of age labels can be considered in the feature extraction by using the similarity of fuzzy labels to define the weight matrices. Secondly, the unbalanced distribution of samples, which is normal in facial age estimation, can be eased since the samples can contribute to multiple ages according to the weight defined by the similarity of fuzzy labels. Finally, the definition of appearance fuzziness can be seen as an adjustment of age labels. As aforementioned, there may exist some outliers whose appearance does not match the biological age because of the intrinsic and extrinsic factors and such outliers may affect the extraction of age related features. Fortunately, the definition of the appearance fuzziness can alleviate this problem by combining the fuzzy labels of a sample's neighbors to adjust the mismatching of appearance and age label.

EXPERIMENTAL RESULTS

This section presents a toy example to demonstrate the effectiveness of the proposed method in characterizing the fuzziness of facial age labels. And then, we conduct age estimation experiments on two widely used facial aging databases, FGNET and MORPH databases, to verify the effectiveness of the proposed method.

A Toy Example

To demonstrate the effectiveness of the proposed method in characterizing the fuzziness of facial age labels, we conduct experiments on a synthetic dataset containing 4 classes according to the following distribution:

$$\begin{cases} x_k^i = x_0^i + \delta_1(k) \\ y_k^i = y_0^i + \delta_2(k) \end{cases} \tag{14}$$

where $i = 1, 2, 3, 4$ denotes the class index, (x_0^i, y_0^i) is the center of class i and $\delta_1(k) \sim N(0, 0.5)$ and $\delta_2(k) \sim N(0, 1)$. We assume the biological age labels of the four classes are 1, 8, 9 and 10, denoted by circle, square, star and triangle in Fig. (**2**).

LDA, OPLDA and the proposed Fuzzy LDA are conducted on the dataset and the resulted projection directions are shown in Fig. (**2**). Generally, we want to find a direction that can project the samples with larger age label difference more separately than those with smaller age label difference. LDA considers each class equally and cannot find such a projection direction. As is shown in Fig. (**2**), the projections of age 1 are overlapped with those of age 8. OPLDA considers the ordinary information, *i.e.* the difference of age labels, and can find a projection better than LDA. As is shown in Fig. (**2**), OPLDA can also projects the points of age 1 separately from the larger ages. However, the performance of OPLDA is sensitive to the distribution of sample age, the classes have more samples of larger age difference will have more contributions to the calculation of the projection matrix. As is demonstrated in the experiment, age 1 have more samples of larger age difference in the dataset and thus has more affection on the calculation of the projection matrix. Thus, the OPLDA finds a project direction approximates to the direction of x axes to minimize the within-class scatter of age 1 and cannot separate the samples of age 8, 9 and 10. Different from the above two methods, the proposed FuzzyLDA can find the optimal direction that can separate all the classes as possible and the data points of age 1 is projected more separately from those of age 8, 9 and 10. This is because in FuzzyLDA, the contribution of different sample pairs is measured by the similarity of fuzzy labels which is normalized to [0, 1] and thus is more robust to the distribution of samples.

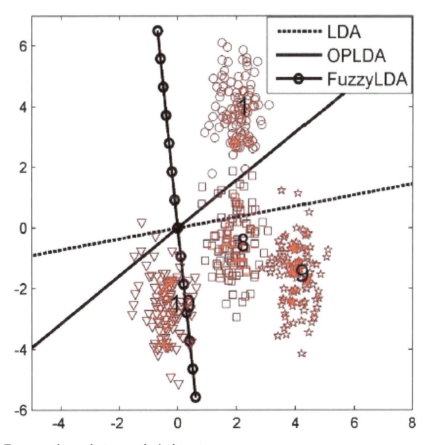

Fig. (2). Toy examples on the two synthetic datasets.

Facial Age Estimation Results

Databases

In order to investigate the performance against different scales of database, two publicly available databases, FG-NET aging database [18] and MORPH Album 2 [19], are used in the experiments.

The FG-NET database is a publicly available facial aging database containing 1002 face images of 82 Europeans within the age range 0-69. Individuals in the database have 6 to 18 images at different ages. The images in FG-NET are obtained by scanning and contain extreme variations in pose, expression and lighting.

MORPH Album 2 is a large database of about 55000 images in the age range of 16 to 77. It is a multi-ethnic database containing about 77% black faces, 19% white faces and 4% other races. Because of the unbalanced distribution of ethnic groups, we randomly select 10000 images from each of the white and black races respectively to construct two subsets for age estimation. The gender distribution of each subset is about Female:Male=1:3 to make full use of the available females.

It should be pointed out that both of the two databases are unbalanced in terms of age distributions. FG-NET has about 70% images aged from 0 to 20. And almost 60% images in MORPH are within the age range of [20, 40].

Experimental Setting

Although support vector regression has best performance in age estimation, it is sensitive to the setting of parameters. Hence, we utilize quadratic regression as an age estimator to have a fair comparison of the methods. Two measures, the mean absolute error (MAE) and cumulative score (CS), are used to evaluate the performance of the methods.

MAE is defined as the average of the absolute errors:

$$MAE = \frac{1}{N} \sum_{i=1}^{N} |\hat{a}_i - a_i| \qquad (15)$$

where $\hat{a}_i$ and a_i are the estimated age and ground truth age of the ith sample respectively. Cumulative score can be calculated as Eq. (16), it reflects the accuracy of age estimator at different error tolerance and higher accuracy at lower error levels indicates better age estimation performance. In our experiments, we consider the error level from 0 to 10 because it is unacceptable to have an estimation error larger than 10 in real cases.

$$CumScore(\theta) = \frac{N_{e \leq \theta}}{N_t} \times 100\% \qquad (16)$$

We compare the proposed fuzzy methods with some related crisp methods, including LDA, OPLDA and MFA. All of the compared methods utilize the biological age labels to find a discriminative subspace. MFA is sensitive to the size of intra-class and inter-class neighbors, thus we tuned the parameters $k1$ and $k2$ for MFA, and report the best results to provide a fair comparison. In all the experiments, the values T are set as 2. FG-NET has fewer samples per-class, thus a smaller size of neighborhoods ($k = 3$) is used to calculate the appearance fuzziness while a larger size of neighborhoods ($k = 10$) is used for MORPH. For the supervised methods, we retain $C - 1$ features for age estimation, where C is the number of classes.

Experiments on the FGNET Database

The images in FGNET database contain variations in lighting, pose and expression. Following the suggestions of [8], we apply active appearance model (AAM) to eliminate such distortions. 200 dimensional AAM features are calculated and utilized as the raw features for further discriminant analysis. The leave-one-person-out (LOPO) strategy is adopted in the experiments to prevent the same person being included in both the training and the test set.

The original 200 dimensional AAM features are also evaluated as the baseline. The MAEs of the methods are summarized in Table **1**. These results confirm that the proposed fuzzy labels are more effective than crisp age labels in exploring the facial aging properties. Furthermore, the definition of fuzzy labels considers both the similarity of biological age labels and facial appearance.

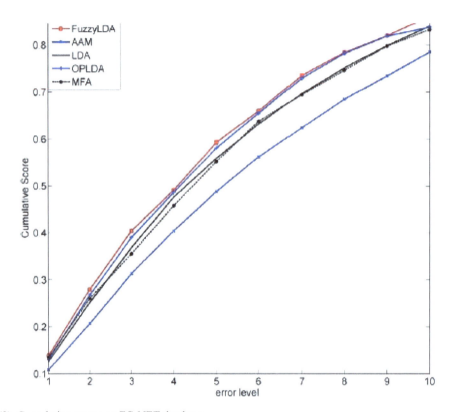

Fig. (3). Cumulative scores on FG-NET database.

Table 1. MAEs on FG-NET database.

Methods	AAM	LDA	MFA	OPLDA	Fuzzy LDA
MAE (years)	6.65	5.90	5.75	5.72	5.54

Thus FuzzyLDA can even achieve a smaller MAE than MFA which considers only the similarity of facial appearance between samples. The cumulative scores shown in Fig. (**3**) also confirm the efficiency of the proposed methods.

Experiments on the MORPH Database

We conduct experiments on black and white subset of MORPH separately to evaluate the performance of the proposed methods. For each subset, we randomly selected 5000 images to construct the training sets and used the remaining for test. The images are manually cropped and resized to 64*64 gray scale images.

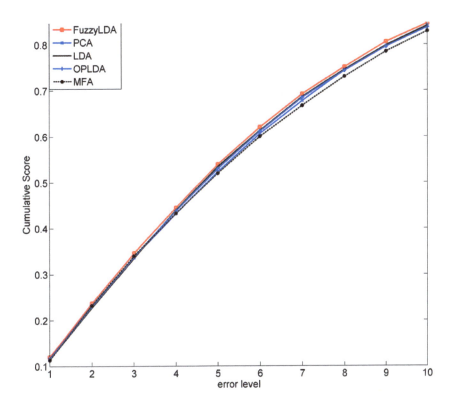

Fig. (4). Cumulative scores on MORPH database.

To avoid the small sample size problems, we first conduct PCA on the two subsets respectively and select the principal components that can retain about 95% energy for further discriminative analysis.

Table **2** tabulates the MAEs of the methods. As demonstrated by the results, FuzzyLDA also outperform the crisp versions on both the black and white subset of MORPH. These results confirm that our fuzzy methods are robust across different sources and scales of database. On the contrary, OPLDA is sensitive to the balances of database and gets a MAE even higher than LDA on the black subset.

Table 2. MAEs on MORPH database.

Methods	PCA	LDA	MFA	OPLDA	Fuzzy LDA
MAE of Black (years)	5.70	5.63	5.66	5.82	5.57
MAE of White (years)	5.72	5.72	5.68	5.76	5.59
Average	5.71	5.68	5.67	5.79	5.58

We combine the results on black and white subset and show the cumulative scores of the supervised methods in Fig. (**4**). We notice that on MORPH database, our methods only bring small improvements. This is because that, with the increase of database scale, all the performance is dominated by the largest age group. Thus, the improvement is not so apparent and most curves of the methods overlap each other. However, our proposed fuzzy methods still outperforms their crisp versions in terms of cumulative score and MAE.

CONCLUSION

To address the fuzziness in facial age labeling, this paper proposes a fuzzy labeling strategy and extend the discriminative manifold analysis into fuzzy ones. The biological age labels are firstly extended into fuzzy ones by introducing a fuzzy membership function to tackle the ongoing prosperity of facial ageing. The fuzziness in facial appearance can then be handled by combining the fuzzy labels of a sample's neighborhoods. By utilizing the fuzzy labels for supervision, we extend LDA into fuzzy ones. The resulted fuzzy method considers both the similarity in biological ages and the similarity of facial appearance in feature extraction and are more effective in extracting age related facial features. Experimental results on both FG-NET and MORPH database confirm that the proposed methods outperform the related crisp methods. To further improve the estimation performance of the proposed methods, we plan to investigate the new definition of neighborhoods in calculating the fuzziness in appearance to remove the affect of other factors of facial variations.

CONFLICT OF INTEREST

The author confirms that author has no conflict of interest to declare for this publication.

ACKNOWLEDGEMENTS

This work is partially supported by National Natural Science Foundation of China under Grant Nos. 61420201, 61373063, 61233011, 61125305, and partially supported by National Basic Research Program of China under Grant No. 2014CB349303.

REFERENCES

[1]   Y. Fu, G. Guo, and T.S. Huang, "Age synthesis and estimation via faces: a survey", *IEEE Trans. Pattern Anal. Mach. Intell*, vol. 32, no. 11, pp. 1955-1976, 2010.
[http://dx.doi.org/10.1109/TPAMI.2010.36] [PMID: 20847387]

[2]   Y. Kwon, and N. Lobo, "Age classification from facial images", In: *IEEE Computer Society Conference on Computer Vision and Pattern Recognition*, 1994, pp. 762-767.
[http://dx.doi.org/10.1109/CVPR.1994.323894]

[3]   Y.H. Kwon, and N. Lobo, "Age classification from facial images", *Comput. Vis. Image Underst*, vol. 74, no. 1, pp. 1-21, 1999.
[http://dx.doi.org/10.1006/cviu.1997.0549]

[4]   A. Lanitis, C. Taylor, and T. Cootes, "Toward automatic simulation of aging effects on face images", *IEEE Trans. Pattern Anal. Mach. Intell,* vol. 24, no. 4, pp. 442-455, 2002.
[http://dx.doi.org/10.1109/34.993553]

[5]   A. Lanitis, C. Draganova, and C. Christodoulou, "Comparing different classifiers for automatic age estimation", *IEEE Trans. Syst. Man Cybern. B Cybern.,* vol. 34, no. 1, pp. 621-628, 2004.
[http://dx.doi.org/10.1109/TSMCB.2003.817091] [PMID: 15369098]

[6]   A. Lanitis, "Comparative evaluation of automatic age-progression methodologies", *EURASIP J. Adv. Signal Process.,* pp. 1-10, 2008.

[7]   T. Cootes, G. Edwards, and C. Taylor, "Active appearance models", *IEEE Trans. Pattern Anal. Mach. Intell.,* vol. 23, no. 6, pp. 681-685, 2001.
[http://dx.doi.org/10.1109/34.927467]

[8]   X. Geng, Z.H. Zhou, and K. Smith-Miles, "Automatic age estimation based on facial aging patterns", *IEEE Trans. Pattern Anal. Mach. Intell.,* vol. 29, no. 12, pp. 2234-2240, 2007.
[http://dx.doi.org/10.1109/TPAMI.2007.70733] [PMID: 17934231]

[9]   Y. Fu, Y. Xu, and T. Huang, "Estimating human ages by manifold analysis of face pictures and regression on aging features", In: *IEEE International Conference on Multimedia and Expo*, 2007, pp. 1383-1386.

[10]   G. Guo, Y. Fu, C.R. Dyer, and T.S. Huang, "Image-based human age estimation by manifold learning and locally adjusted robust regression", *IEEE Trans. Image Process.,* vol. 17, no. 7, pp. 1178-1188, 2008.
[http://dx.doi.org/10.1109/TIP.2008.924280] [PMID: 18586625]

[11]   S. Yan, D. Xu, B. Zhang, H-J. Zhang, Q. Yang, and S. Lin, "Graph embedding and extensions: a

general framework for dimensionality reduction", *IEEE Trans. Pattern Anal. Mach. Intell.,* vol. 29, no. 1, pp. 40-51, 2007.
[http://dx.doi.org/10.1109/TPAMI.2007.250598] [PMID: 17108382]

[12]   Y. Fu, M. Liu, and T.S. Huang, "Conformal embedding analysis with local graph modeling on the unit hypersphere", In: *IEEE Conference on Computer Vision and Pattern Recognitionl CWorkshop Component Analysis,* 2007.
[http://dx.doi.org/10.1109/CVPR.2007.383410]

[13]   G.D. Guo, G.W. Mu, and Y. Fu, "Human age estimation using bio-inspired features", In: *IEEE Conference on Computer Vision and Pattern Recognition,* 2009, pp. 112-119.

[14]   G.D. Guo, and C. Zhang, "A study on cross-population age estimation", In: *IEEE Conference on Computer Vision and Pattern Recognition,* 2014, pp. 4257-4263.

[15]   C.S. Li, Q.S. Liu, and J. Liu, "Learning ordinal discriminative features for age estimation", In: *IEEE Conference on Computer Vision and Pattern Recognition,* 2012, pp. 2570-2577.

[16]   J.W. Lu, and Y-P. Tan, "Ordinal preserving manifolds analysis for human age estimation", In: *IEEE International Conference of Computer Vision and Pattern Recognition, Workshop Biometrics,* 2010, pp. 90-95.

[17]   J. Lu, and Y-P. Tan, "Ordinal preserving manifolds analysis for human age and head pose estimation", *IEEE Trans. Hum. Mach. Syst.,* vol. 43, no. 2, pp. 249-258, 2013.
[http://dx.doi.org/10.1109/TSMCC.2012.2192727]

[18]   T. Cootes, and A. Lanitis, *"The FG-NET aging database" in http://www.fgnet.rsunit.com/.*

[19]   K. Ricanek, and T. Tesafaye, "MORPH: A longitudinal image database of normal adult age-progression", In: *IEEE International Conference on Automatic Face Gesture Recognition,* 2006, pp. 341-345.
[http://dx.doi.org/10.1109/FGR.2006.78]

[20]   H. Hu, "Orthogonal neighborhood preserving discriminant analysis for face recognition", *Pattern Recognit.,* vol. 41, no. 6, pp. 2045-2054, 2008.
[http://dx.doi.org/10.1016/j.patcog.2007.10.029]

CHAPTER 11

Facial Image-Based Age Estimation

Ammar Assoum[*], **Jouhayna Harmouch**

LaMA Laboratory, Lebanese University, Tripoli, Lebanon

Abstract: Automatic age estimation consists of using a computer to predict the age of a person based on a given facial image. The age prediction is built on distinct patterns emerging from the facial appearance. The interest of such process has increasingly grown due to the wide range of its potential applications in law enforcement, security control, and human-computer interaction. However, the estimation problem remains challenging since it is influenced by a lot of factors including lifestyle, gender, environment, and genetics. Many recent algorithms used for automatic age estimation are based on machine learning methods and have proven their efficiency and accuracy in this domain. In this chapter, we present an empirical study on a complete age estimation system built around label sensitive learning [1]. Experimental results conducted on FG-NET and MORPH Album II face databases are presented.

Keywords: Age classification, Age estimation, Age prediction, Dimensionality reduction, Facial feature extraction, Gabor filter, K-nearest neighbors, Label-sensitive, Local binary pattern, Local regression, Locality preserving projections, Machine learning, Marginal fisher analysis, Mean absolute error, Partial least square regression, Preprocessing, Recognition rate, Support vector regression.

INTRODUCTION

Despite of its relative newness, automatic age estimation from facial images has recently emerged among the interesting new technologies due to its multiple potential applications. Indeed, taking advantage of rapid progress in computer vision, pattern recognition and machine learning, this technique can be widely used in such areas as age-based access control, age-adaptive human computer interaction, person identification, data mining and organization, multimedia communication and age-targeted advertising and entertainment [2, 3]. Automatic

---

[*] **Address to Corresponding Author Ammar Assoum:** Lebanese University, Faculty of Science, Section III, Tripoli, Lebanon; Tel: +9613069591; Fax: +9616386365; E-mail: a.assoum@ul.edu.lb

Fadi Dornaika (Ed)

age estimation is achieved using computers and is useful in scenarios where one does not need to explicitly find the identification of the individual, but wants to know his or her age.

However, estimating accurately the age from facial images is a particularly challenging task since it depends on many complicated and unrelated factors, such as ethnic origin, working environment, living style, health condition and sociality [4, 5]. On the other hand, visual facial features used in the age estimation process are affected by pose, illumination and imaging conditions [6, 7]. Thus, face aging is uncontrollable and personalized [8, 9].

In addition to the challenges cited above, three other factors should also be considered when developing a consistent age estimation system. Firstly, the ordinal relationship that exists between age labels; for instance, age 40 is closer to age 35 than to age 15. This fact makes the age determination learning task more complicated than the traditional classification problem since this latter assumes there is no correlations between classes. Indeed, most of the dimensionality reduction algorithms and distance metric learning techniques ignore this kind of correlations and are well suited, due to their original design, to the traditional classification problems. That is why, techniques like regression and cost-sensitive learning are usually used in order to consider the ordinal relationship between the ages in their objective functions. Secondly, it may not be easy to detect the aging effects on human faces by a single classifier or regressor [10]. Finally, it is often hard to gather a large aging database that contains chronometrical image series for the same individuals which implies that the number of images available for each age label can be very different. This would lead to a serious imbalance during the learning phase and to a degradation in the global performance of the estimation process.

AGE ESTIMATION ALGORITHMS

An age estimation algorithm is composed mainly of two processing stages: feature extraction and age determination. In the first stage, a compact representation of facial images is built by extracting facial features related to human ages or facial appearance change; in the second stage, the age corresponding to the input facial image is estimated by an age determination function based on the extracted features. We can eventually add other processing blocks such as input images preprocessing, distance metric adjustment and dimensionality reduction in order to solve some aspects related to the algorithm or to improve its performance (see Fig. (**1**)). In the following, we present a review of the previous work related to each of the processing stages.

Fig. 1. The full flowchart of age estimation process (some of the blocks may not exist).

Input Images Preprocessing

In the context of automatic age estimation, the preprocessing step consists in preparing the input images and putting them in a common and homogeneous form. This process includes operations such as cropping, resizing, reshaping of the set of input images. The output of this step is generally composed of an ($m \times n \times p$) array corresponding to the preprocessed image ($p = 1$ for grayscale images and $p = 3$ for color ones). Depending on how the next processing methods are implemented, the preprocessed images can be reshaped as 1D vectors that contain the pixels and that can be gathered to form a huge matrix corresponding to the input data.

Feature Extraction

In the terminology related to image processing and computer vision domains, a feature is a particular information suitable for solving the computational task related to a given application. In general, features are intended to be informative and non redundant. They serve as a starting point for numerous computer vision algorithms and should facilitate the subsequent learning and generalization steps, in some cases leading to better human interpretations. In practice, features may consist of specific structures in the image such as points, edges or objects but may also be the result of an intermediate processing stage such as general neighborhood operation or feature detection applied to the input image [11]. During the feature extraction process, it is important to define a set of features, or image characteristics, that will most efficiently represent the information and that will be used for analysis and classification. The extraction process should help in improving the efficiency of analysis and classification processes. This may be achieved by:

• Eliminating redundancy that may exist in the image data.
• Removing variability in the image data that has a little or no impact on classification – even throwing entire images away if necessary.
• Optimizing the performance of the classifier and/or regressor by rebuilding the data (in feature space).
• Retrieving spatial information which is important to target identification. Examples of spacial information could be size, texture, shape, etc.

Examples of features extraction methods are Active Appearance Model (AAM) [12], Local Binary Patterns (LBP) [13] and Matrix-based Complex Principal Component Analysis (MCPCA) [14].

The feature extraction process can be applied to the input image considered as a whole or on a part of it after its decomposition into a set of blocks. In the latter case, the features of all the blocks are concatenated together to build the final features set corresponding to the input image.

Since the major problems encountered when performing analysis of complex data come from the number of variables involved, feature extraction is, in general, associated to dimensionality reduction.

Distance Metric Adjustments

In the domain of age estimation, the neighbors of a particular observation consist of samples that have close facial appearance change resulted from human ages. Nevertheless, most of the features extracted from facial images are relevant to poses and expressions rather than to human ages [1]. This means that, neighbors resulting from the application of traditional techniques such as Euclidean metric are mainly those with similar poses or expressions, but not with similar change of appearances caused by human ages. This will have negative consequences not only on the performance of the dimensionality reduction process built on the erroneous neighborhood, but also on the global precision of age estimation. to overcome the problem described above, a distance metric adjustment stage can be added in order to reweigh the strengths of features. Among the methods that can be used for this purpose can be mentioned Relevant Component Analysis (RCA) [15] and its label-sensitive variant lsRCA [1].

Dimensionality Reduction

When dealing with pattern recognition and computer vision problems, the large amount of input data, such as images and videos, are computationally challenging to manipulate. In these cases, it is preferable to reduce the dimensionality of the data without radically altering the original information in the data distribution. This would mostly result in in more efficient learning and inference. A large number of approaches have been proposed in this domain [16]. These latter are mostly categorized by their linearity. Among the linear methods we can mention Multi-Dimensional Scaling (MDS) [18], Principal Component Analysis (PCA) [17], Locality Preserving Projections (LPP) [19], Marginal Fisher Analysis (MFA) [20] and their label-sensitive variants lsLPP and lsMFA [1]. These methods are characterized by their efficiency in observing the Euclidean structure. On the other hand, the nonlinear methods such as Laplacian Eigenmaps [22], Locally Linear Embedding (LLE) [21] and Isomap [23] focus on preserving the geodesic distances.

As mentioned before, feature extraction and dimensionality reduction can be combined in one single step [17, 23, 24]. In machine learning this process is also called low-dimensional embedding [25].

Age Determination

Given an aging feature representation, eventually followed by a dimensionality reduction, the next step is to estimate the age. The estimation process can be considered as a multi-class classification problem. This means that traditional classification algorithms such as the k-Nearest Neighbor (kNN) classifier [26], Support Vector Machines (SVM) [28, 29] and Learning Vector Quantization (LVQ) [27] can be directly applied for age determination. These algorithms, nevertheless, do not consider the ordinal relationship and correlations among age labels. Indeed, a uniform penalty is assigned to any misclassification case even when the output class is so close to the true one; For example, wrongly predicting a 40-year-old person either as 35-year-old or 15-year-old is the same from a classifier point of view, which is not the case in real life application. On the other hand, owing to the set of sequential values 0, 1, 2, ..., *etc.* to which age numbers belong, age estimation can also be seen as a regression problem. In fact, regressors, because of their indigenous mode of operation, could take the ordinal relationship and correlations that exist among the ages into account and could probably give better estimation results. Regression algorithms such as the Least Square Regression (LSR) [30], the Kernel Regression [31], the Support Vector Regression (SVR) [33] and the Partial Least Square Regression (PLSR) [32] all have been applied and tested in previous work [34 - 36].

Recently, a hybrid classification-regression method has been tested and consists of the so-called local regression and is inspired by the local classification technique [37]. Given a testing sample, the method first searches its nearest neighbors among a training set, and trains a regressor based on these neighbors before applying the learned regressor to the test sample for age estimation. The main advantage of such local regressions consists in their ability to capture the complicated facial aging process since they can generate comparably sophisticated mapping functions. The algorithm of kNN-SVR [38] is one of the techniques that use this paradigm.

AGE ESTIMATION FRAMEWORK AND EXPERIMENTS PERFORMED

The age estimation framework used to perform the experiments is built on the general block diagram given in Fig. (**1**). For comparison purposes, several combinations/scenarios are considered and, for each block of the framework, several methods are tested. Table **1** summarizes the set of blocks combinations tested during the experiments (each row corresponds to a combination). The age determination process (last block of the framework) is achieved by a regressor in the first eight combinations and by a classifier in the remaining ones.

On the other hand, in order to investigate the effect of twinning multiple feature extraction techniques on the performance, the scenarios of Table **1** were tested with and without applying a preliminary Gabor filter on the input image before running the proper features extracting process (the LBP method in our case).

Table 1. The combination of processing blocks tested during experiments.

Feature extraction	Metric adjustment	Dimensionality reduction	Age determination
LBP–PCA	–	lsLPP	kNN–SVR
LBP–PCA	lsRCA	lsLPP	kNN–SVR
LBP–PCA	–	lsLPP	PLSR
LBP–PCA	lsRCA	lsLPP	PLSR
LBP–PCA	–	lsMFA	kNN–SVR
LBP–PCA	lsRCA	lsMFA	kNN–SVR
LBP–PCA	–	lsMFA	PLSR
LBP–PCA	lsRCA	lsMFA	PLSR
LBP–PCA	–	lsLPP	kNN
LBP–PCA	lsRCA	lsLPP	kNN
LBP–PCA	–	lsMFA	kNN
LBP–PCA	lsRCA	lsMFA	kNN

EXPERIMENTAL SETTING

Datasets

The age estimation experiments are conducted on two face databases. The first is the FG-NET aging database. It contains 1,002 color and grayscale face images of 82 individuals with large variations of pose, expression and lighting. Each subject has 6-18 face images taken at different ages from 0 to 69. In addition, each face image has 68 labeled landmark points that characterize its shape information [39].

The second is the MORPH II database containing 55,132 color face images from more than 13,000 subjects with about three aging images per person ranging from 16 to 77 with a median age of 33 [40].

Age range distributions and examples of face images from the two databases are shown in Table **2** and Fig. (**2**), respectively.

We randomly divide each of the face datasets into ten splits of train/test subsets. For every split, two groups of experiments are conducted and correspond to a train/test percentage of 80% − 20% and 20% − 80% respectively.

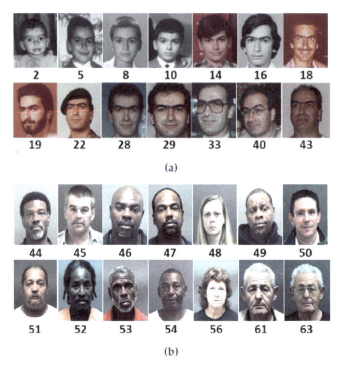

Fig. 2. Sample images of FG-NET database **(a)** and MORPH II database. **(b)** The chronological ages are given below the images.

Table 2. Age range distribution (%) for FG-NET and MORPH II face databases.

Age Range	FG-NET (%)	MORPH II (%)
0–9	37.03	0
10–19	33.83	8.94
20–29	14.37	26.04
30–39	7.88	32.16
40–49	4.59	24.58
50–59	1.50	7.37
60–69	0.80	0.82
70–77	0	0.09

The results are then averaged, for each experiment, over those obtained for different splits.

Performance Scores

The performance of the experiments is measured in two metrics. The first one is the Mean Absolute Error (MAE) and is used when the age estimation process is built on a regression. The MAE measures the average error over a given test sample of the absolute values of the differences between prediction and the corresponding observation. Practically, if the test dataset is composed of n images, and if y_i and $\hat{y}_i$ denote the true age and the estimated one respectively, then the MAE is given by

$$MAE = \frac{1}{n}\sum_{i=1}^{n}|y_i - \hat{y}_i| \tag{1}$$

The second metric is the Recognition Rate RR and is used when the age estimation is performed by a classifier. It measures the percentage of success during classification. If n denotes the number of testing images and n_s that of points successfully recognized, then RR is defined as

$$RR = 100\frac{n_s}{n} \tag{2}$$

RESULTS

The results obtained for the set of experiments (scenarios) listed in Table **1** are given in Tables **3-8** and Figs. (**3-6**) for an age determination performed by a regressor and a classifier respectively.

Since the performance of the experiments is measured either in term of Mean Absolute Error (MAE) or as a Recognition Rate (RR), it is obvious that the less MAE is and the greater RR is, the better the performance and the results are.

Table 3. MAE (years) obtained for FG-NET dataset without Gabor filter (LBP mono-block).

	80% learn & 20% test		20% learn & 80% test	
	PLSR	**KNN-SVR**	**PLSR**	**KNN-SVR**
LBP-PCA-lsRCA-lsLPP	8.06	8.30	10.02	9.77
LBP-PCA-lsRCA-lsMFA	8.06	8.42	10.02	10.34

(Table 3) contd.....

	80% learn & 20% test		20% learn & 80% test	
	PLSR	**KNN-SVR**	**PLSR**	**KNN-SVR**
LBP-PCA-lsLPP	8.05	8.17	10.02	9.89
LBP-PCA-lsMFA	8.04	8.09	10.01	10.04

Table 4. MAE (years) obtained for FG-NET dataset with Gabor filter (LBP mono-block).

	80% learn & 20% test		20% learn & 80% test	
	PLSR	**KNN-SVR**	**PLSR**	**KNN-SVR**
LBP-PCA-lsRCA-lsLPP	8.95	9.04	10.80	10.21
LBP-PCA-lsRCA-lsMFA	8.95	9.06	10.80	10.60
LBP-PCA-lsLPP	8.95	8.96	9.95	10.05
LBP-PCA-lsMFA	8.95	8.89	10.97	10.30

Table 5. MAE (years) obtained for FG-NET dataset with Gabor filter (LBP multi-block).

	80% learn & 20% test		20% learn & 80% test	
	PLSR	**KNN-SVR**	**PLSR**	**KNN-SVR**
LBP-PCA-lsRCA-lsLPP	8.95	9.04	10.80	10.21
LBP-PCA-lsRCA-lsMFA	8.95	9.06	10.80	10.62
LBP-PCA-lsLPP	8.95	9.96	10.80	9.94
LBP-PCA-lsMFA	8.95	8.89	10.80	10.22

Table 6. MAE (years) obtained for MORPH II dataset without Gabor filter (LBP mono-block).

	80% learn & 20% test		20% learn & 80% test	
	PLSR	**KNN-SVR**	**PLSR**	**KNN-SVR**
LBP-PCA-lsRCA-lsLPP	9.18	9.44	9.47	9.73
LBP-PCA-lsRCA-lsMFA	9.18	9.48	9.47	9.81
LBP-PCA-lsLPP	9.18	9.32	9.47	9.65
LBP-PCA-lsMFA	9.17	9.35	9.47	9.70

Table 7. MAE (years) obtained for MORPH II dataset with Gabor filter (LBP mono-block).

	80% learn & 20% test		20% learn & 80% test	
	PLSR	**KNN-SVR**	**PLSR**	**KNN-SVR**
LBP-PCA-lsRCA-lsLPP	8.58	9.03	9.01	9.33
LBP-PCA-lsRCA-lsMFA	8.58	9.06	9.01	9.52
LBP-PCA-lsLPP	8.58	8.84	9.01	9.02
LBP-PCA-lsMFA	8.58	8.84	9.01	9.11

Table 8. MAE (years) obtained for MORPH II dataset with Gabor filter (LBP multi-block).

	80% learn & 20% test		20% learn & 80% test	
	PLSR	**KNN-SVR**	**PLSR**	**KNN-SVR**
LBP-PCA-lsRCA-lsLPP	8.81	9.37	9.14	9.37
LBP-PCA-lsRCA-lsMFA	8.81	9.43	9.14	9.58
LBP-PCA-lsLPP	8.81	9.01	9.14	9.01
LBP-PCA-lsMFA	8.81	9.10	9.13	9.39

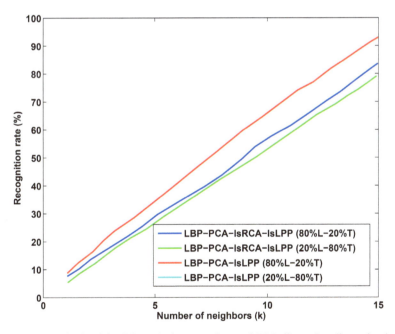

Fig. 3. Recognition rate obtained for FG-NET dataset using an lsLPP dimensionality reduction and a kNN classifier.

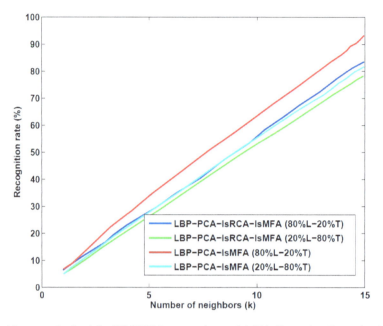

Fig. 4. Recognition rate obtained for FG-NET dataset using an lsMFA dimensionality reduction and a kNN classifier.

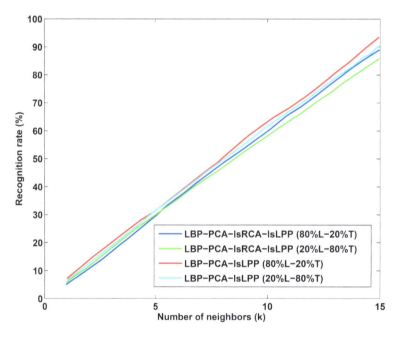

Fig. 5. Recognition rate obtained for FG-NET dataset (with Gabor prefiltering) using an lsLPP dimensionality reduction and a kNN classifier.

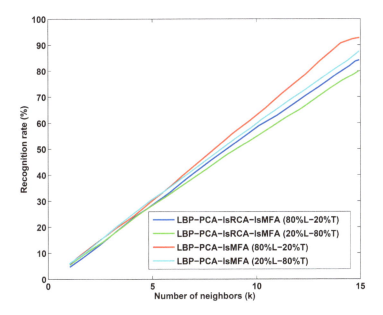

Fig. 6. Recognition rate obtained for FG-NET dataset (with Gabor prefiltering) using an lsMFA dimensionality reduction and a kNN classifier.

The results depicted in Tables **3-8** and Figs. (**3-6**) allow to conclude the following remarks:

- Performance improves with the increasing of the train percentage which is normal since the size of data used for learning is bigger.
- Contrary to what is expected, the distance metric adjustment made by lsRCA did not improve the performance.
- The results obtained when performing dimensionality reduction by lsLPP are slightly better than those of lsMFA.
- The global performance improves after the application of Gabor filter for MORPH II dataset but rather deteriorates for FG-NET.
- The decomposition of the image into blocks before running features extraction process does not improve the results of FG-NET and contrarily deteriorates those of MORPH II.

CONCLUSION

In this chapter, we presented a complete age estimation system based on machine learning methods. The features of the preprocessed input face image were extracted using Local Binary Pattern (LBP) method, eventually preceded by a Gabor prefiltering and followed by a Principal Component Analysis (PCA) scheme. The obtained features have been subject to a distance metric adjustment performed by lsRCA then to a dimensionality reduction using either label sensitive Locality Preserving Projections (lsLPP) or labelsensitive Marginal Fisher Analysis (lsMFA). The age determination process was carried out either through a classification using kNN method or a regression (local Support Vector Regression – SVR or Partial Least Square Regression – PLSR). The results of the experiments that have been conducted on FG-NET and MORPH II face databases showed the beneficial effect of using Gabor filter and that lsLPP provided better performance than lsMFA.

CONFLICT OF INTEREST

The author confirms that author has no conflict of interest to declare for this publication.

ACKNOWLEDGEMENTS

Declared none.

REFERENCES

[1]   W-L. Chao, J-Z. Liu, and J-J. Ding, "Facial age estimation based on label-sensitive learning and age-oriented regression", *Pattern Recognit.,* vol. 46, no. 3, pp. 628-641, 2013.
[http://dx.doi.org/10.1016/j.patcog.2012.09.011]

[2]   A. Lanitis, C. Draganova, and C. Christodoulou, "Comparing different classifiers for automatic age estimation", *IEEE Trans. Syst. Man Cybern. B Cybern.,* vol. 34, no. 1, pp. 621-628, 2004.
[http://dx.doi.org/10.1109/TSMCB.2003.817091] [PMID: 15369098]

[3]   G. Guo, Y. Fu, C.R. Dyer, and T.S. Huang, "Image-based human age estimation by manifold learning and locally adjusted robust regression", *IEEE Trans. Image Process.,* vol. 17, no. 7, pp. 1178-1188, 2008.
[http://dx.doi.org/10.1109/TIP.2008.924280] [PMID: 18586625]

[4]   A. Stone, "The aging process of the face and techniques of rejuvenation", *[Online]. Available: http://www. aaronstonemd.com/Facial_Aging_Rejuvenation.shtm.*accessed February 10, 2015

[5]   D.S. Berry, and L.Z. McArthur, "Perceiving character in faces: the impact of age-related craniofacial changes on social perception", *Psychol. Bull.,* vol. 100, no. 1, pp. 3-18, 1986.
[http://dx.doi.org/10.1037/0033-2909.100.1.3] [PMID: 3526376]

[6]   W.L. Braje, D. Kersten, M.J. Tarr, and N.F. Troje, "Illumination effects in face recognition", *J. Psychol.,* vol. 26, no. 4, pp. 371-380, 1998.

[7]   G. Riegler, D. Ferstl, M. RA1/4ther, and H. Bischof, "Hough networks for head pose estimation and facial feature localization", In: *Proceedings of the British Machine Vision Conference.* BMVA Press, 2014.
[http://dx.doi.org/10.5244/C.28.66]

[8]   X. Geng, Z.H. Zhou, and K. Smith-Miles, "Automatic age estimation based on facial aging patterns", *IEEE Trans. Pattern Anal. Mach. Intell.,* vol. 29, no. 12, pp. 2234-2240, 2007.
[http://dx.doi.org/10.1109/TPAMI.2007.70733] [PMID: 17934231]

[9]   N. Ramanathan, and R. Chellappa, "Face verification across age progression", *IEEE Trans. Image Process.,* vol. 15, no. 11, pp. 3349-3361, 2006.
[http://dx.doi.org/10.1109/TIP.2006.881993] [PMID: 17076395]

[10]   G. Guo, Y. Fu, C.R. Dyer, and T.S. Huang, "Image-based human age estimation by manifold learning and locally adjusted robust regression", *IEEE Trans. Image Process.,* vol. 17, no. 7, pp. 1178-1188, 2008.
[http://dx.doi.org/10.1109/TIP.2008.924280] [PMID: 18586625]

[11]   M. Nixon, and A. Aguado, "Feature Extraction and Image Processing", *Elsevier,* 2008.

[12]   T.F. Cootes, G.J. Edwards, and C.J. Taylor, "Active appearance models", *IEEE Trans. Pattern Anal. Mach. Intell.,* vol. 23, no. 6, pp. 681-685, 2001.
[http://dx.doi.org/10.1109/34.927467]

[13]   T. Ojala, M. Pietikäinen, and D. Harwood, "A comparative study of texture measures with classification based on featured distributions", *Pattern Recognit.,* vol. 29, pp. 51-59, 1996.
[http://dx.doi.org/10.1016/0031-3203(95)00067-4]

[14]   Y. Xu, D. Zhang, and J-Y. Yang, "A feature extraction method for use with bimodal biometrics", *Pattern Recognit.,* vol. 43, pp. 1106-1115, 2010.
[http://dx.doi.org/10.1016/j.patcog.2009.09.013]

[15]   N. Shental, and D. Weinshall, "Learning Distance Functions using Equivalence Relations", In: *International Conference on Machine Learning,* 2003, pp. 11-18.

[16]   L. van der Maaten, E. Postma, and J. van den Herik, "Dimensionality Reduction: A Comparative Review", *J. Mach. Learn. Res.,* 2008.

[17]   I. Borg, and P. Groenen, *Modern Multidimensional Scaling: Theory and Applications..* Springer, 2005.

[18]   M. Turk, and A. Pentland, "Eigenfaces for recognition", *J. Cogn. Neurosci.,* vol. 3, no. 1, pp. 71-86, 1991.
[http://dx.doi.org/10.1162/jocn.1991.3.1.71] [PMID: 23964806]

[19]   X. He, and P. Niyogi, "Locality Preserving Projections", In: *Advances in Neural Information Processing Systems.* 2003.

[20]   S. Yan, D. Xu, B. Zhang, H-J. Zhang, Q. Yang, and S. Lin, "Graph embedding and extensions: a general framework for dimensionality reduction", *IEEE Trans. Pattern Anal. Mach. Intell.,* vol. 29, no. 1, pp. 40-51, 2007.

[http://dx.doi.org/10.1109/TPAMI.2007.250598] [PMID: 17108382]

[21]   M. Belkin, and P. Niyogi, "Laplacian Eigenmaps and Spectral Techniques for Embedding and Clustering", In: *Neural Information Processing Systems.* 2001, pp. 585-591.

[22]   S.T. Roweis, and L.K. Saul, "Nonlinear dimensionality reduction by locally linear embedding", *Science,* vol. 290, no. 5500, pp. 2323-2326, 2000.
[http://dx.doi.org/10.1126/science.290.5500.2323] [PMID: 11125150]

[23]   J.B. Tenenbaum, V. de Silva, and J.C. Langford, "A global geometric framework for nonlinear dimensionality reduction", *Science,* vol. 290, no. 5500, pp. 2319-2323, 2000.
[http://dx.doi.org/10.1126/science.290.5500.2319] [PMID: 11125149]

[24]   P.N. Belhumeur, J.P. Hespanha, and D.J. Kriegman, "Eigenfaces vs. Fisherfaces: Recognition Using Class Specific Linear Projection", *IEEE Trans. Pattern Anal. Mach. Intell.,* vol. 19, pp. 711-720, 1997.
[http://dx.doi.org/10.1109/34.598228]

[25]   B. Shaw, and T. Jebara, "Structure Preserving Embedding", In: *International Conference on Machine Learning*, 2009, pp. 118-944.
[http://dx.doi.org/10.1145/1553374.1553494]

[26]   E. Fix, and J. Hodges, "Discriminatory analysis, nonparametric discrimination: Consistency properties", In: *USAF School of Aviation Medicine, Randolph Field, Texas, Technical Report 4.* 1951.

[27]   C.J. Burges, "A Tutorial on Support Vector Machines for Pattern Recognition", *Data Min. Knowl. Discov.,* vol. 2, pp. 121-167, 1998.
[http://dx.doi.org/10.1023/A:1009715923555]

[28]   C. Cortes, and V. Vapnik, "Support-vector networks", *Mach. Learn.,* vol. 20, pp. 273-297, 1995.
[http://dx.doi.org/10.1007/BF00994018]

[29]   T. Kohonen, "The self-organizing map", *Neurocomputing,* vol. 21, pp. 1-6, 1998.
[http://dx.doi.org/10.1016/S0925-2312(98)00030-7]

[30]   Y. Fu, and T.S. Huang, "Human Age Estimation With Regression on Discriminative Aging Manifold", *IEEE Trans. Multimed.,* vol. 10, pp. 578-584, 2008.
[http://dx.doi.org/10.1109/TMM.2008.921847]

[31]   H. Takeda, S. Farsiu, and P. Milanfar, "Kernel regression for image processing and reconstruction", *IEEE Trans. Image Process.,* vol. 16, no. 2, pp. 349-366, 2007.
[http://dx.doi.org/10.1109/TIP.2006.888330] [PMID: 17269630]

[32]   H. Drucker, C.J. Burges, L. Kaufman, A.J. Smola, and V. Vapnik, "Support Vector Regression Machines", In: *Neural Information Processing Systems.* 1996, pp. 155-161.

[33]   V.E. Vinzi, W.W. Chin, J. Henseler, and H. Wang, *Handbook of Partial Least Squares: Concepts, Methods and Applications in Marketing and Related Fields..* European Planning Studies, 2008.

[34]   S. Yan, H. Wang, X. Tang, and T.S. Huang, "Learning Auto-Structured Regressor from Uncertain Nonnegative Labels", In: *International Conference on Computer Visio.* 2007, pp. 1-8.
[http://dx.doi.org/10.1109/ICCV.2007.4409050]

[35]   P. Bouboulis, S. Theodoridis, and C. Mavroforakis, "Complex support vector regression", In: *IEEE International Conference on Digital Ecosystems and Technologies*, 2012.

[36]   M. Ratsch, P. Quick, P. Huber, T. Frank, and T. Vetter, "Wavelet Reduced Support Vector Regression for Efficient and Robust Head Pose Estimation", In: *Canadian Conference on Computer and Robot Vision*, 2012.

[37]   J. Fox, and S. Weisberg, *An R Companion to Applied Regression..* SAGE Publications, 2010.

[38]   H. Zhang, A.C. Berg, M. Maire, and J. Malik, "SVM-KNN: Discriminative Nearest Neighbor Classification for Visual Category Recognition", In: *Computer Vision and Pattern Recognition,* vol. 2. 2006, pp. 2126-2136.
        [http://dx.doi.org/10.1109/CVPR.2006.301]

[39]   T. Cootes, "The FG-NET aging Database", *Available: http://www-prima.inrialpes.fr/FGnet/ html/home.html,* 2002.accessed February 3, 2015 [Online]

[40]   K. Ricanek, and T. Tesafaye, "MORPH: A longitudinal image database of normal adult age-progression", In: *Seventh IEEE International Conference on Automatic Face and Gesture Recognition (FG 2006)*, 10-12 April 2006 , Southampton, UK, 2006.
        [http://dx.doi.org/10.1109/FGR.2006.78]

SUBJECT INDEX

2

2D shape landmarks 155, 156

3

3D Face matching 109, 126, 127

3D Face model 119, 154, 155, 159, 160, 166, 173, 174

3D Face recognition 106, 119, 120, 124, 125, 127-130

3D Face Registration 107, 114, 129

3D Rotation 86, 88, 166

A

Affinity matrix 27, 29, 30, 41, 66, 68, 69, 71, 72, 81, 82

Age classification 232

Age estimation 67, 84, 132, 152, 227, 228, 242, 246-249

Age Information 217, 220

Age prediction 132, 234

Aging pattern subspace 217, 218

Alex-Net architecture 3, 13

Appearance age 217, 219, 220, 222, 224

B

Backpropagation algorithm 3

Belief function 181, 188, 189, 194

Biological Age 217, 224, 225, 228, 229, 231

Biometric 86, 87, 109, 110, 128

C

Cautious rule 181, 197, 198, 200

CK-Regianini dataset 3, 11, 12, 14-17

CK-Zheng dataset 3, 13-16

Classification accuracy 3, 39, 42, 101, 102

CMU-Pittsburgh dataset 3, 13, 17

Combined features 3

Complete Kernel Fisher Discriminant method 39, 43, 55

Computer vision 20, 21, 37, 40, 63, 64, 67, 84, 129, 130, 132, 151, 152, 181, 182, 236, 238, 250

Conformal embedding analysis 64, 217, 218, 233

Conjunctive rule 181, 189, 190, 197, 199-201

Convolutional neural networks 3, 4, 21

Cumulative score 217, 227, 228, 231

Curvature descriptors 109, 120

D

Deep learning 3, 4

Deformable model backprojection 155, 165, 166

Dempster-Shafer 181, 185, 191, 203, 214, 215

Depth data 86, 89, 90, 93, 94, 99, 104

Dimensionality reduction 33, 36, 37, 62, 63, 66, 67, 83, 84, 86, 88, 99, 102, 107, 132, 133, 135, 136, 138, 143, 144, 146, 150, 240, 244-249

Distance diffusion mapping 39, 42, 48, 50, 53, 61

Distance metric learning 39, 42, 64, 107, 235

E

Eigenface 86, 102

Eigen problem 86, 100, 101

Eigenvalue problem 23, 30, 31, 70, 71

Ellipse fitting 86, 95

Exponential discriminant analysis 39, 43, 54

www.ingramcontent.com/pod-product-compliance
Lightning Source LLC
Chambersburg PA
CBHW041434050326
40690CB00003B/538